POSTCARD HISTORY SERIES

Concord and Cabarrus County

IN VINTAGE POSTCARDS

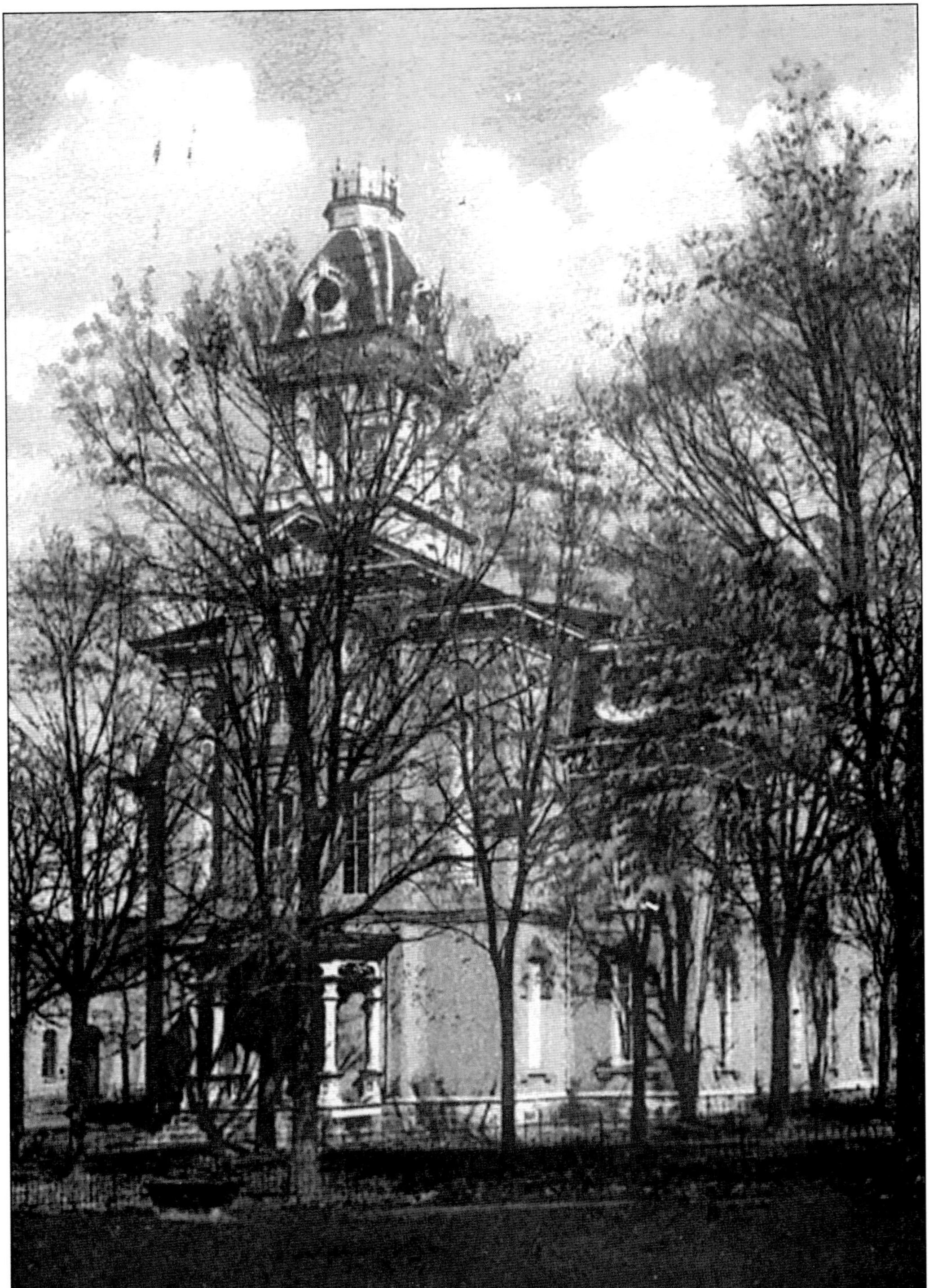

An early postcard of the Cabarrus County Court House, postmarked March 9, 1909, was published by Fetzer Drug Store and was colorized in Germany. In the image, the stucco building was painted a reddish color to give the impression of being of brick.

POSTCARD HISTORY SERIES

Concord and Cabarrus County IN VINTAGE POSTCARDS

George Michael Patterson

ARCADIA PUBLISHING

ISBN 978-0-7385-1382-9

Published by Arcadia Publishing
Charleston, South Carolina

Printed in the United States of America

Library of Congress Catalog Card Number: 200109126

For all general information contact Arcadia Publishing at:
Telephone 843-853-2070
Fax 843-853-0044
E-mail sales@arcadiapublishing.com
For customer service and orders:
Toll-Free 1-888-313-2665

Visit us on the Internet at www.arcadiapublishing.com

Dedication

This author wishes to extend special gratitude to Ryan Michael and Brittany Catherine Patterson and especially to my wife, Janet Troutman Patterson, for support, for encouragement, and for being there for me while this book was being created. Also, to my mom, Nan Justice Patterson, and my dad, the late Louis Allen Patterson, for whom I thank God for their leadership, patience, guidance, and understanding. This book is dedicated to you.

Contents

ACKNOWLEDGMENTS

When I first thought of doing a book on postcards from Cabarrus County, I doubted that I would ever find enough cards to complete this project. I was pleasantly surprised to find such a large number of collectors who were willing to share their favorite postcards of Cabarrus County so that this book could become a reality. My sincere appreciation is extended to each of the many people who generously loaned postcards for this project (their names appear in this book with their cards).

I want to express my sincere appreciation to Wayne Chapman who introduced me to my first five postcards of Concord less than four years ago. Wayne set the hook for my passion for collecting "Concord" cards. I also offer my sincere appreciation to Mike Coltrane for the use of his personal collection, and for allowing me to use *The Progress Magazine* published by The Concord Telephone Company as a reference text.

A word of thanks also goes to Kathryn Bridges of Concord and Norris Dearmon of Kannapolis with the Charles A. Cannon Memorial Library for giving their support and helping with research as well as the use of postcards. My thanks to Carolyn Ritchie and Linda Grist of Historic Cabarrus and to Debbie Robb and Vicki Cline of the Eastern Cabarrus Historical Society for their invaluable help in finding cards with descriptions.

A very special thank you also goes to my dear friend Clarence E. Horton Jr. for sharing his vast knowledge of Cabarrus County history and for proofreading my work for accuracy. Finally, I want to thank Susan G. Sides for her guidance in this project and also Marian Harter and Jim Ramseur for generously allowing the use of their collections.

Introduction

In the early part of the 20th century picture-postcards became one of our nations most popular means of communicating. Between 1907 and 1914 more than a billion cards were manufactured. Thanks to the many traveling photographers and to people like O.V. Foust and Matthews Studio, which were just two of the firms located in Concord, today we can enjoy the views that their cameras captured more than 80 years ago.

Every image you will find within the pages of this book are, in fact, from a postcard. It is amazing to see the number of Cabarrus County cards that were produced so many years ago and the large number of these cards that still exist today. It seems that every time I check, I find another postcard and, often, one I didn't know existed. With the large number of people traveling by rail at the turn of the century, it is no wonder that many visitors to Cabarrus County would take the time to stop for a meal, to rest for the night, or to visit with friends or family, and, upon seeing a rack of postcards, would purchase one to send news back home of sights seen along their journey. People often would have picture postcards made of their children or other family members, and these served as a very inexpensive way to send pictures to relatives and friends.

Thus, one can understand the vast numbers of postcards in circulation today. It makes me wonder what it will be like a hundred years from now with our computer communications and e-mail messages. Will people be able to compile a book of things that happen way back in 2001 based on computer images? It certainly makes you want to be careful what you put into your computer or on that $3^{1}/_{2}$-inch floppy disk.

My hope in creating this book is to express through the medium of postcards a little bit of what Cabarrus County, North Carolina—its street life, buildings, and the people themselves—was like in the early 20th century. Many of the sites depicted no longer exist and most of the people are gone forever. Hopefully, this book will be a pleasant reminder of times that have slowly faded away.

One

Novelties

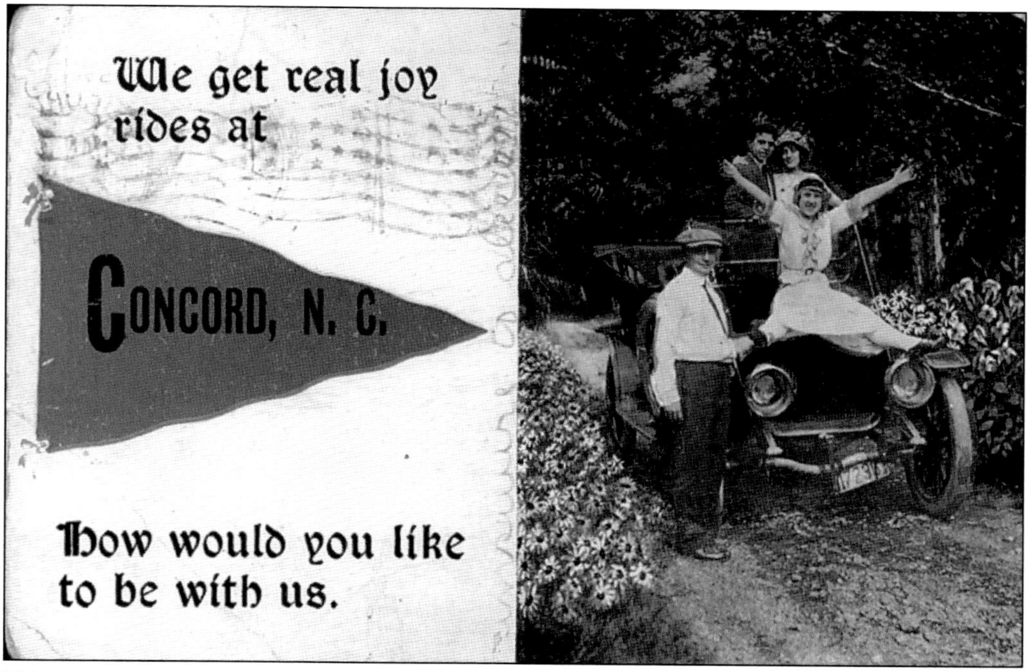

This generic postcard,with a postmark of 1915, features Concord, North Carolina, although it could be Anytown, U.S.A. The people in this card have nothing to do with Concord other than they are young and enjoying life. (Courtesy of Don and Vicki Cline.)

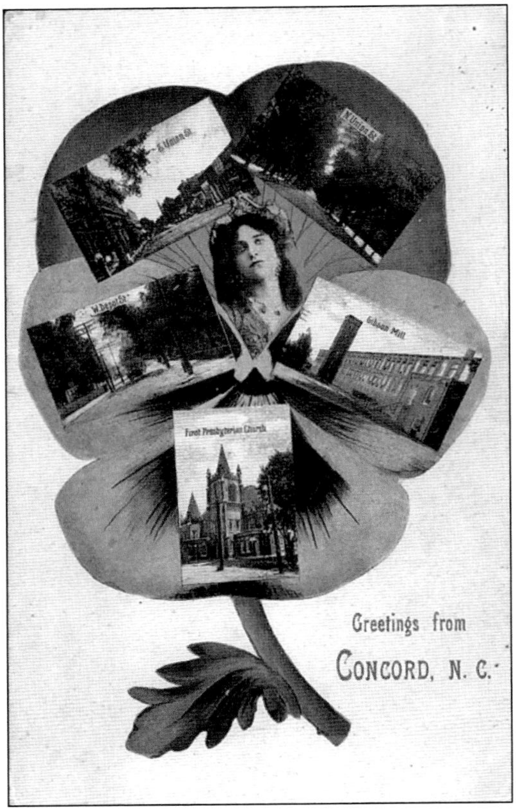

The Paul Koebler Publishing firm was responsible for this Pansy Lady format, which features, from top left clockwise, South Union Street, North Union Street, Gibson Mill, First Presbyterian Church, and Depot Street. (Courtesy of Mike Coltrane.)

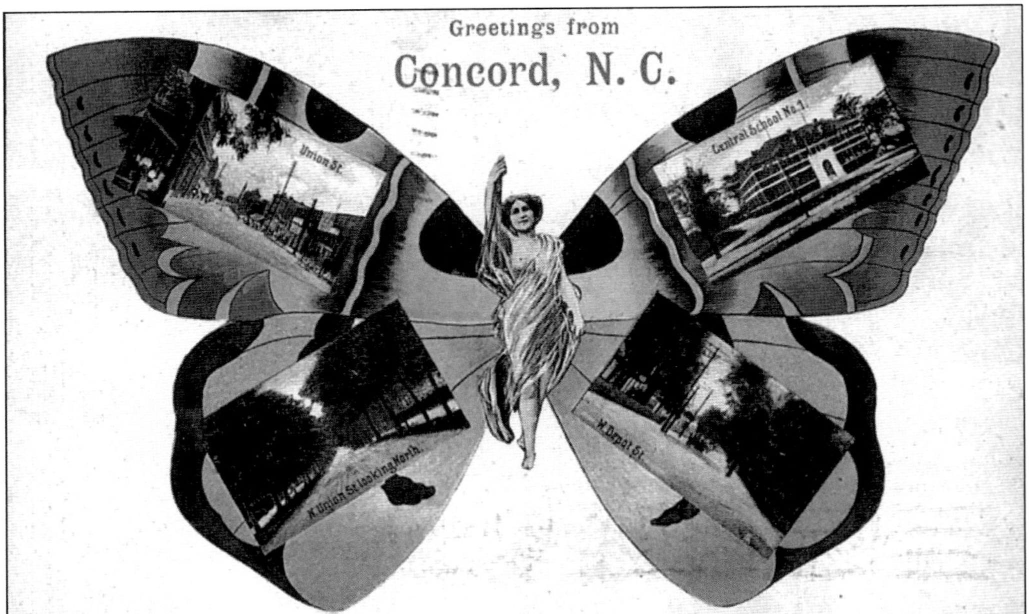

A card postmarked 1908 in the Butterfly format by the Paul Koebler Publishing firm features in its design downtown Union Street, Central School # 1, West Depot, and North Union Street. This card was distributed by H.L. Parks & Co. (Courtesy of Wayne Chapman.)

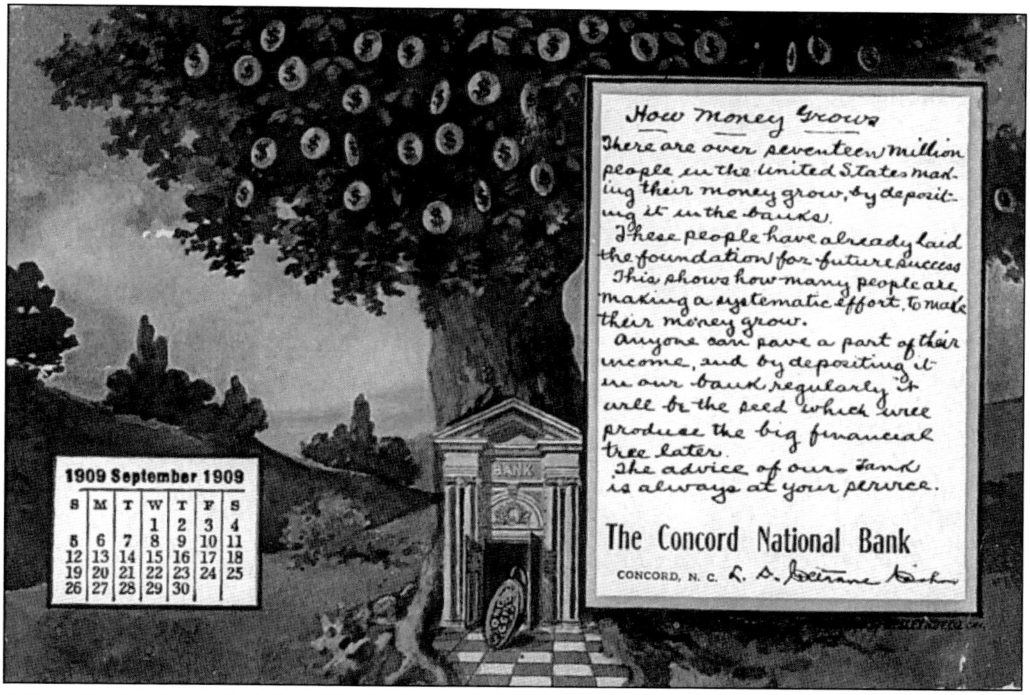

Offered by the Concord National Bank, this postcard was handy in that it utilized a monthly calendar. The card features a note from bank president L.D. Coltrane on "How Money Grows," and its calendar is for the month of September 1909. (Courtesy of Mike Coltrane.)

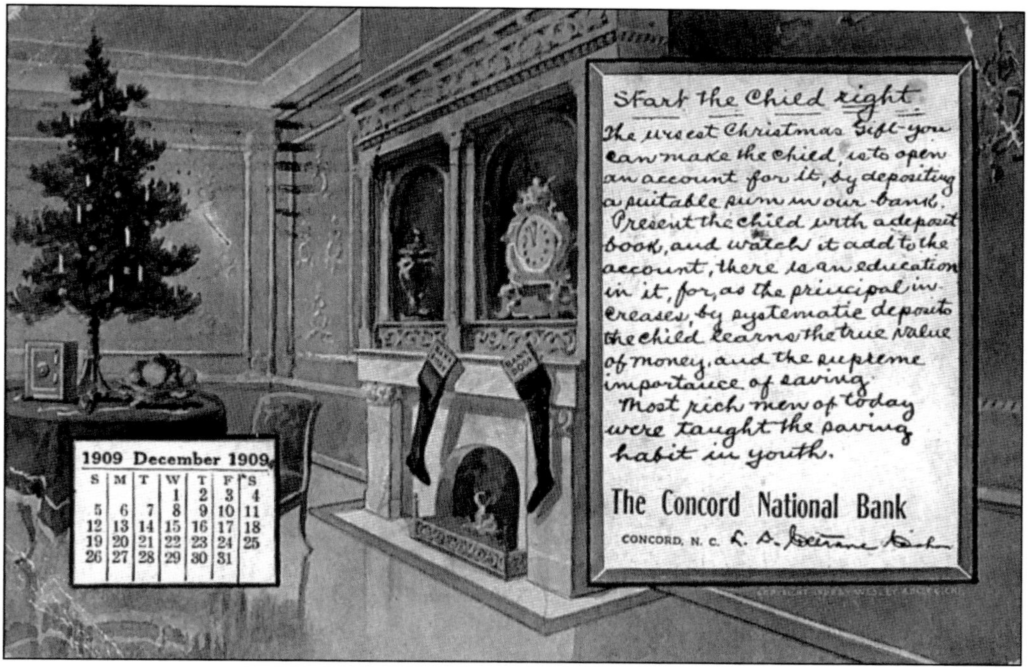

Another Concord National Bank postcard for the month of December 1909 spotlights Christmas and "Start the Child Right" as the lesson. (Courtesy of Marian Harter.)

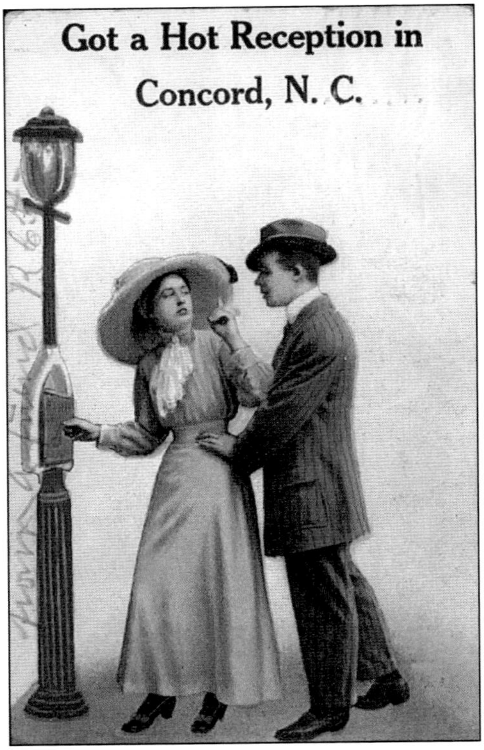

An early generic card features Concord and is postmarked 1912. Note the wording in the title as well as the couple's clothing. (Courtesy of Don and Vickie Cline.)

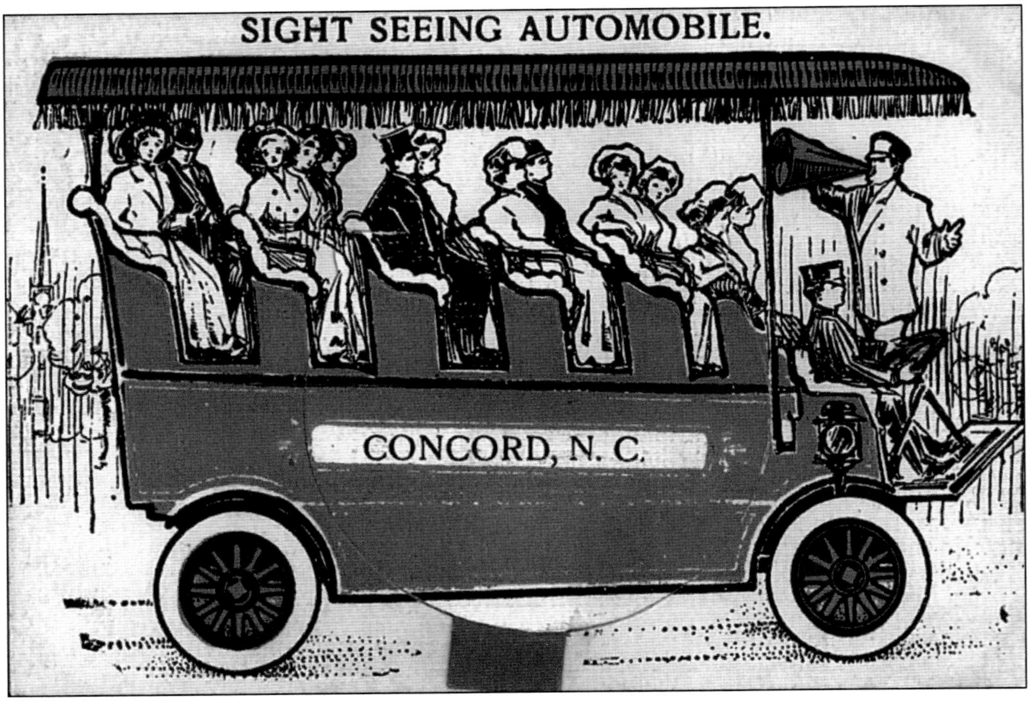

A most unusual generic card shows a "Sight Seeing" automobile. This card had an opening on the face, which when opened would allow for a group of "miniature" pictures of Concord to unfold like a private sightseeing tour of Concord. This card dates to around 1909 and was published by O.V. Foust.

Many companies used a generic design for postcards that were sold across the country. It is interesting to note the subject matter in postcards. This early card features Kannapolis and shows a relaxed couple enjoying the moment. (Courtesy of Marian Harter.)

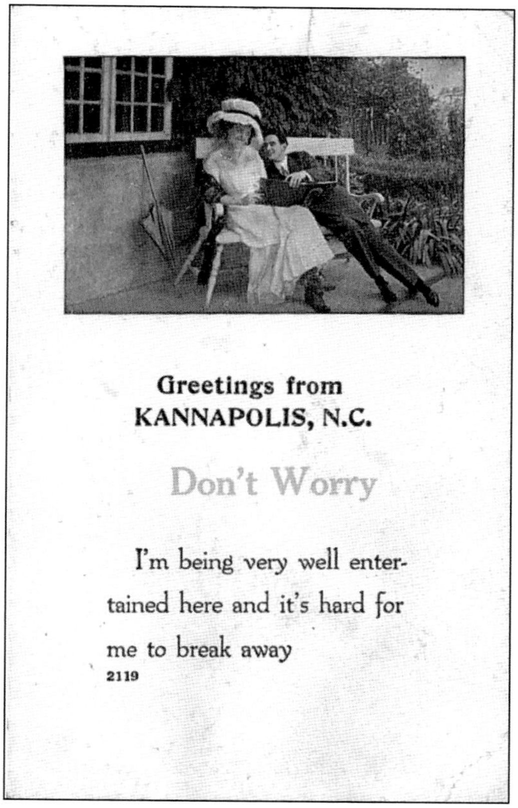

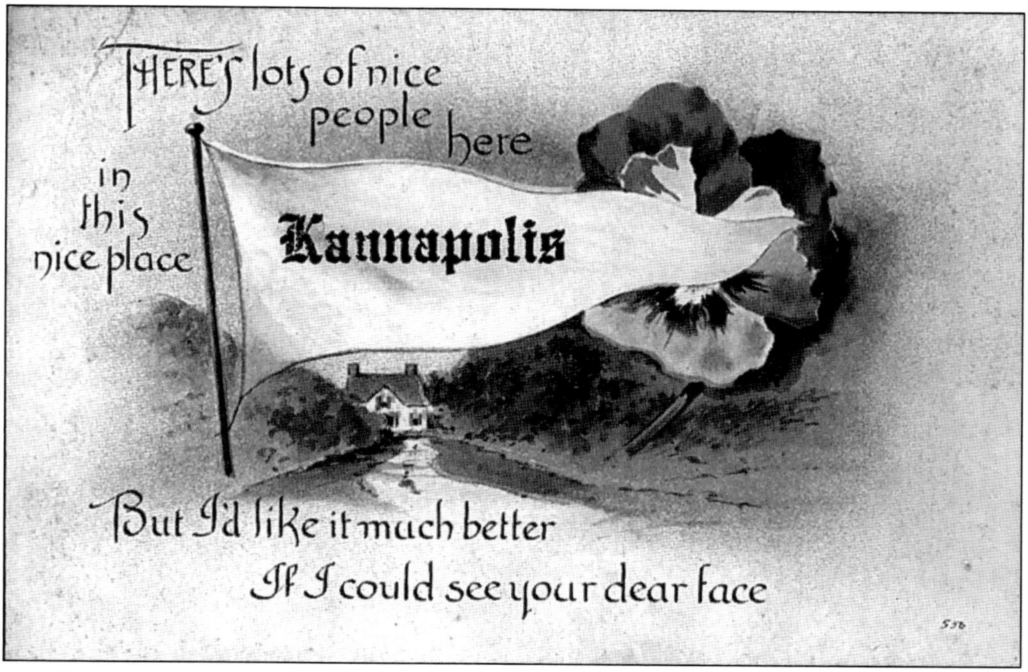

Does this postcard make you want to visit Kannapolis? The makers of this card sure would hope so. (Courtesy of Susan G. Sides.)

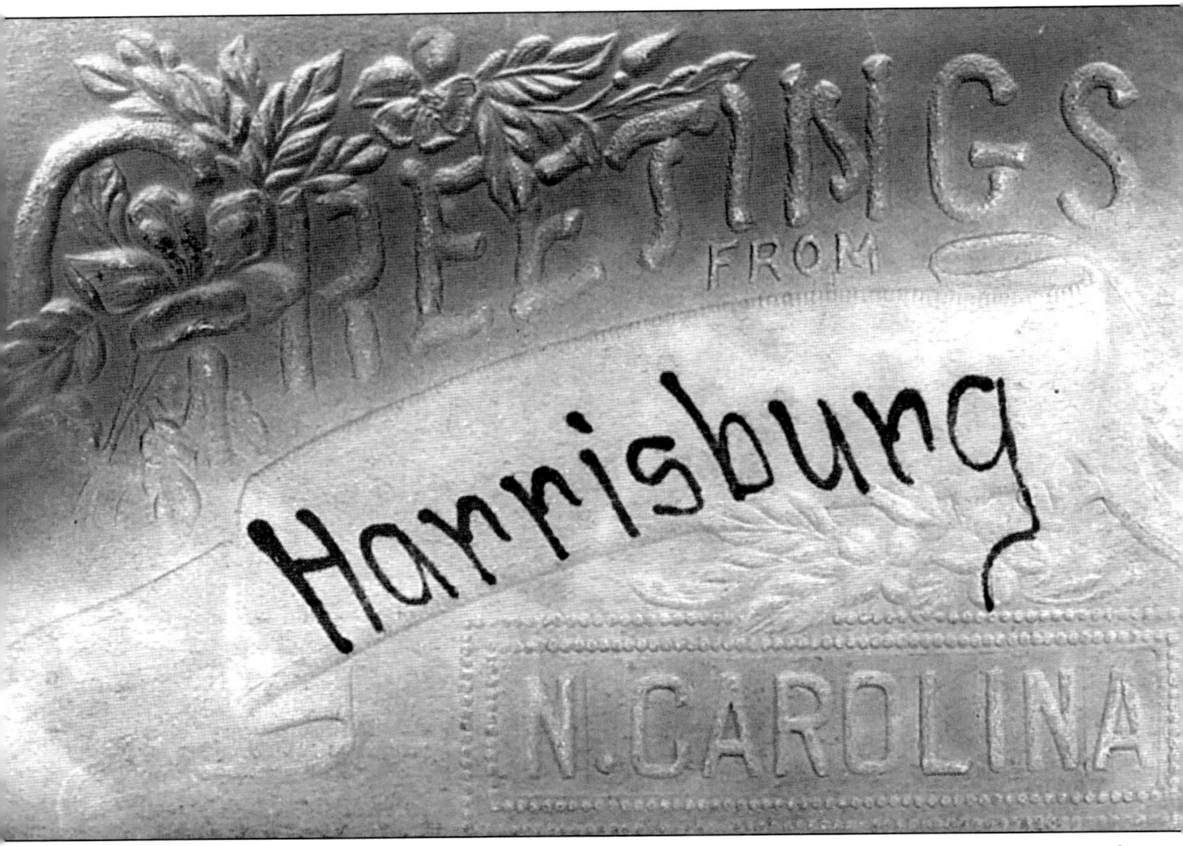

Postmarked in 1910, the word "Harrisburg" is in bold, bright, red ink and the card has a pastel blue top and a rich, pink bottom. In raised letters are the words "Greetings from Harrisburg, N. Carolina."

Two

Residential Street Scenes

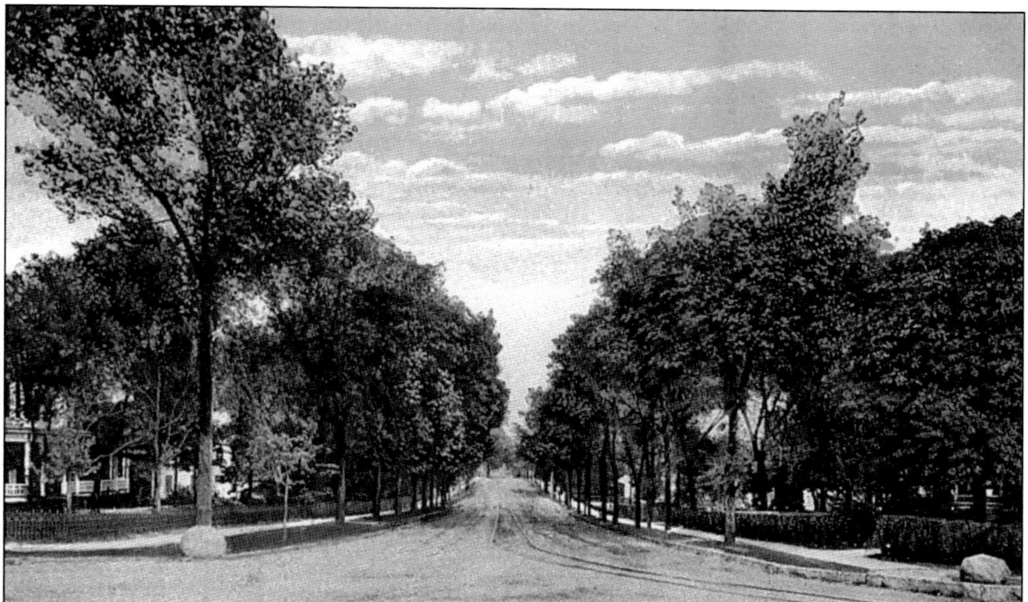

North Union Street at the Odell Mill was located in the area known as the Forest Hill Community. Notice the streetcar track turning off North Union Street at Buffalo Street (Beattie Road) and going west to the Gibson Mill community. (Courtesy of the Charles A. Cannon Memorial Library.)

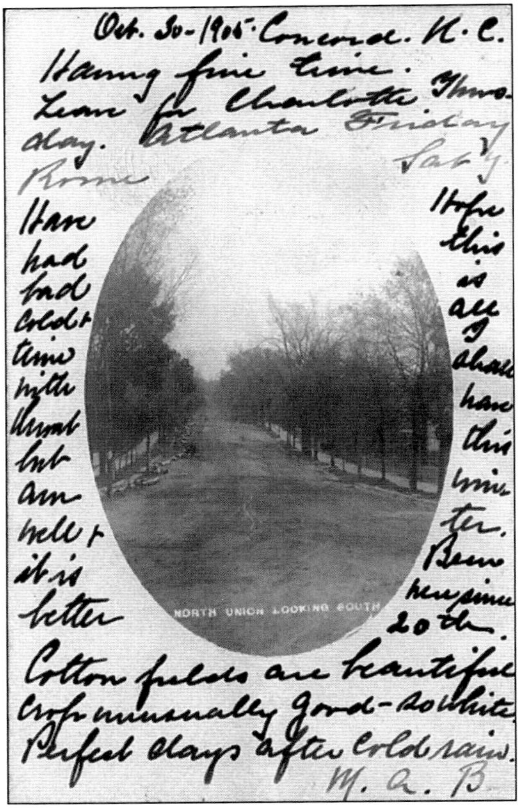

Postmarked 1905, this card shows the same shot of North Union Street as does the image on page 15. The image uses a popular oval format, and the sender in this case used the front to scribble a message.

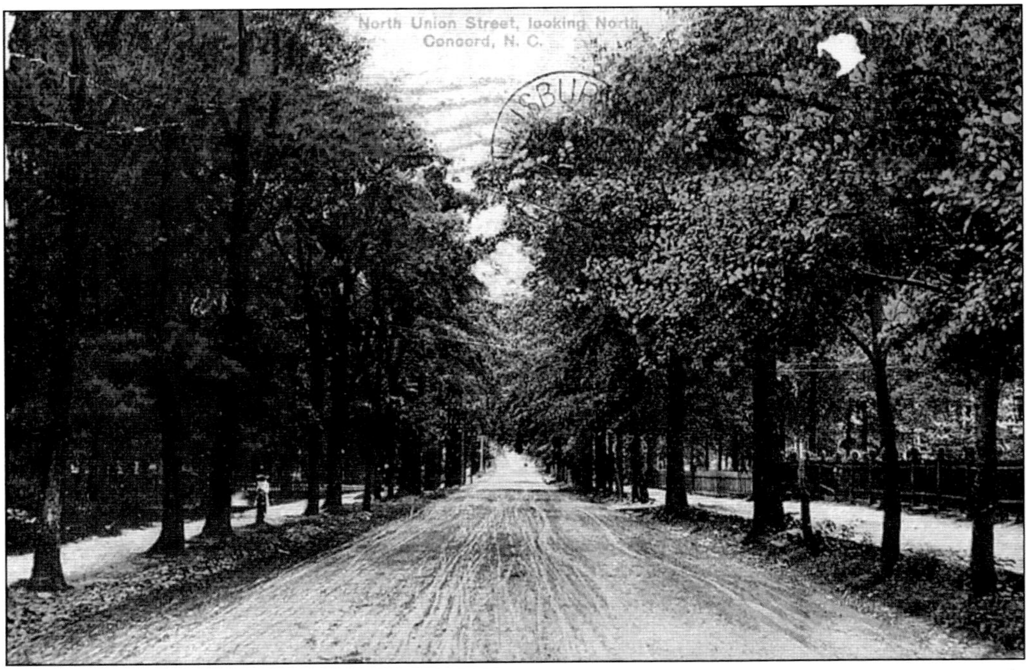

A beautiful tree-lined North Union Street has a tranquil look much as it does today. This image was made around 1906 and was captured by O.V. Foust, a local photographer. (Courtesy of Jim Ramseur.)

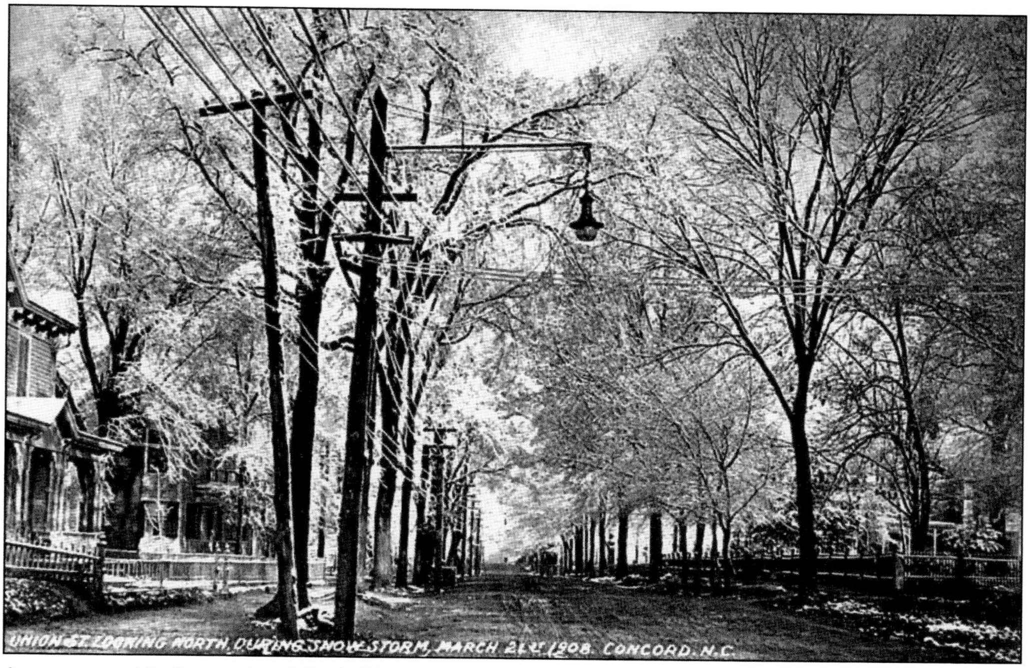

A snowstorm hit Concord on March 21, 1908, as depicted in this view of Union Street looking north. The first house on the left is that of Dr. Robert S. Young whose father was a great soldier in the Army of the Confederacy. This property was adjacent to that of Victor Barringer to the south. Attention should be given to the peace and beauty of the scene even in winter. (Courtesy of Wayne Chapman.)

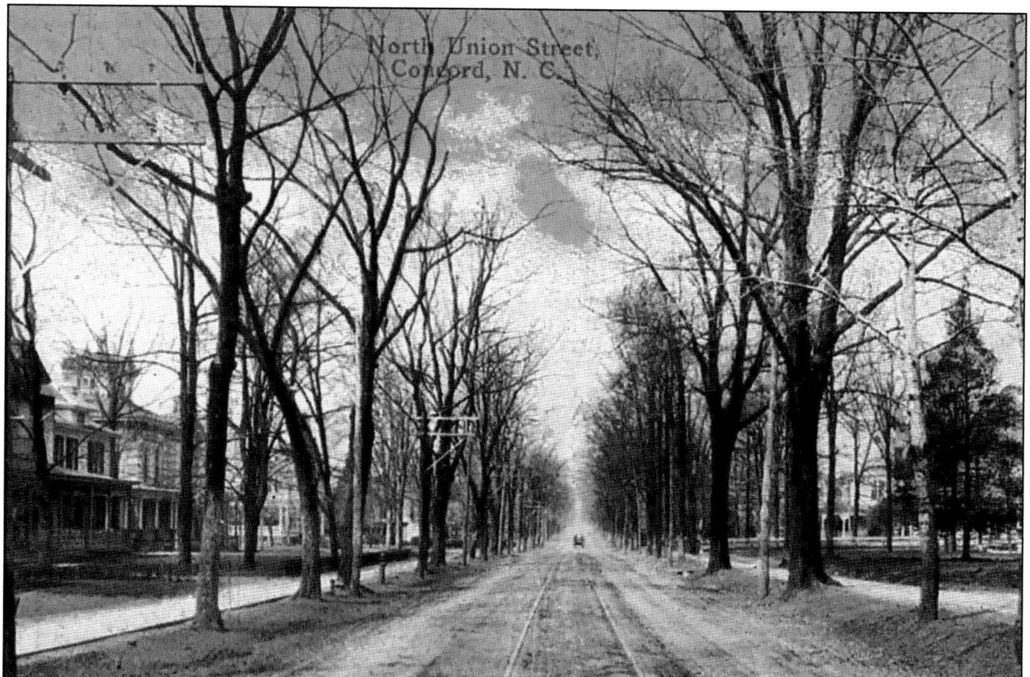

North Union Street, located just at the edge of the business section, is shown in this view looking north. (Courtesy of the Charles A. Cannon Memorial Library.)

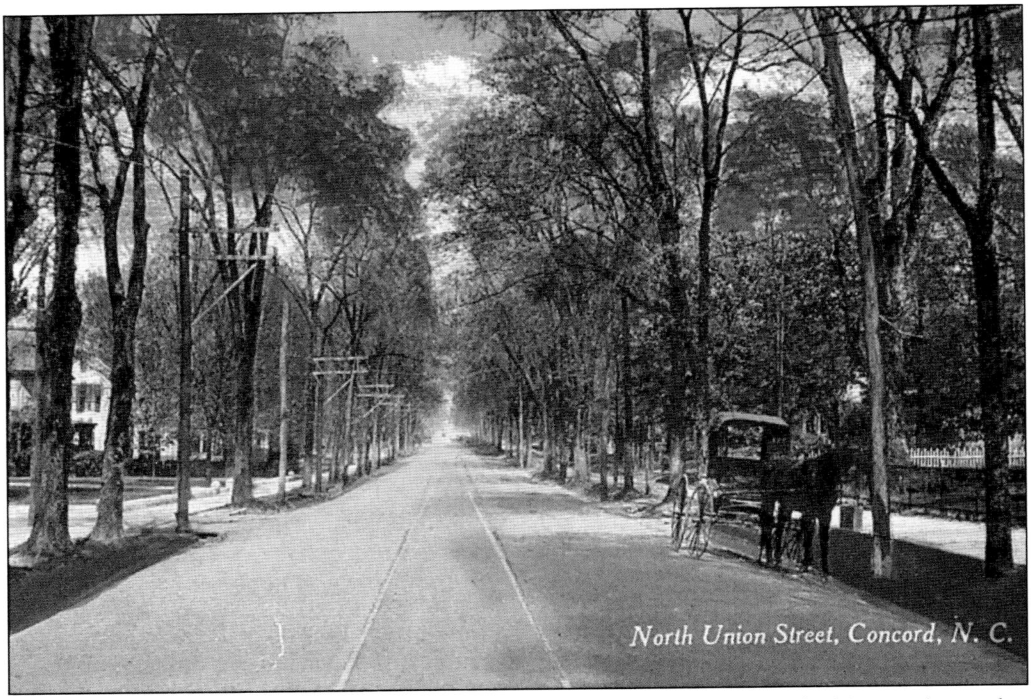

The photographer of this interesting postcard, made about 1913 of Union Street looking north, stood at today's Killarney Street to snap this image. In the middle of Union Street the street car tracks can be seen running up North Union to the Odell Mill. Dr. L.M. Archey's house is just on the right and his horse and buggy is hitched to a post in front of his home.

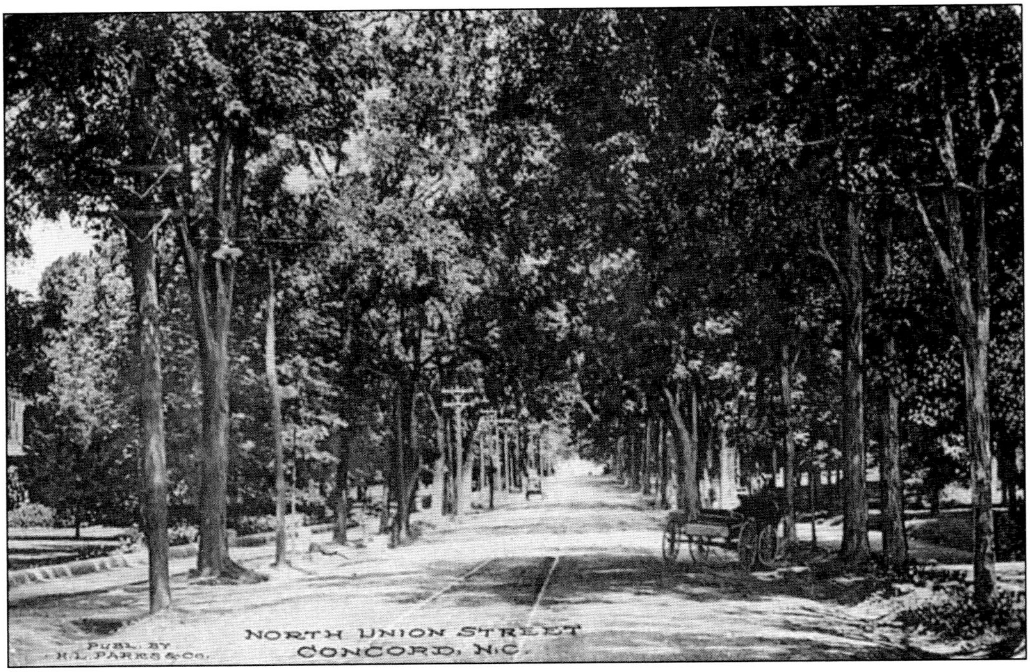

Another image of North Union Street gives onlookers a feeling of the tranquility of this peaceful, quiet, Southern town. (Courtesy of Mike Coltrane.)

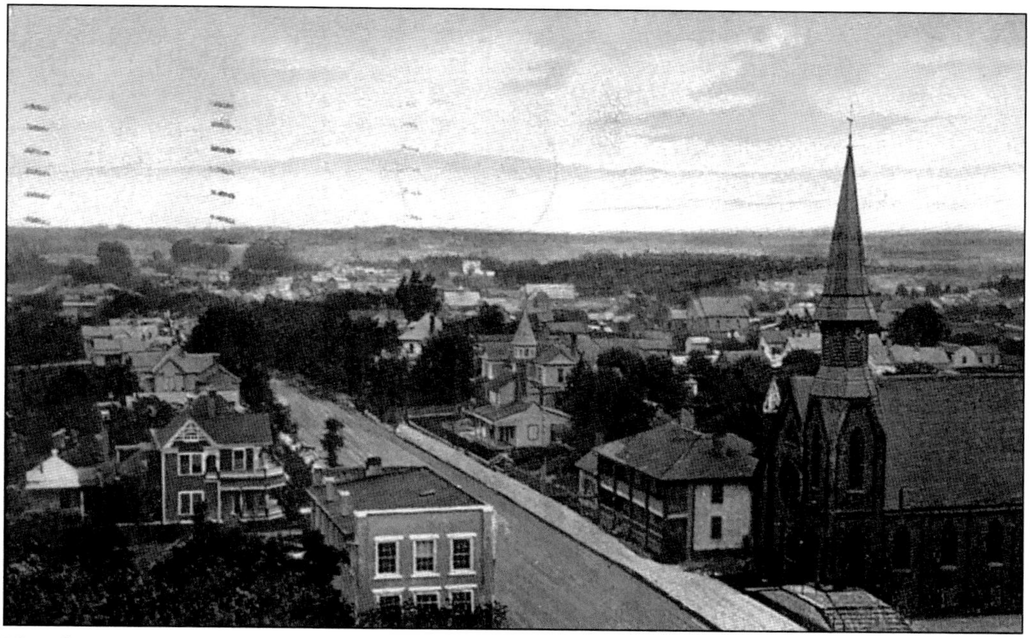

The photographer of this image placed his camera on top of the Allison Building at South Union Street and Corban Street. St. James Lutheran Church is on the right followed by the Foard Boarding House, operated by Robert W. Foard. The small building at the end was used as a tailor shop and was owned by a Mr. Williams. Beyond the tailor shop is the Ransom Winecoff home. (Courtesy of Wayne Chapman.)

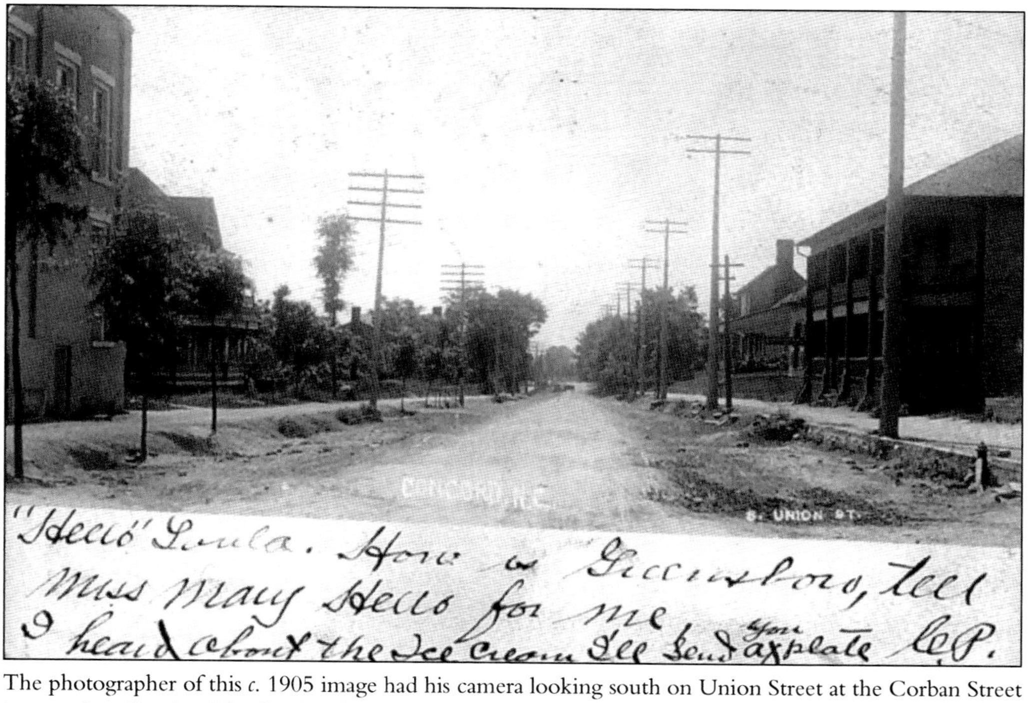

The photographer of this *c.* 1905 image had his camera looking south on Union Street at the Corban Street intersection. On the right the Foard House, built by John Phifer, in 1804 can be seen. On the left you can just see the two-story Masonic Temple, the Zeb Morris home, the Miss Alice Bost home, and then the R. Vic Blackwelder home. (Courtesy of Historic Cabarrus.)

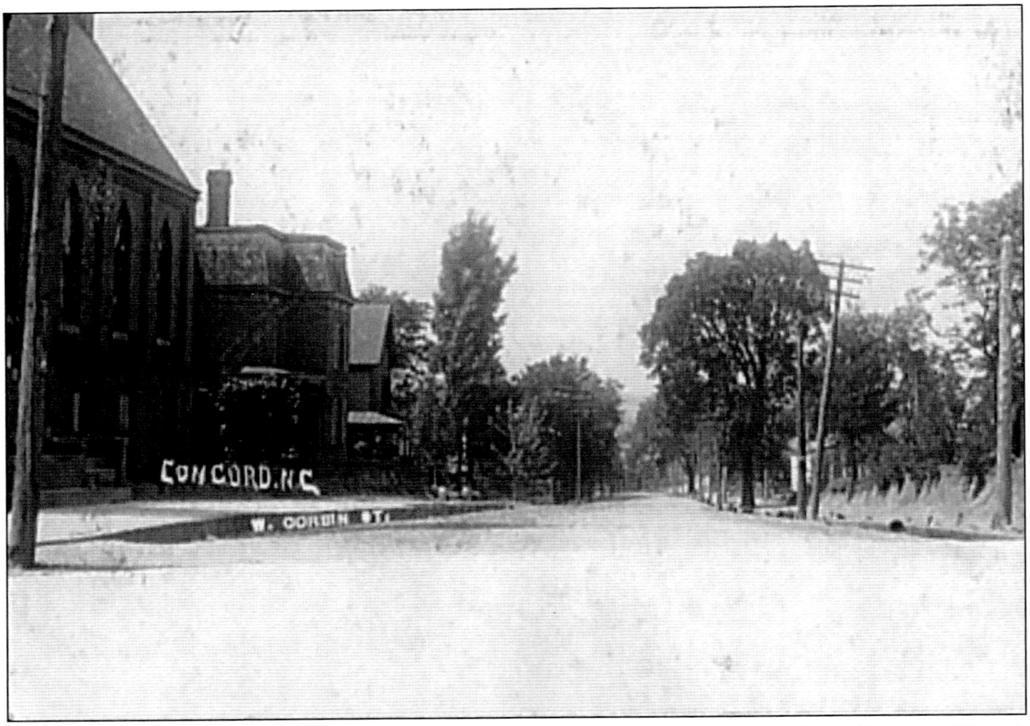

Looking down West Corban Street at South Union Street, this postcard shows St. James Lutheran Church on the left, followed by the church parish. About eight-tenths of a mile down this road was Concord's train depot. This card was published around 1905. (Courtesy of Durwood Barbour.)

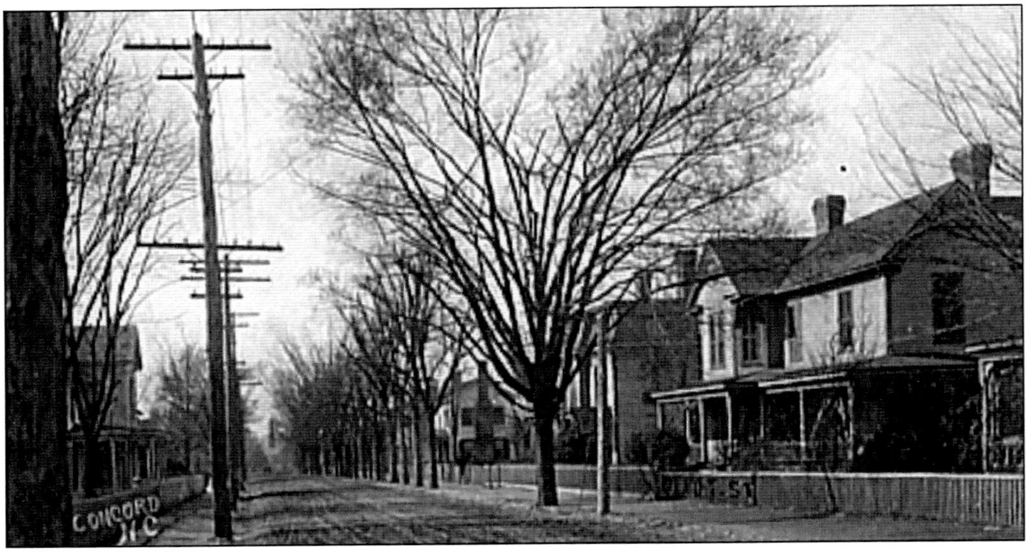

This location, West Depot Street at Spring Street, shows Mrs. J.F. Goodson's home, the first on the right. The third home belonged to Mr. D.B. Morrison. It is of interest that most homes utilized fences to keep stray animals from doing damage to personal property. (Courtesy of Durwood Barbour.)

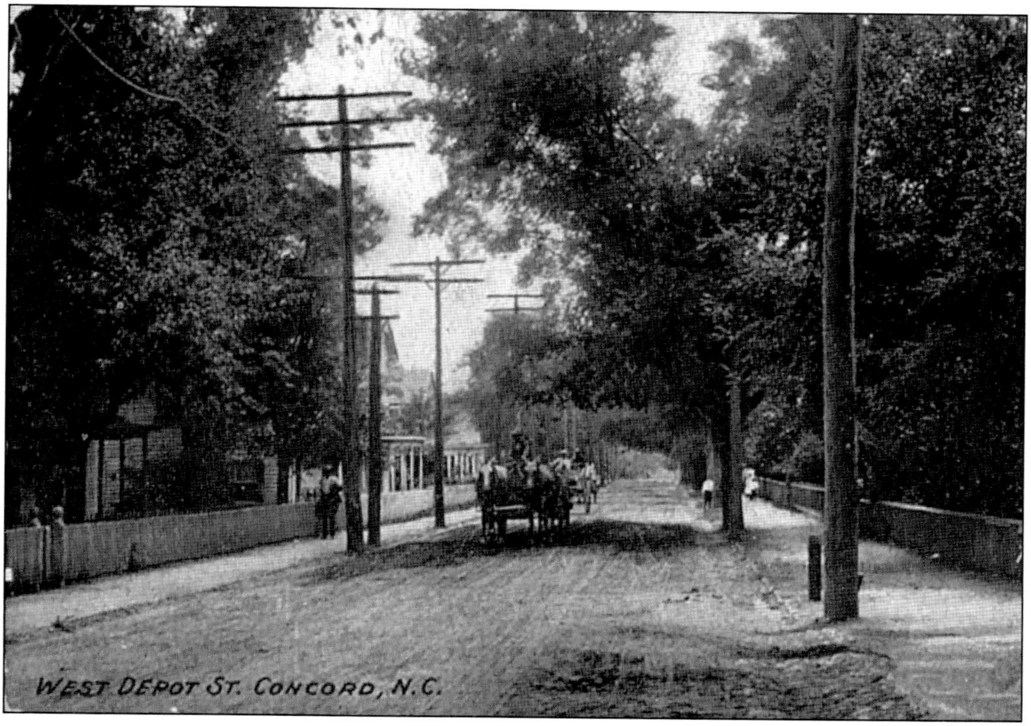

The postmark on this interesting card, published by the White, Morrison, Flowe Company, is 1907. The wagons are heading east towards town on West Depot Street. In three more years the streetcar tracks will run from town to just past the Scotia Seminary, four blocks beyond this point.

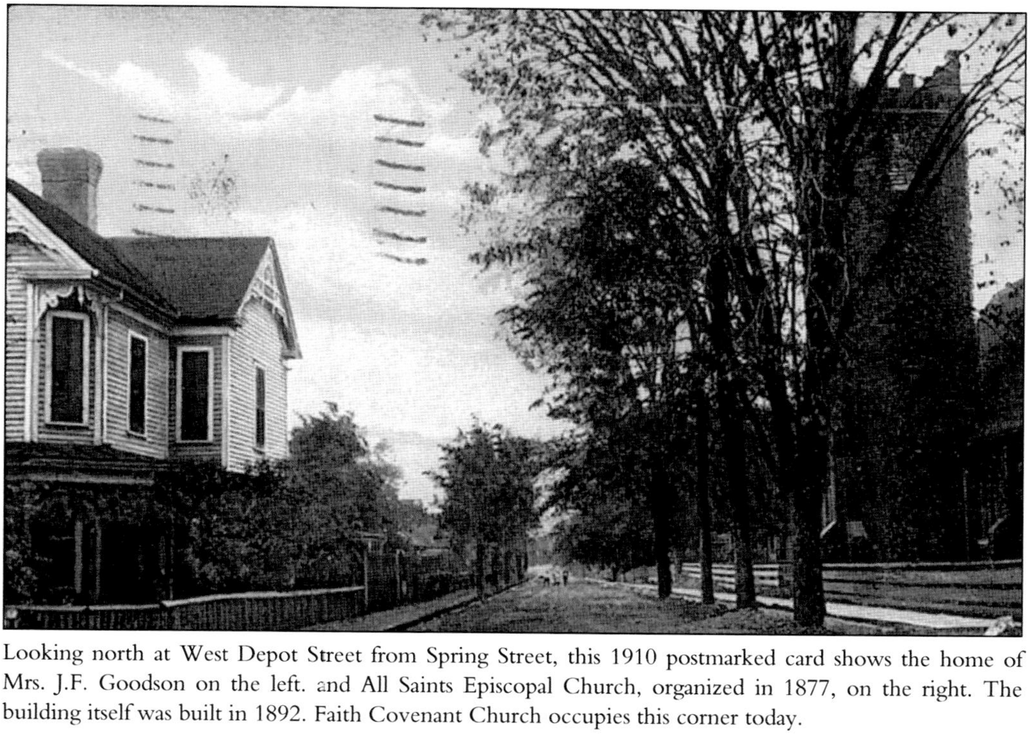

Looking north at West Depot Street from Spring Street, this 1910 postmarked card shows the home of Mrs. J.F. Goodson on the left. and All Saints Episcopal Church, organized in 1877, on the right. The building itself was built in 1892. Faith Covenant Church occupies this corner today.

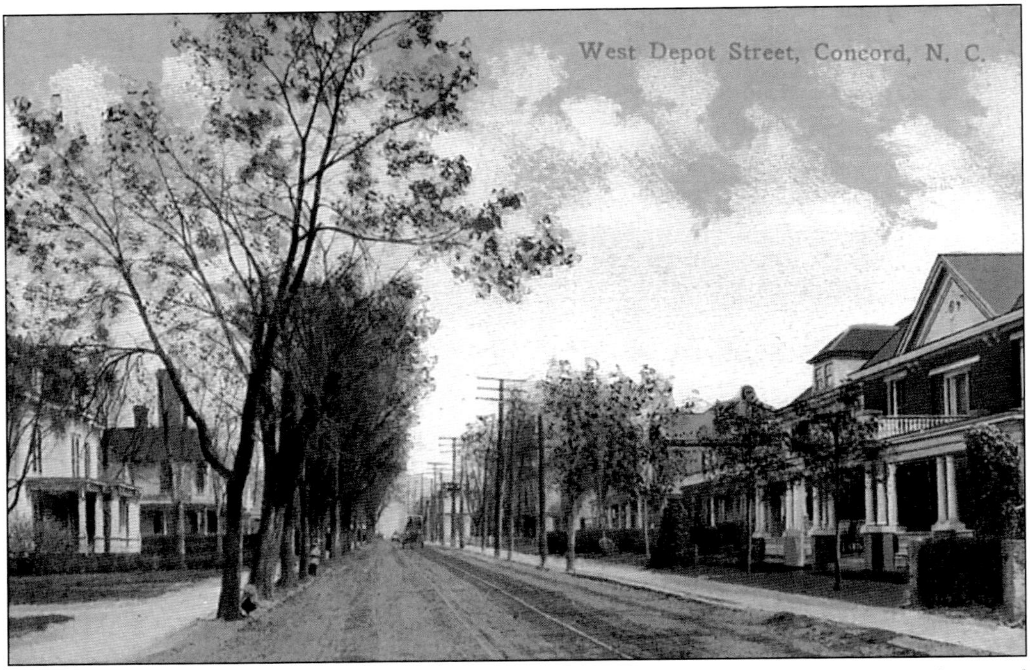

West Depot Street looking east is the subject of this June 1915 postmarked card. The photographer stood about where Yorktown Street joins Depot Street (Cabarrus Avenue) to snap his image. (Courtesy of Marian Harter.)

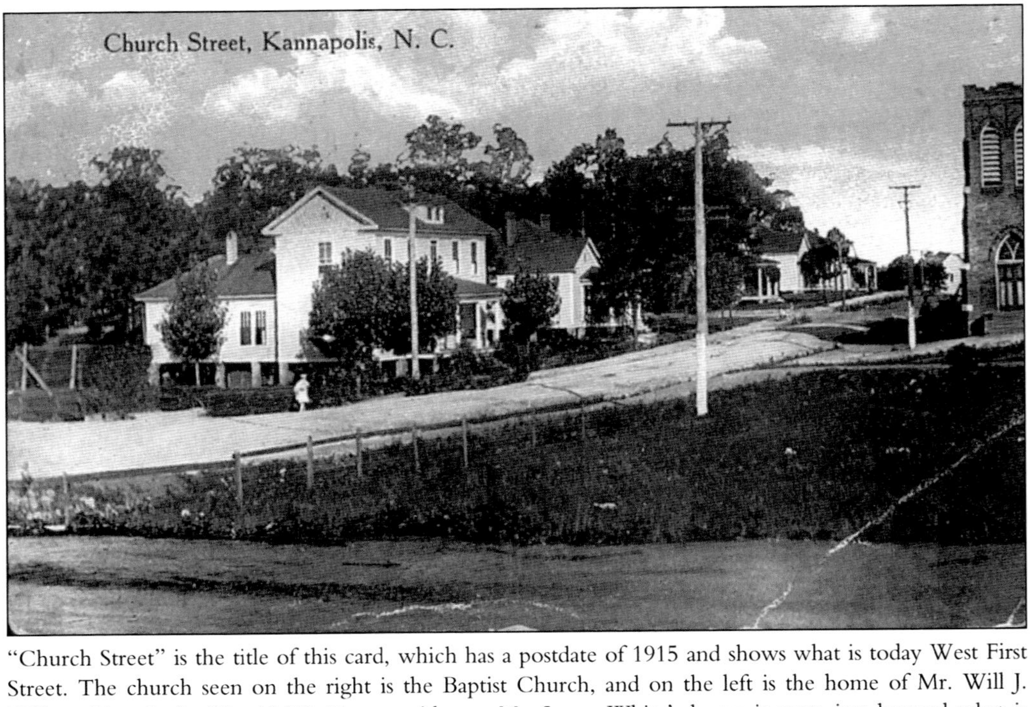

"Church Street" is the title of this card, which has a postdate of 1915 and shows what is today West First Street. The church seen on the right is the Baptist Church, and on the left is the home of Mr. Will J. Willett. Next is the Harold W. Nantz residence. Mr. James White's home is next, just beyond what is today's West Avenue. Mr. G.C. "Grover" Maulden owned a home that sat near this point. (Courtesy of Susan G. Sides.)

Three

Business Scenes

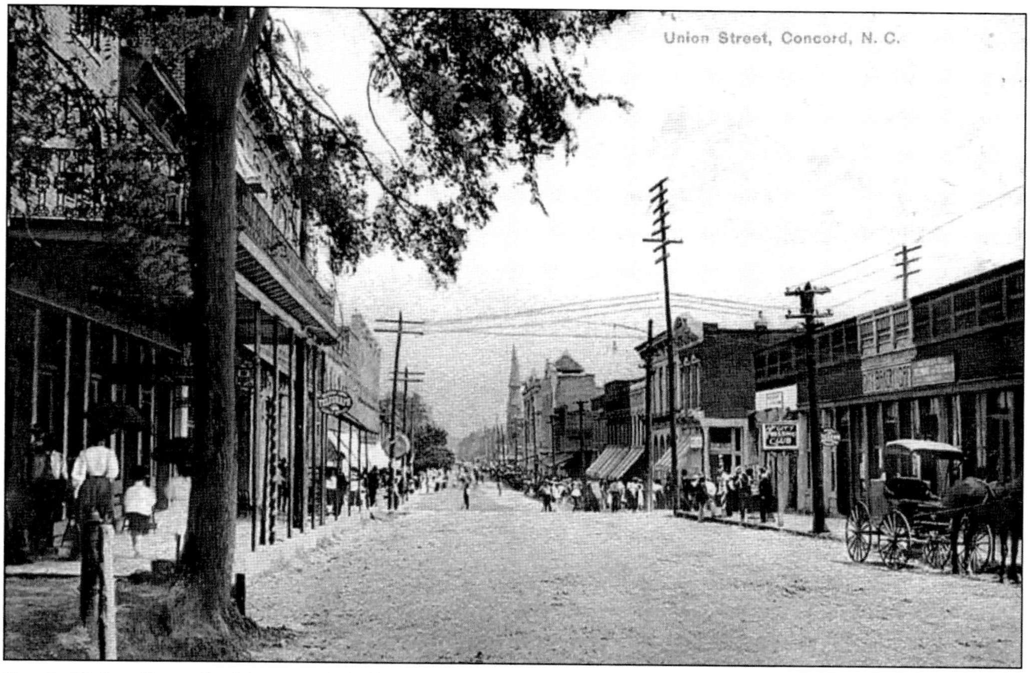

North Union Street looking south is the view shown on this card made around 1905. The photographer set his camera just at the edge of downtown to photograph the St. Cloud Hotel, its balcony being first on the left. On the right is a horse and buggy, which sits in front of the office of Dr. L.M. Archer. St. James Lutheran Church can be seen at the far end of the Concord business district.

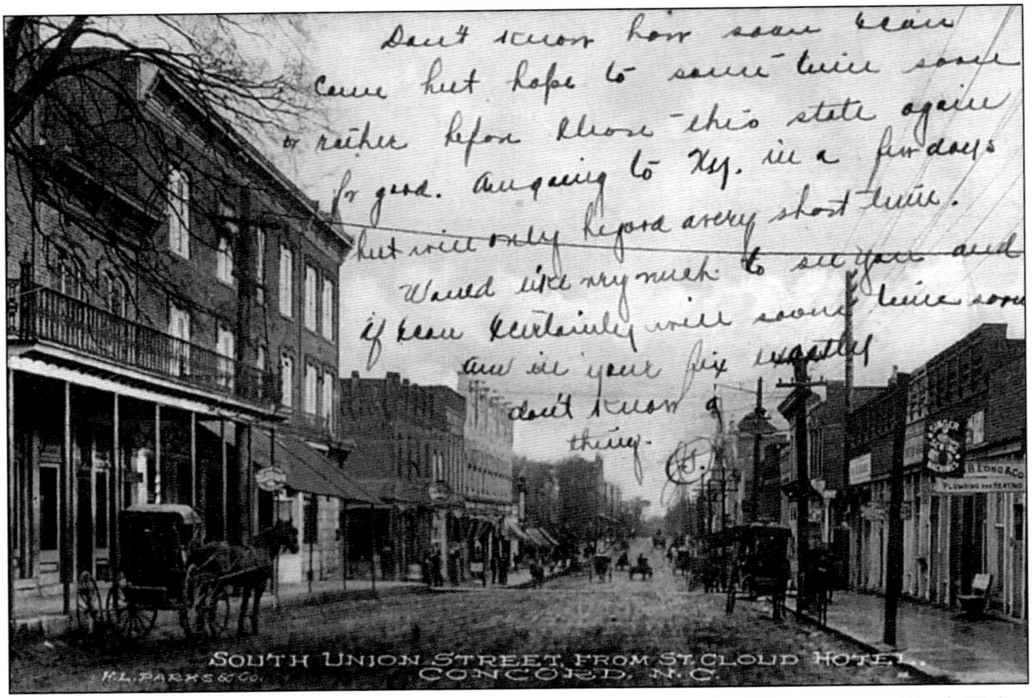

The photographer of this 1910-postmarked card was positioned just north of the square on North Union Street looking south. On the left is the St. Cloud Hotel owned by J.M. Odell, J.W. Cannon, D.F. Cannon, and G.M. Lore. This card was published by H.L. Parks & Co.

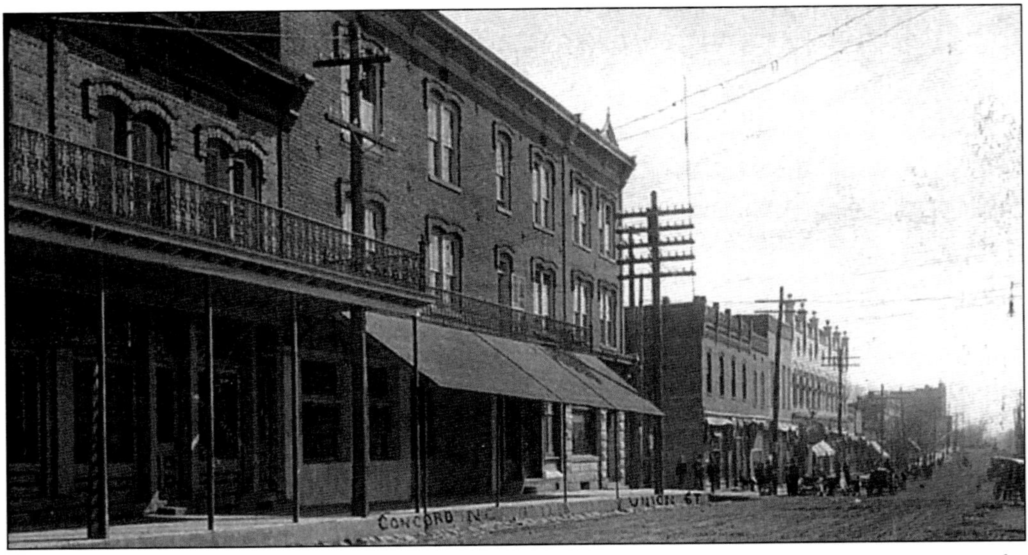

The three-story St. Cloud Hotel was built by one of Concord's finest architects, Mr. A.H. Propst. On the corner at the square was the Concord National Bank. (Courtesy of Durwood Barbour.)

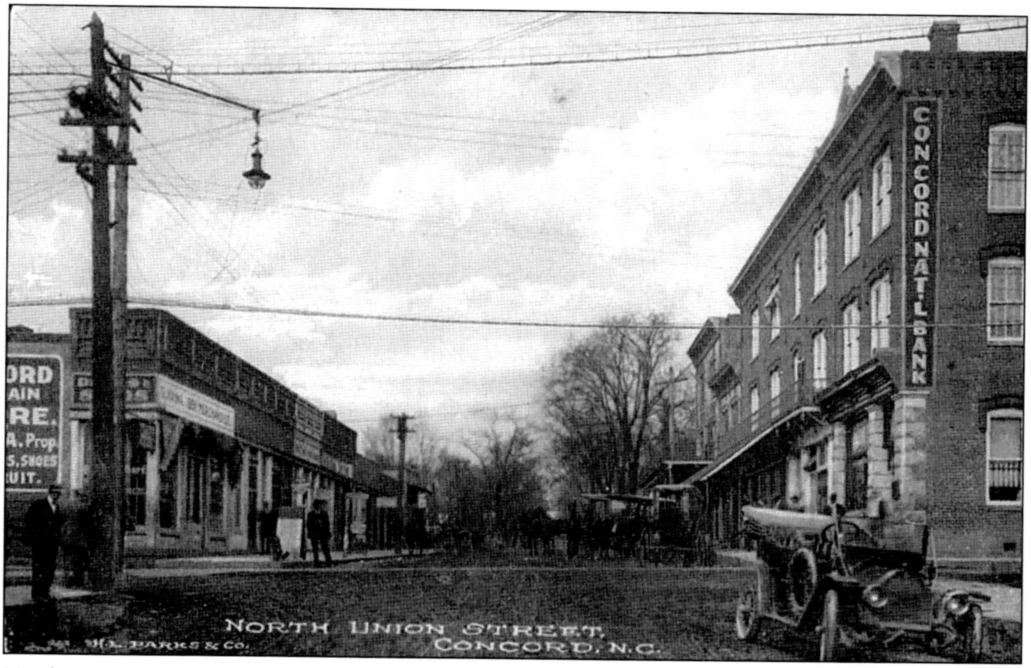

North Union Street at the square is the scene of this card published by H.L. Parks & Co. Concord National Bank can be seen on the right and attention is drawn to the arc light at the square. This type of street lighting was considered to be the best in its time. (Courtesy of Wayne Chapman.)

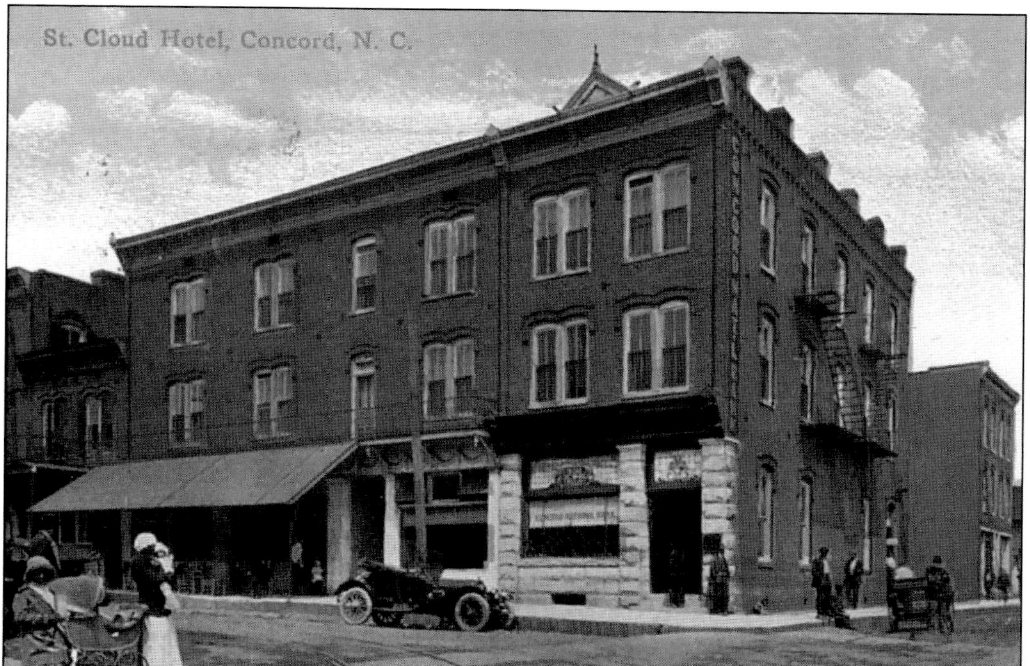

Shown here is a great image of the Concord National Bank. Behind the bank was the Concord Telephone Company followed by the Brown Livery Stable and then William Propst's house. (Courtesy of Bub and Jane Craver.)

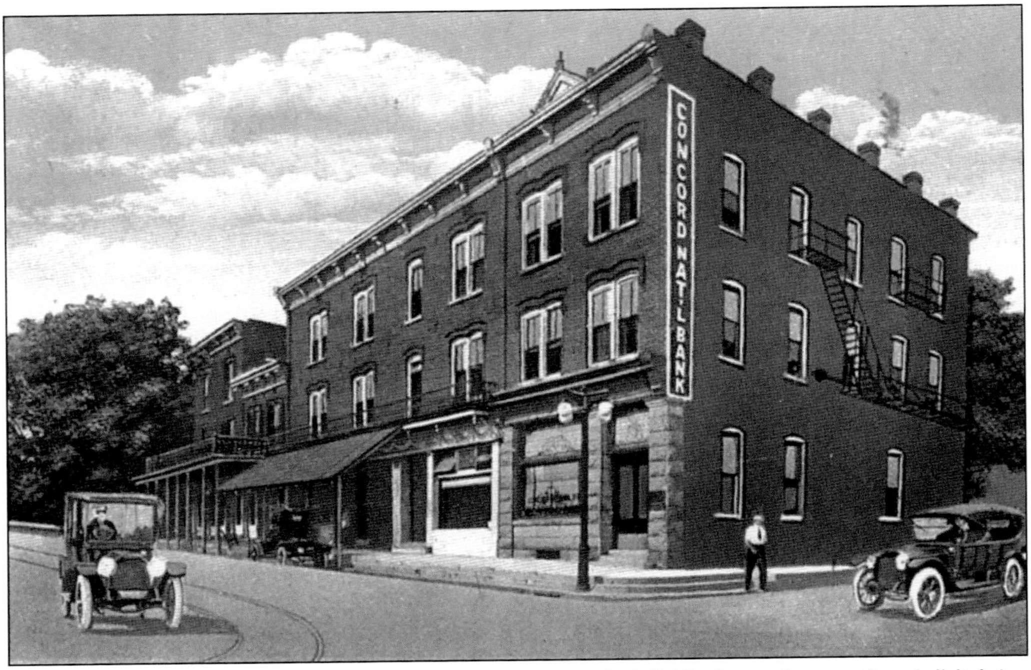

A very similar view of the Concord National Bank, postmarked 1919, shows the new four-ball lighting system. This lighting modernization occurred in the city in 1914. (Courtesy of Marian Harter.)

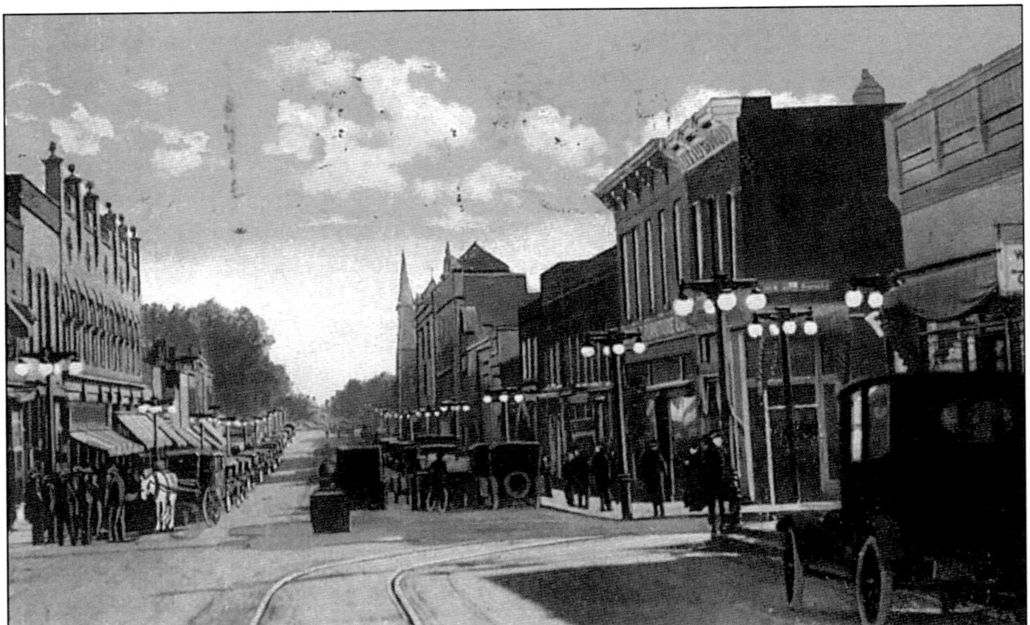

This postcard, looking south on Union Street at the city square in the 1920s, shows Davis Drug Store on the right with Gibsons Drug Store on the left. (Courtesy of Marian Harter.)

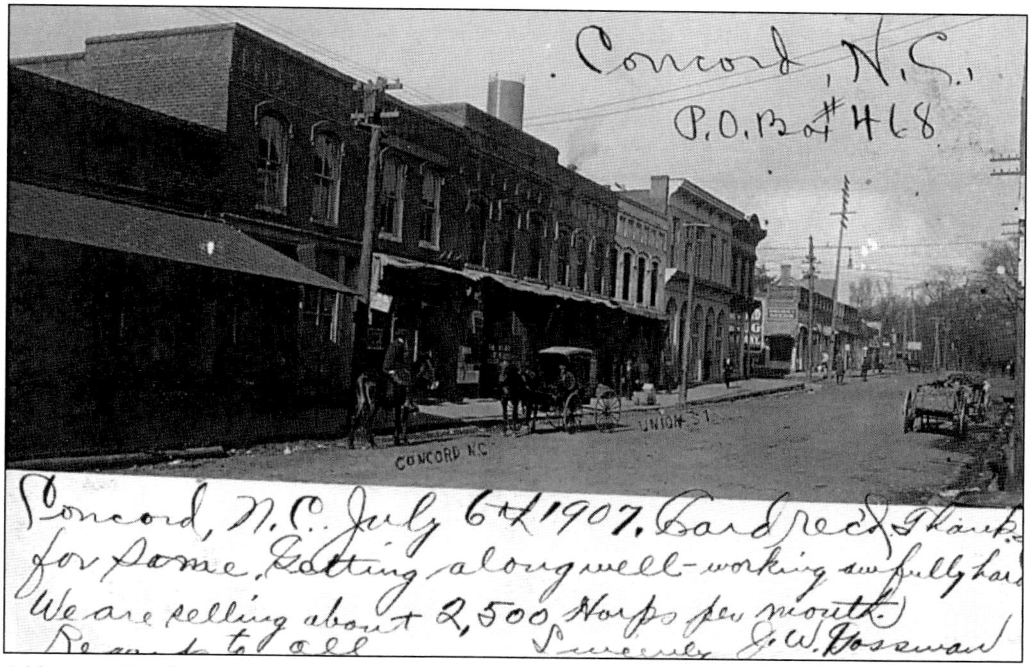

A blue-toned card taken around 1905 shows the west side of South Union Street looking North. The photographer stood just half a block south of the square to catch this image. (Courtesy of Wayne Chapman.)

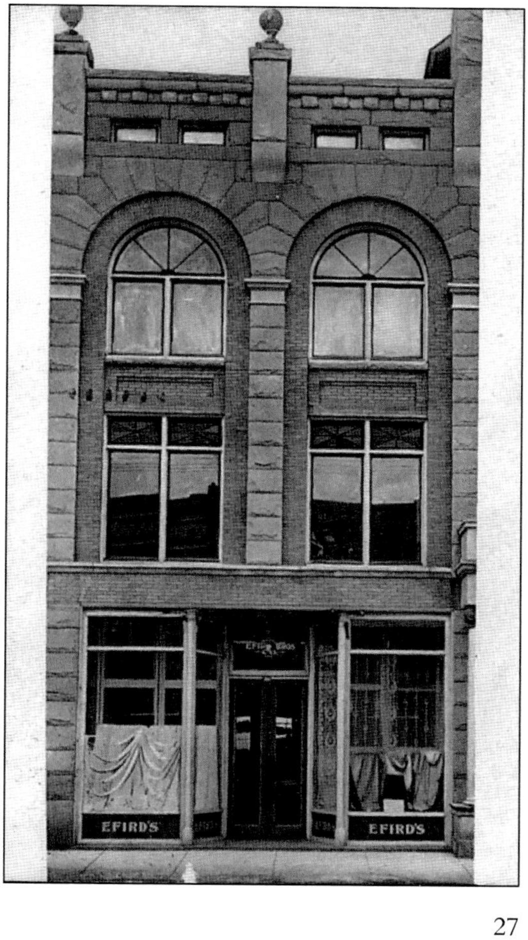

Efird's Department Store, owned by Mr. Joe B. Efird, utilized the south end of the Pythian Building. To the north were stairs leading to the second floor and the Pythian Grand Lodge. (Courtesy of Wayne Chapman.)

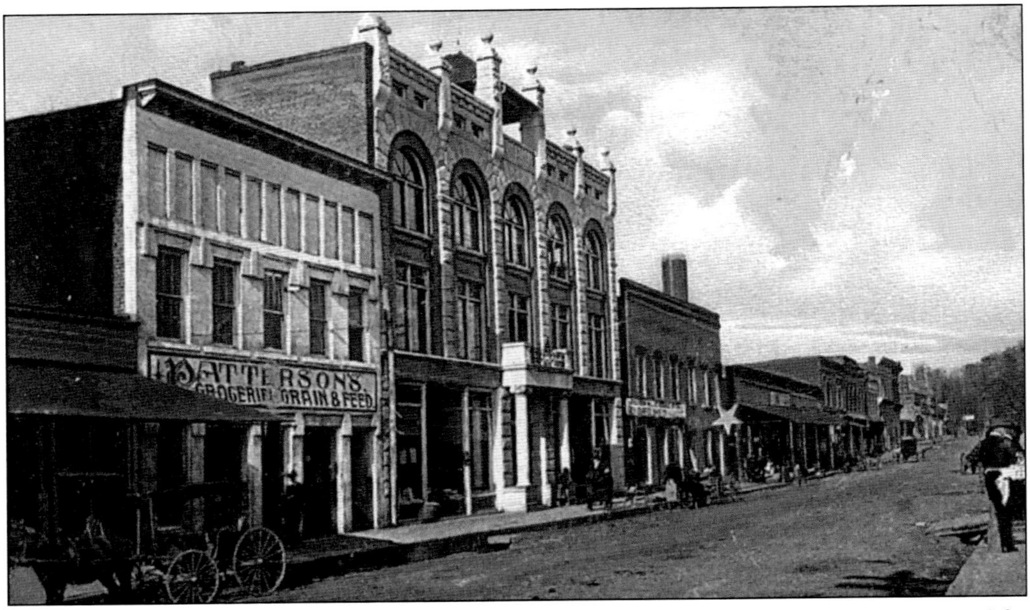

The three-story building in the center of this card is the Pythian Building. Built in 1903, it was named for the Knights of Pythias, a fraternal order. George W. Patterson's Grocery, Grain and Feed is located to the left. Jetting out over the building just to the right of the Pythian Building is the standpipe, which held the city's water supply.

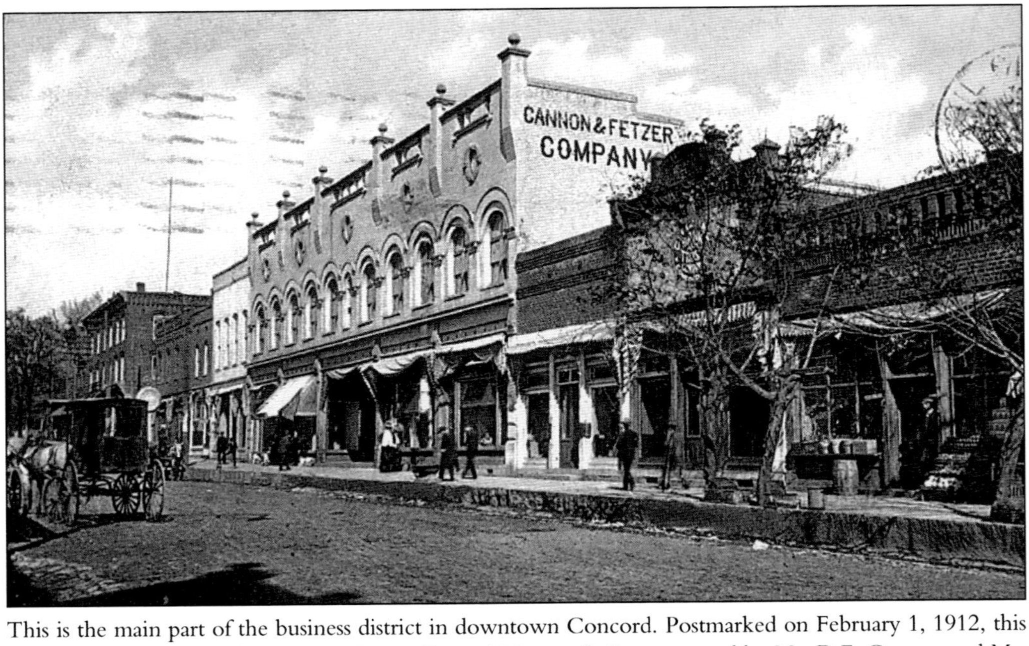

This is the main part of the business district in downtown Concord. Postmarked on February 1, 1912, this postcard is centered on the Cannon-Fetzer General Mercantile Store, owned by Mr. D.F. Cannon and Mr. P.B. Fetzer. The second building below Cannon-Fetzer, seen faintly through the tree, is the Citizens Bank and Trust building.

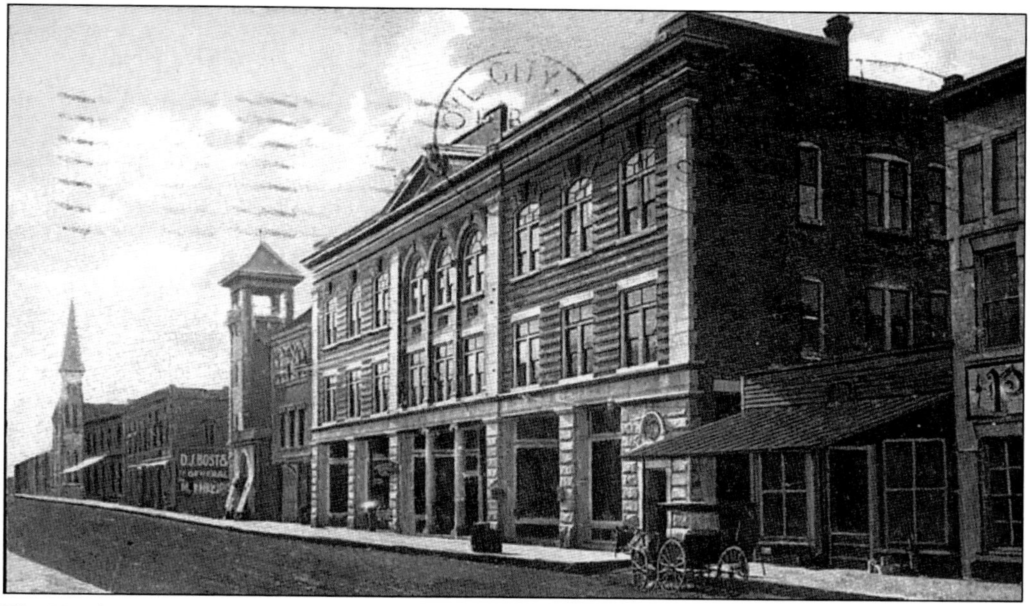

The Hotel Normandy was located in the Morris Building just south of W.J. Hill's Tin Shop. South of the Normandy Hotel was the location of the Ritz's Store owned by Mr. Henry G. Ritz. Beside the Ritz was the city hall. (Courtesy of Jim Ramseur.)

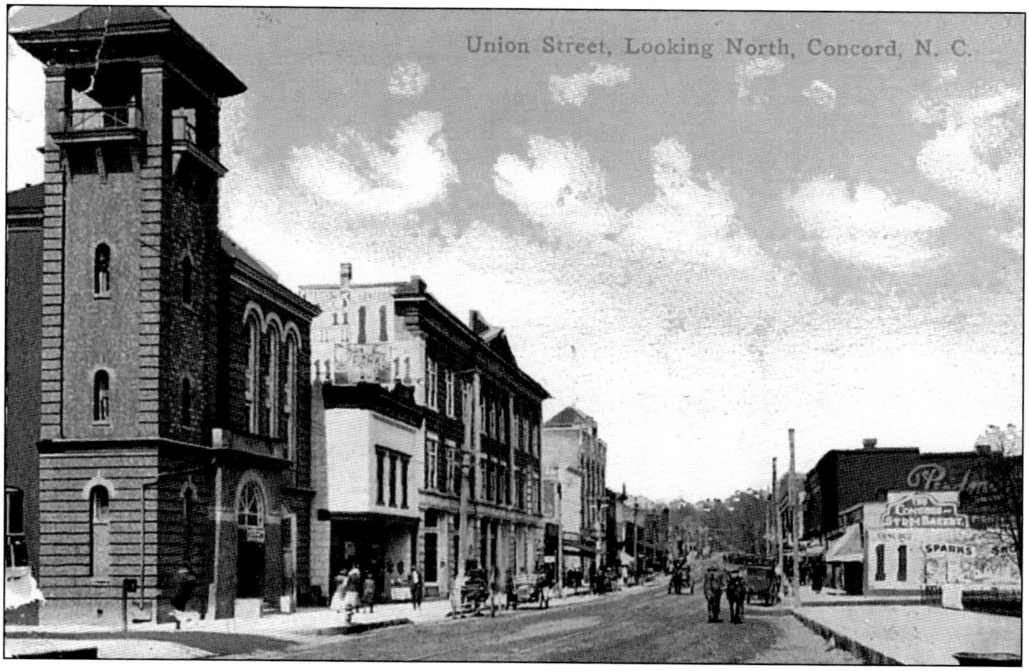

Shown is South Union Street looking north with the first building on the left being city hall. Ritz's Store, a favorite place among children, was next. Henry G. Ritz was known to have one of the largest selections of toys, candies, trinkets, and fruit, as well as a wide variety of peanuts. When Henry Ritz died, a child was overheard saying, "I feel like Santa Claus is dead." (Courtesy of the Charles A. Cannon Memorial Library.)

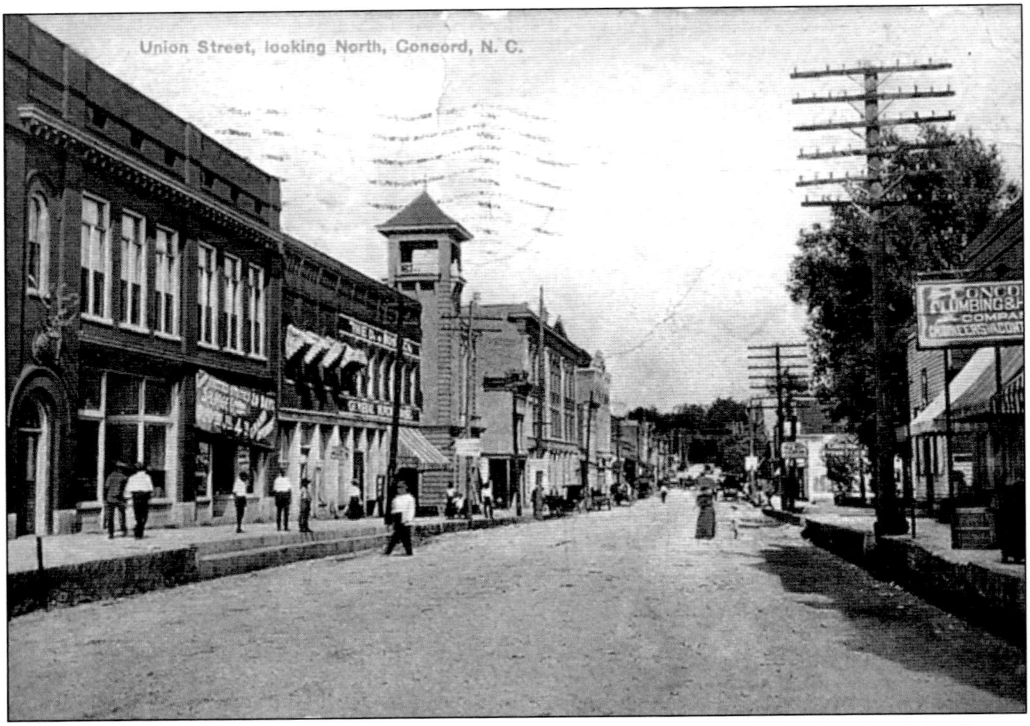

A 1908-postmarked card of South Union Street looks north at the Allison Building. Matthew's Studio was located in the last building on the left side of Union Street just before the city hall building. (Courtesy of Wayne Chapman.)

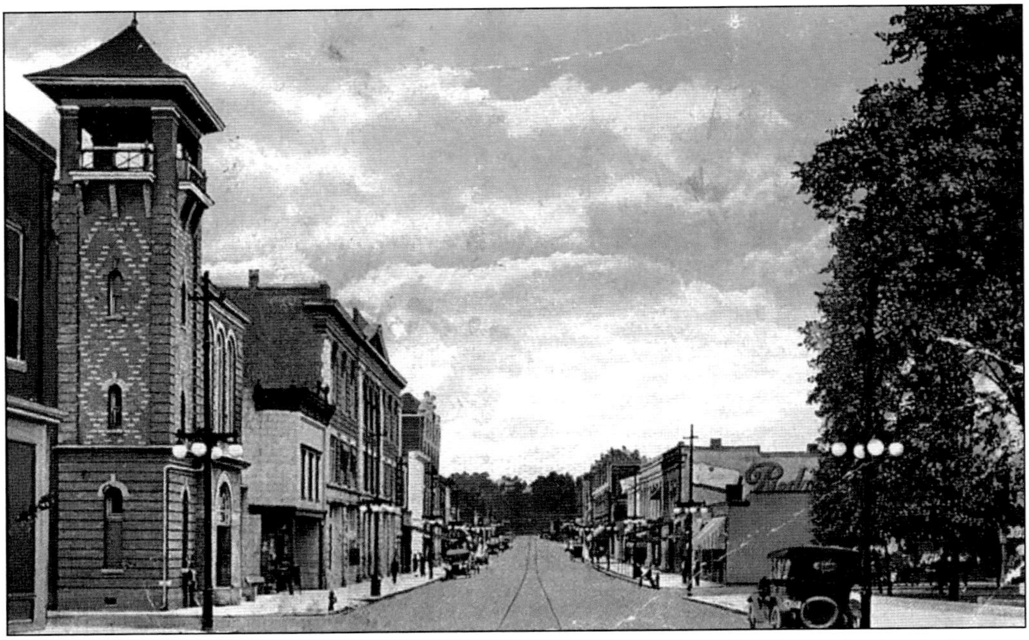

Another similar view shows South Union Street looking north, only this image shows the four-ball globe-lights that were first used in 1914. Also added are the streetcar tracks. The group of trees to the right sit in front of the 1876 courthouse.

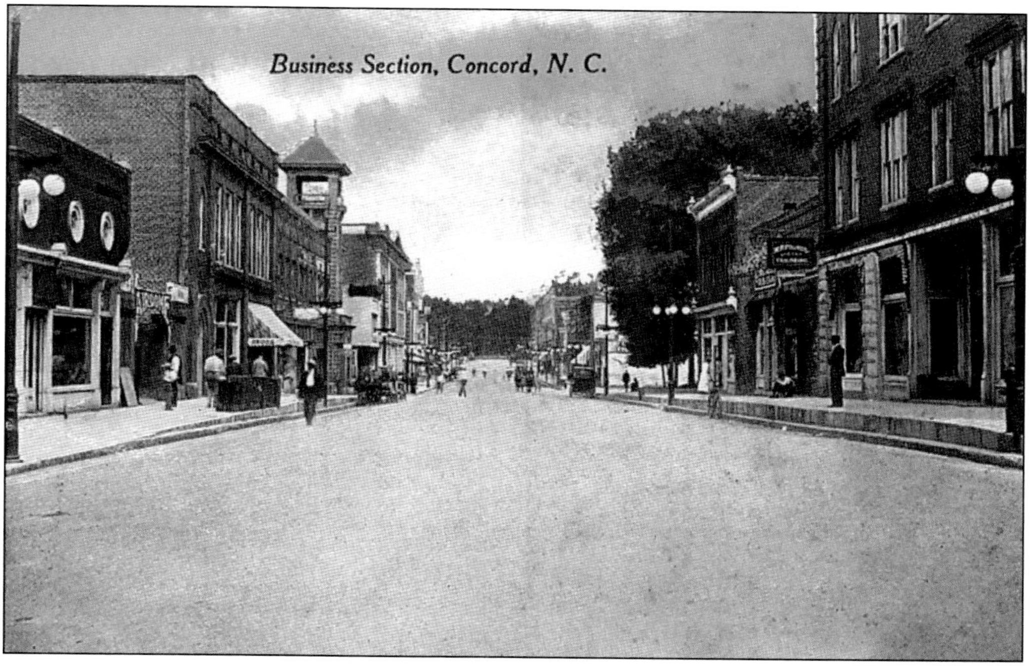

On the right is the three-story Allison Building, which at times housed the Southern Railway Express Co. and A.F. "Gus" Hartsell's Wholesale Grocery. The next building was the Litaker building where Mr. Cephus Litaker conducted a printing business in half of the building and the other half housed several different tenants, including Reed's Drug Store, Ritz Fireworks Store, and Earnest Shepherd's Shoe Hospital.

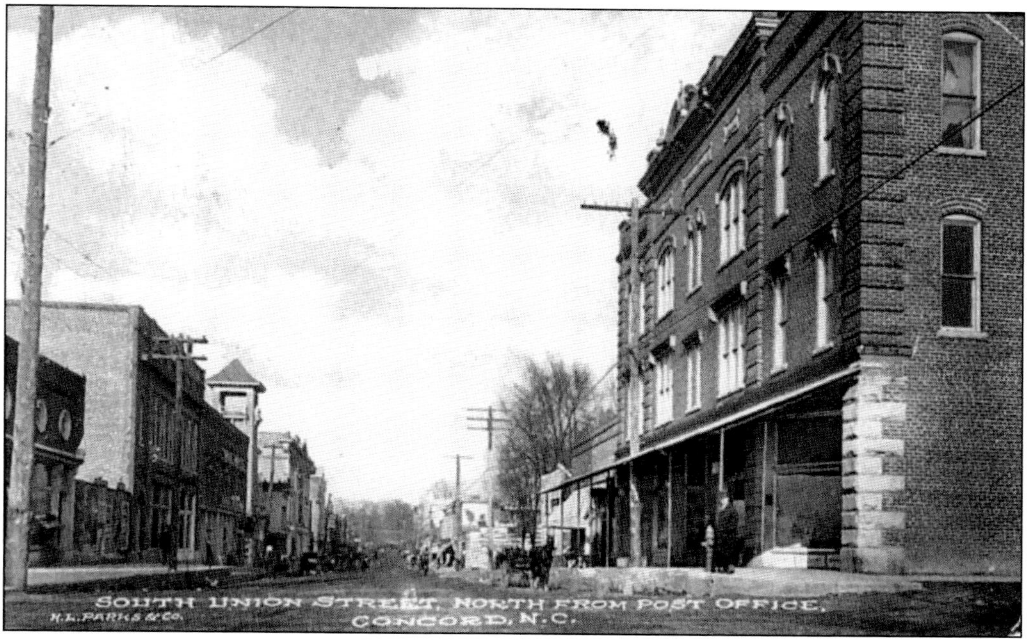

A 1910-postmarked card where the photographer stood on Union Street in front of St. James Lutheran Church shows the Archey Building, the last building on the right before the clump of trees. At one time this building housed one of Concord's early hospitals. This card was the product of the H.L. Parks & Co.

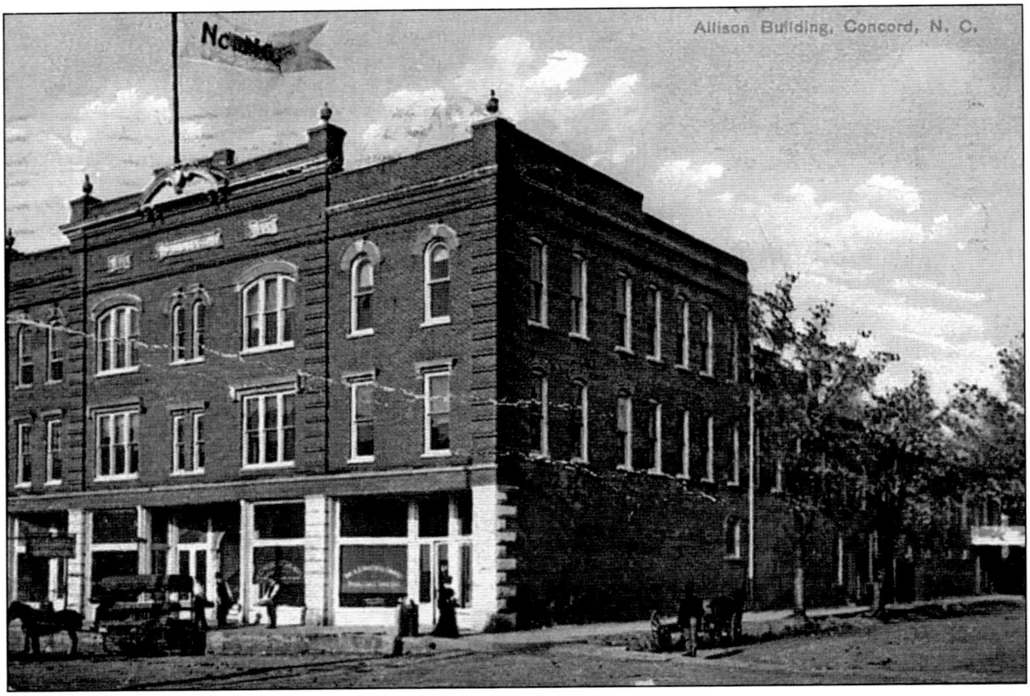

This card shows the Allison Building on South Union at Corban Street. The building has a flag over the center top stating "NC National Guard." This armory was located on the third floor of the Allison Building. (Courtesy of Wayne Chapman.)

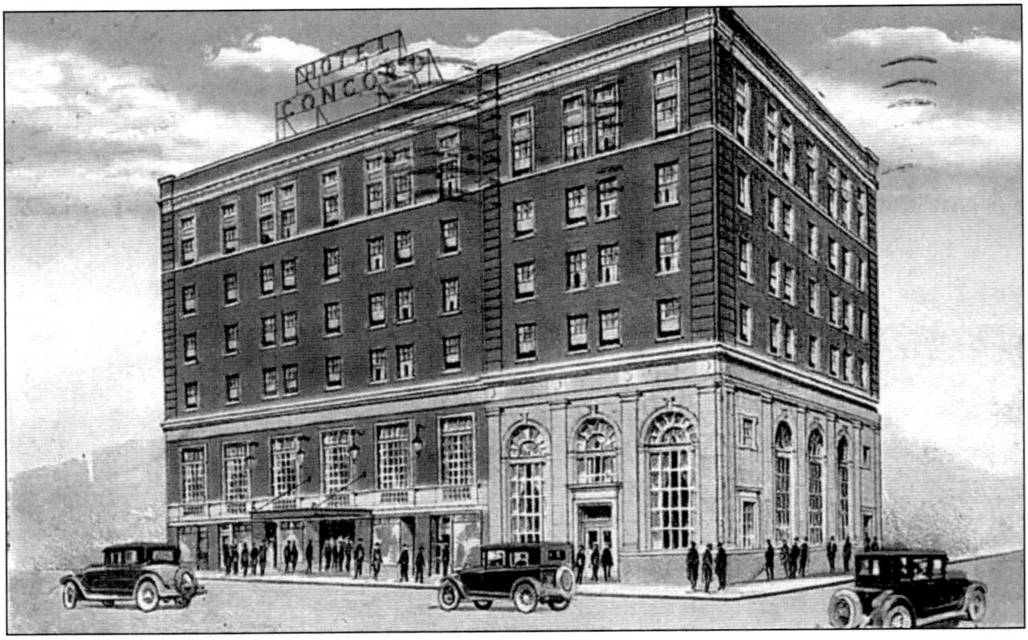

In 1927 the St. Cloud Hotel was replaced with the Hotel Concord. This is a 1934-postmarked card of the hotel when its sign was located on the roof. The white marble building on the square was the Concord National Bank. Capt. John M. Odell and D.B. Coltrane, along with his son L.D. Coltrane, organized this bank in 1888. D.B. Coltrane served as its president and was succeeded by his son, L.D. Coltrane.

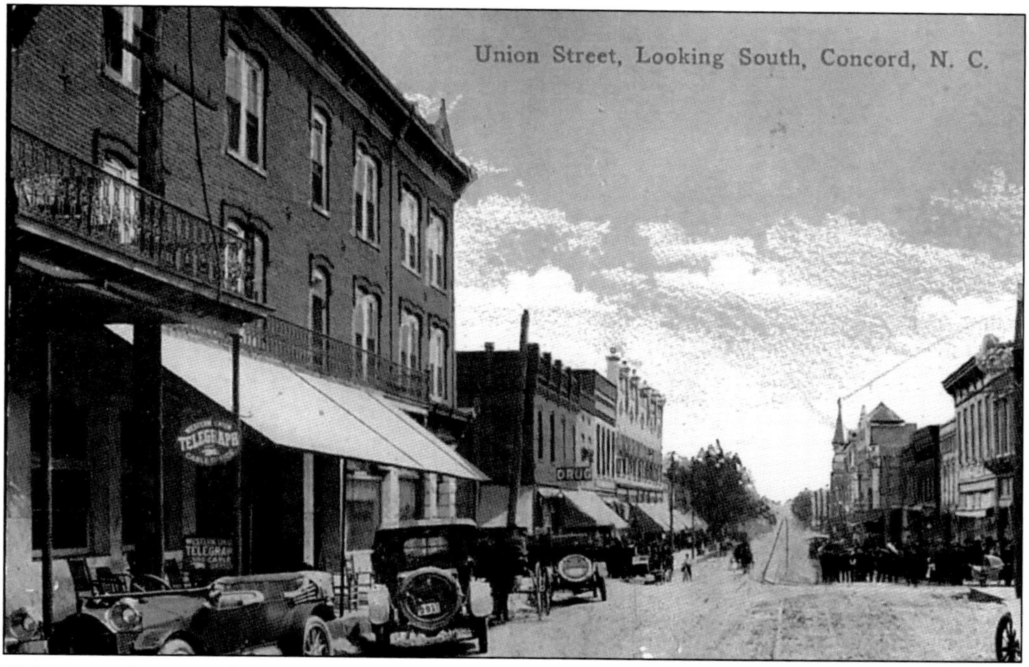

This image taken around the 1920s shows Union Street looking south from just north of the square. Concord was certainly becoming quite a busy little community.

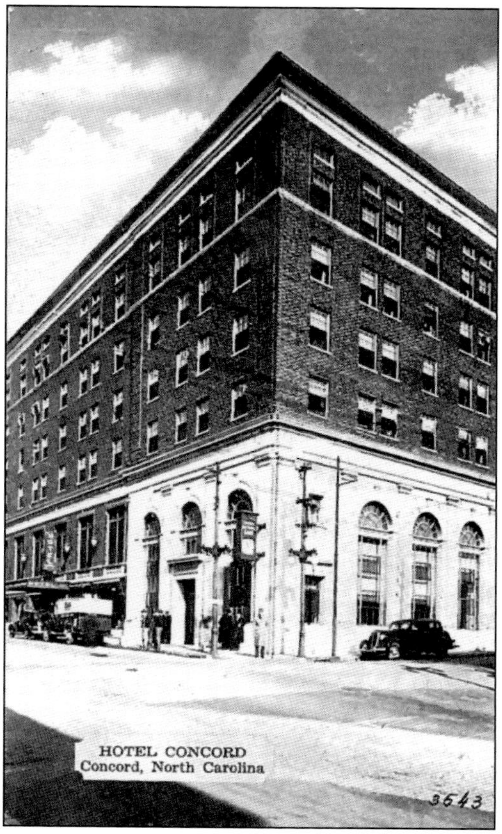

This is another view of the Hotel Concord with emphasis placed on the Concord National Bank. This card is attributed to Dexter Press, a popular postcard publishing company.

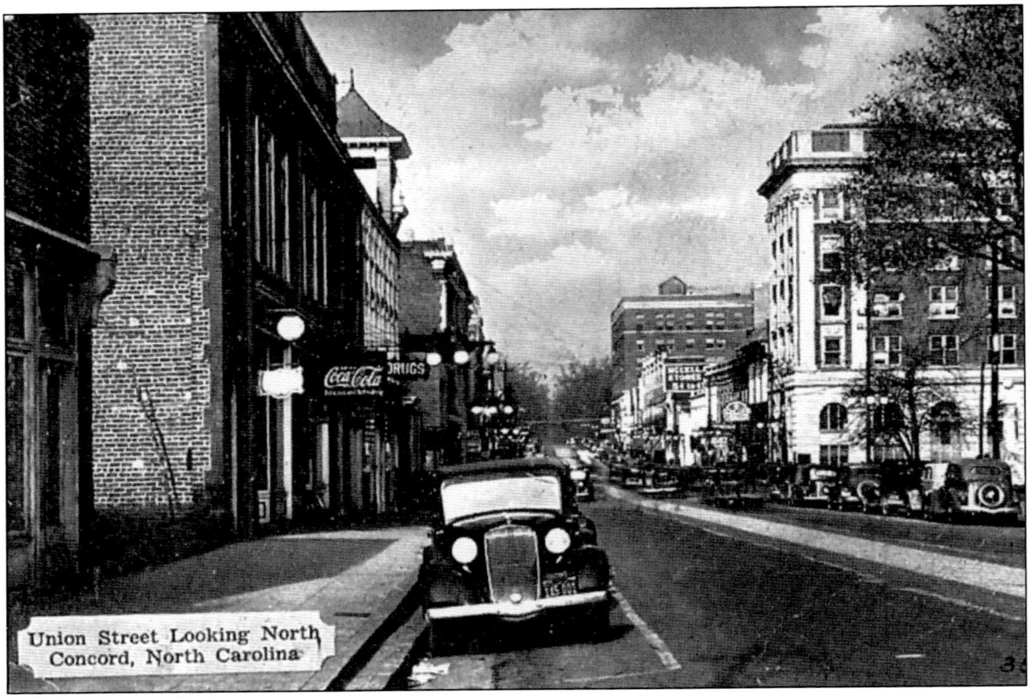

This card dates to the 1930s and shows South Union Street from just north of Corban Street. The Cabarrus Bank (today's First Union) is the large, five-story building on the right and in the distance is the Hotel Concord. (Courtesy of Alex and Jane Patterson.)

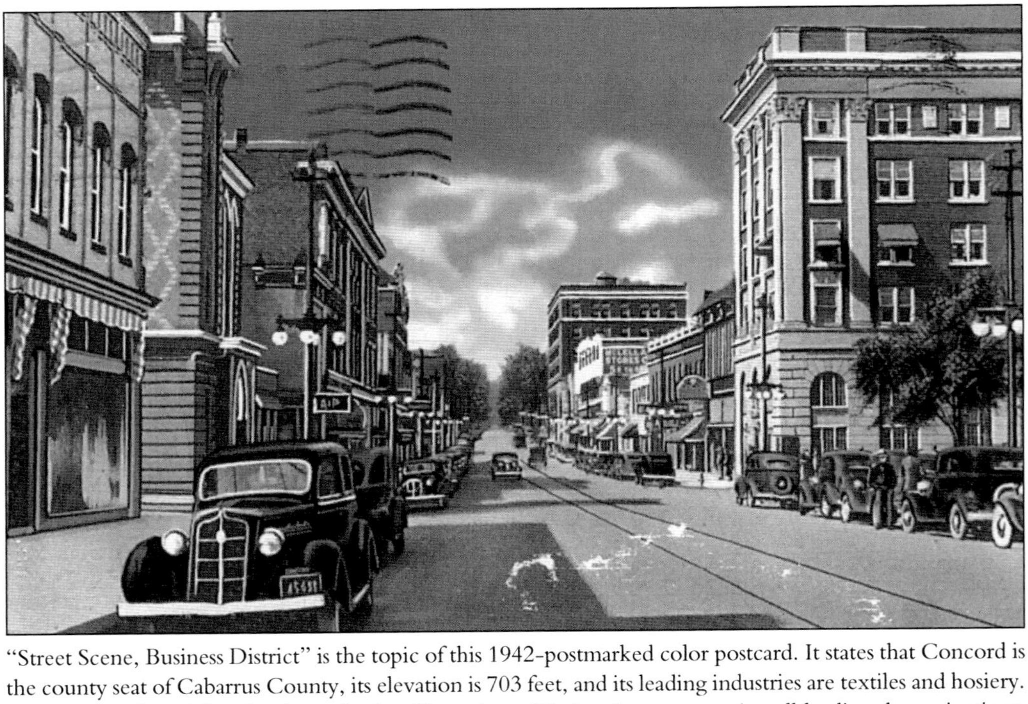

"Street Scene, Business District" is the topic of this 1942-postmarked color postcard. It states that Concord is the county seat of Cabarrus County, its elevation is 703 feet, and its leading industries are textiles and hosiery. The city has six public schools employing 90 teachers, 25 churches representing all leading denominations, and 2 daily newspapers.

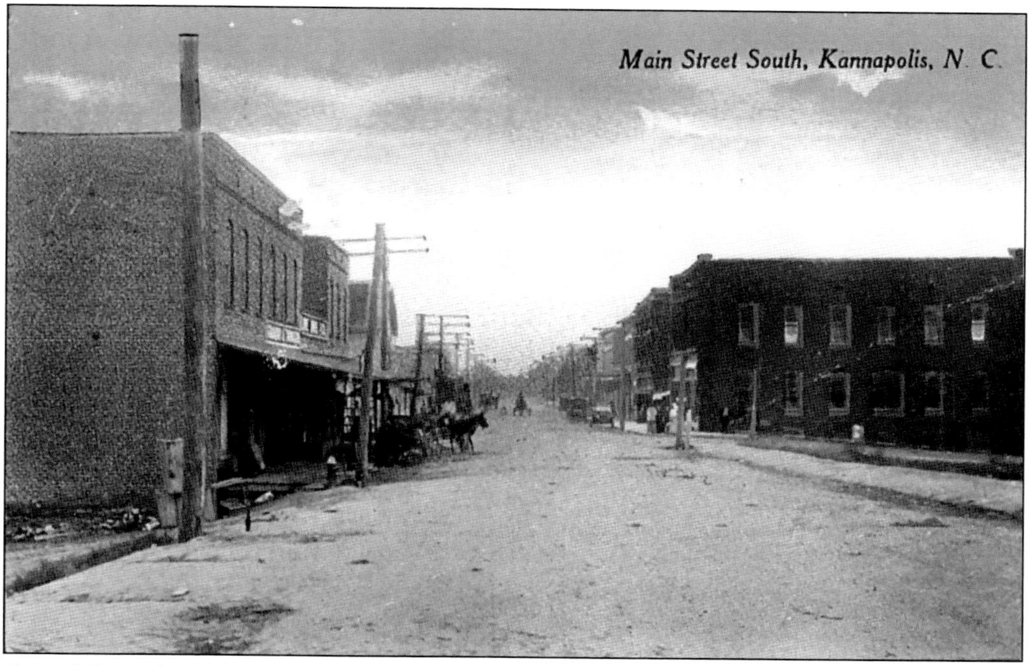

One of the earliest postcards of Kannapolis, North Carolina, made around 1910, is shown here. The photographer's tripod and camera were set up on Main Street a short distance north of the square. (Courtesy of Marian Harter.)

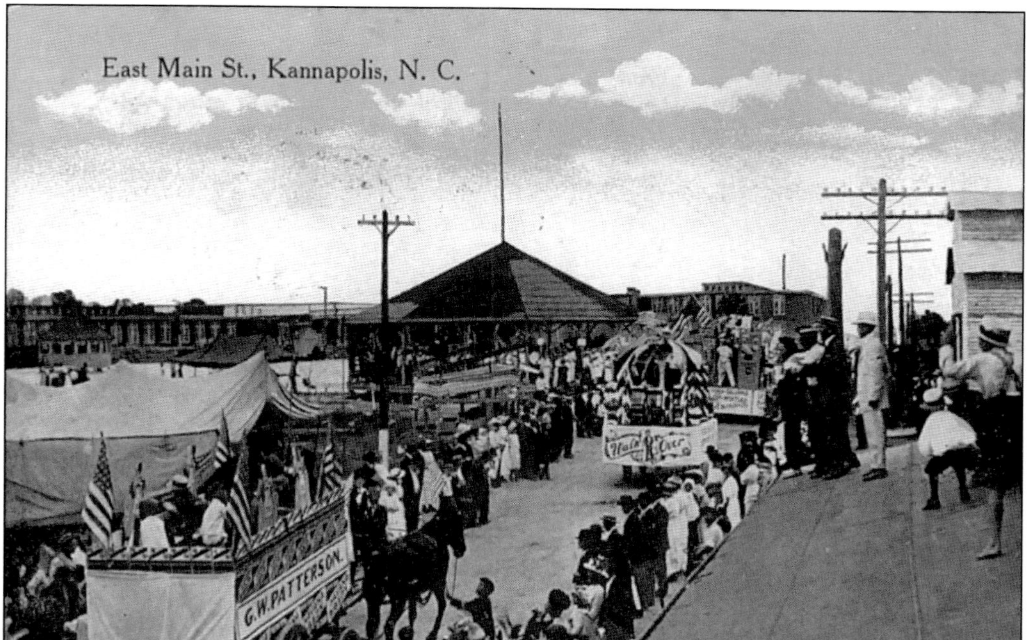

A parade goes along North Main Street sometime around 1912. A wagon with G.W. Patterson, who had a general store in Concord, can be seen heading north in the festivities. Spectators watching the parade stand on an awning of the Lowe Brothers Building on the right of this image. (Courtesy of Wayne Chapman.)

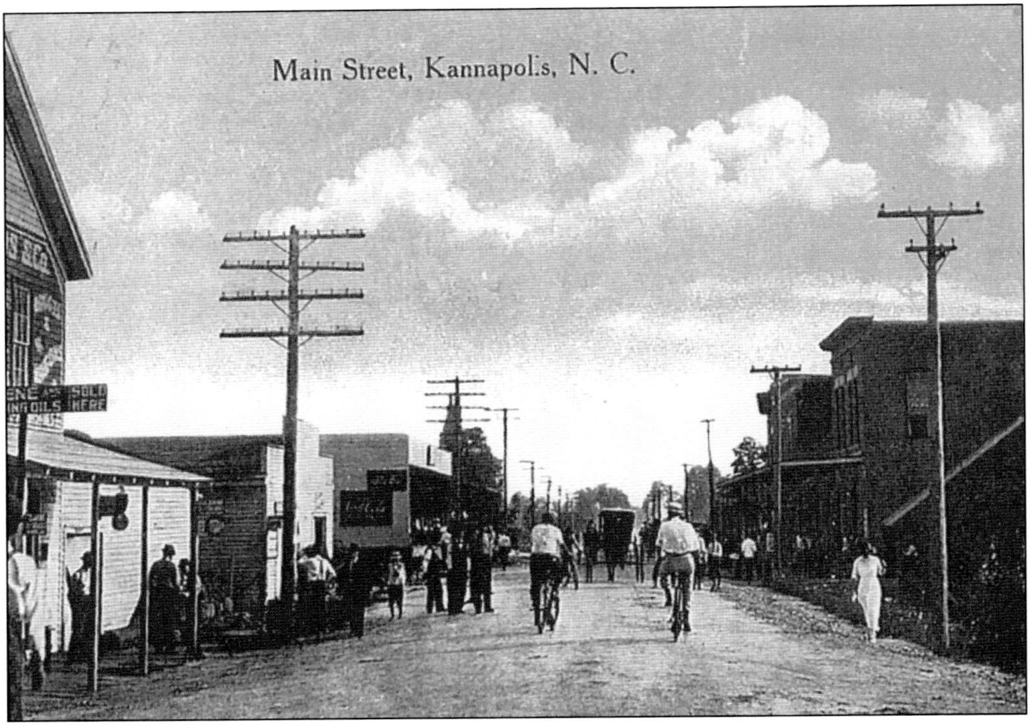

Everyday life in a small, Southern town includes pedestrians, bicycle riders, and a horse and buggy. The card is not dated, but it is estimated to have been made sometime around 1911. (Courtesy of Durwood Barbour.)

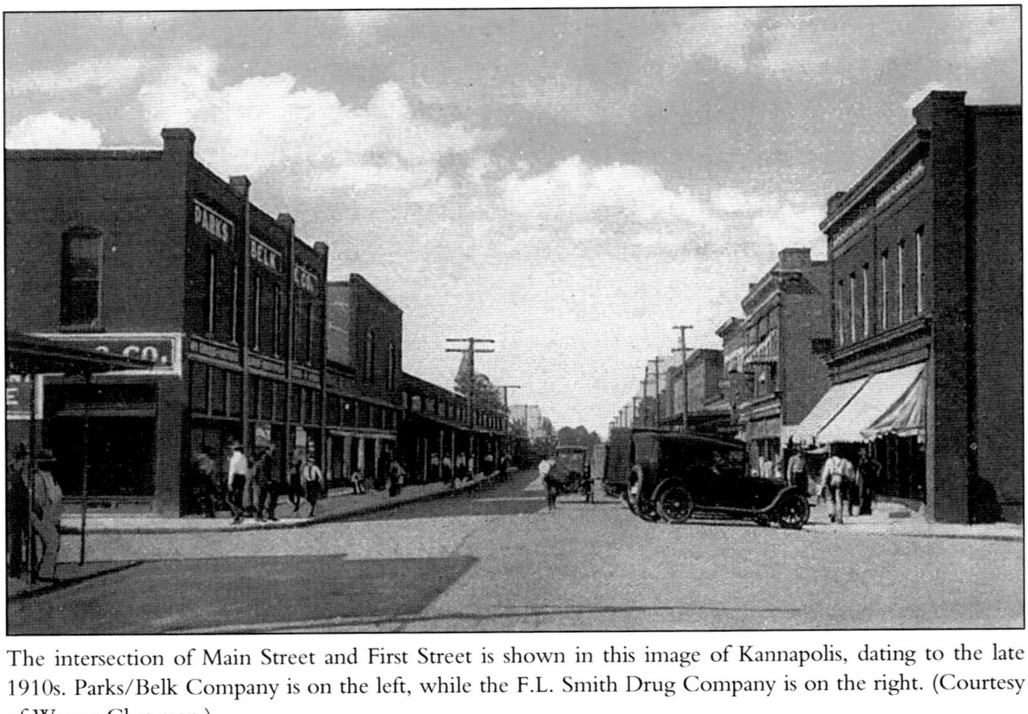

The intersection of Main Street and First Street is shown in this image of Kannapolis, dating to the late 1910s. Parks/Belk Company is on the left, while the F.L. Smith Drug Company is on the right. (Courtesy of Wayne Chapman.)

In 1913, H.B. Wilkinson's and Co. opened for business on the west side of Main Street. Wilkinson sold furniture and coffins, which led him to open an undertaking business. In 1918, W.H. Whitley began working for Wilkinson and purchased stock in the company during the early 1920s. The name Wilkinson-Whitley Funeral Home was incorporated in 1923. Records from 1938 show that W.H. Whitley and Sons Funeral Home became incorporated, and it remains in operation today. (Courtesy of Wayne Chapman.)

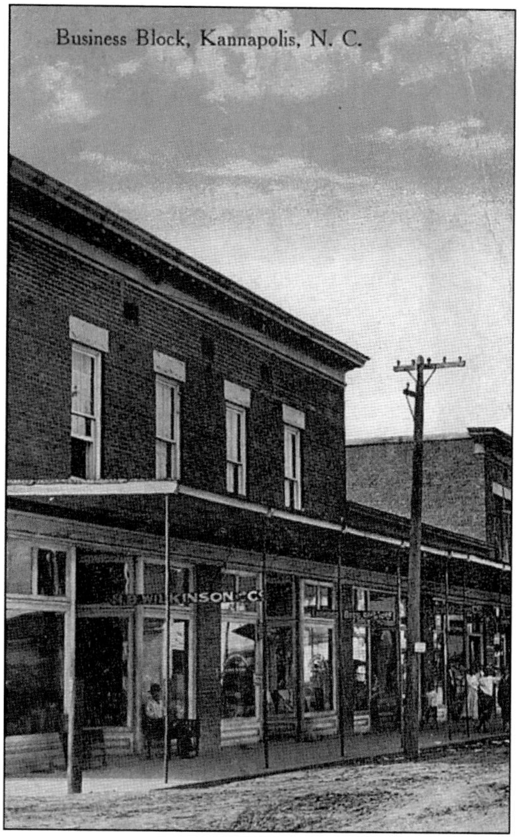

In this view of the "business block" of Kannapolis, taken around 1908, the F.L. Smith Drug Store is on the right, at the corner of Main Street and First Street. The Concord Telephone Company was located on the second floor of the drugstore. Next to Smith's Drug was Richmond and Sloan Company, a popular mercantile store. (Courtesy of Steven E. Massengill and the North Carolina Division of Archives and History.)

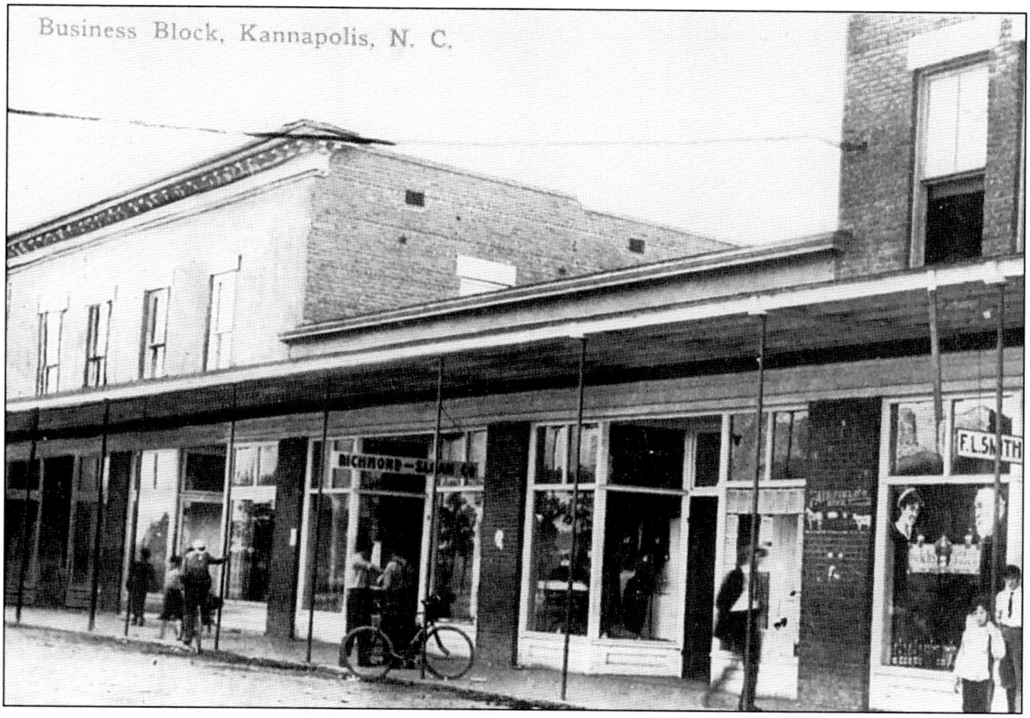

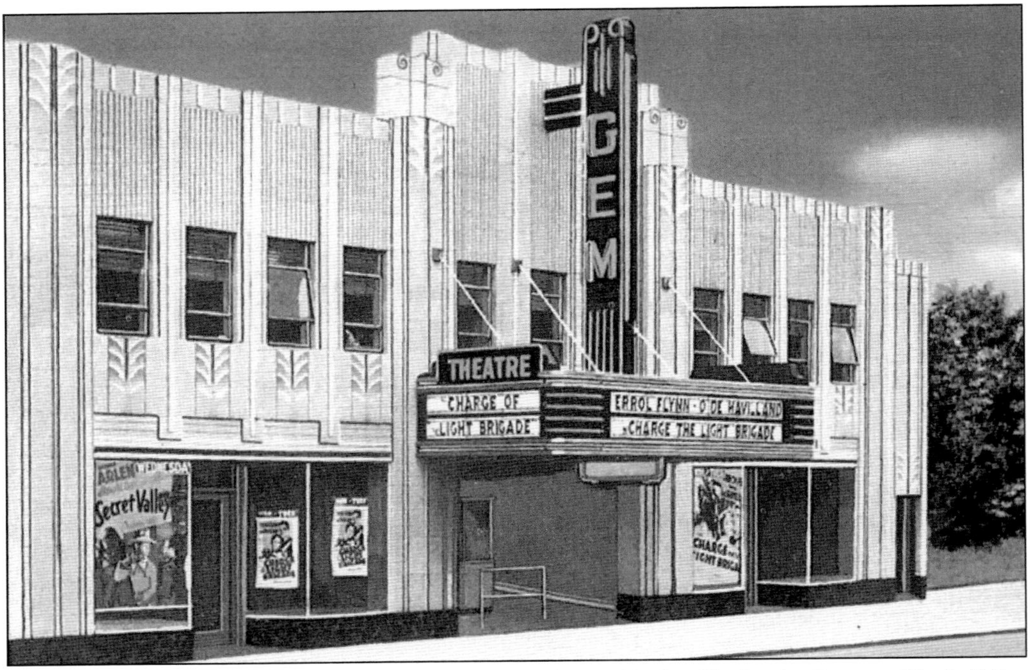

This art deco building is the Gem Theater and was built in 1936 by Charles A. Cannon. The building suffered fire damage around 1942, but it re-opened after 1948. The theater still operates today with Steve Morris as manager. (Courtesy of Marian Harter.)

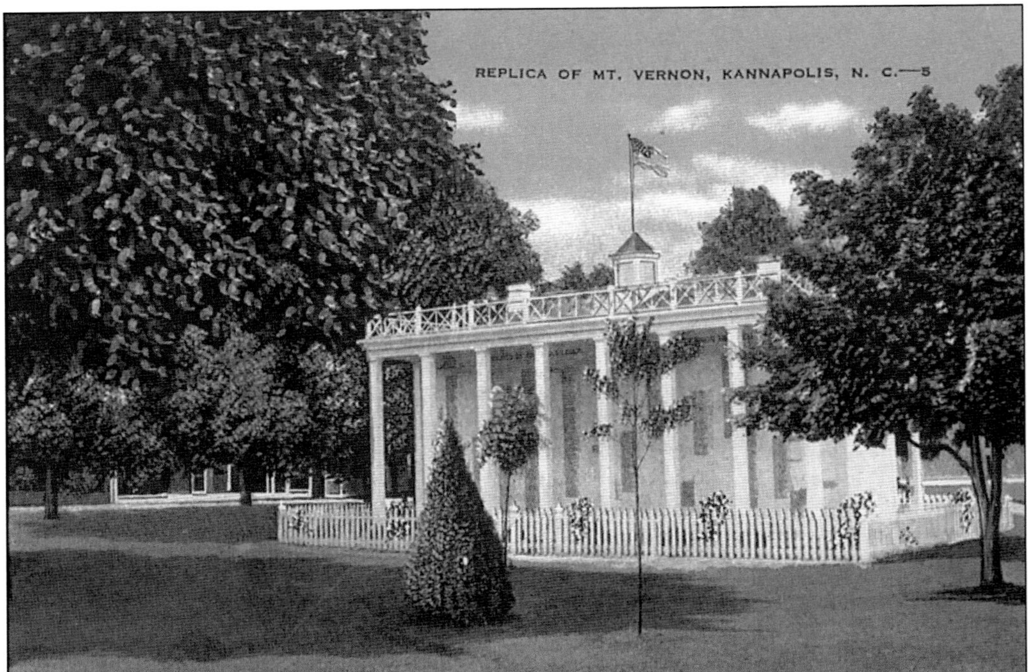

"Little Mt. Vernon" was the name given to this monument, which honored the veterans of Kannapolis. It held the names of every soldier from Kannapolis who fought during World War II. (Courtesy of Whitley's Funeral Home.)

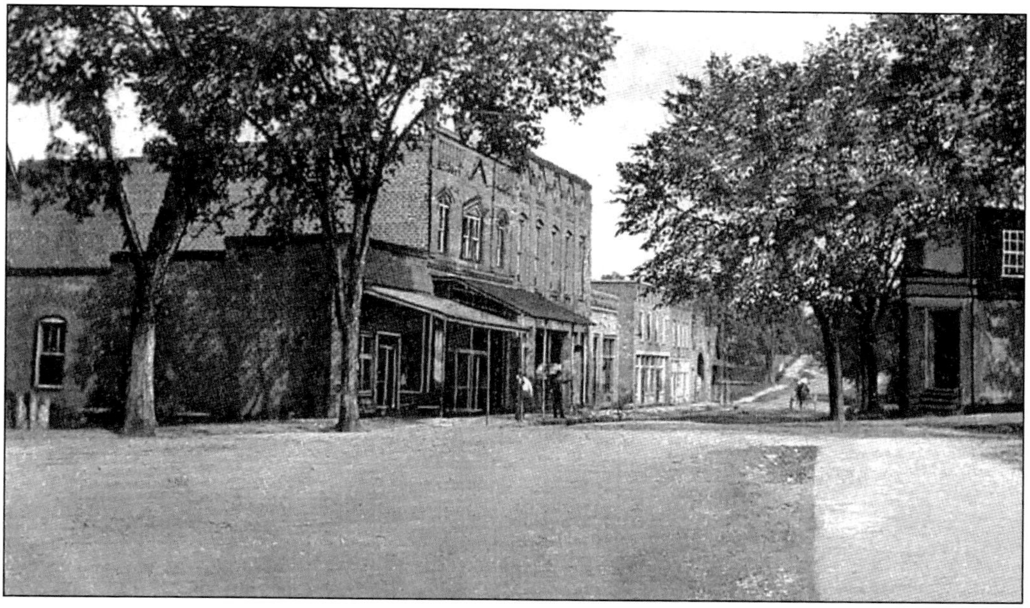

Mt. Pleasant, located in the eastern part of Cabarrus County, is the subject of this image. The photographer had his camera facing west on Franklin Street, with Concord just nine miles ahead. The open door on the right at the square is the entrance to Heilig General Merchandise. (Courtesy of Wayne Chapman.)

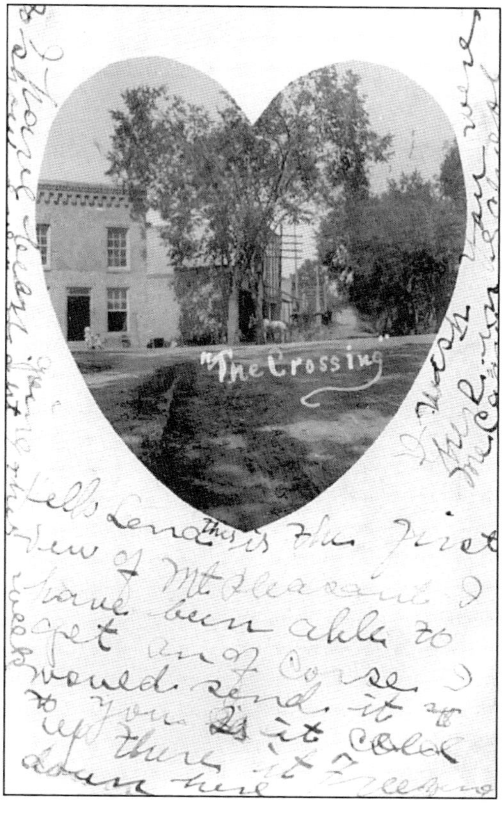

A most unusual card entitled "The Crossing," which was a not-too-familiar term given to the square in Mt. Pleasant, includes Franklin Street and Main Street. The heart-shaped image on this rectangular 1906-postmarked card allowed space for the sender to include a message. (Courtesy of Marian Harter.)

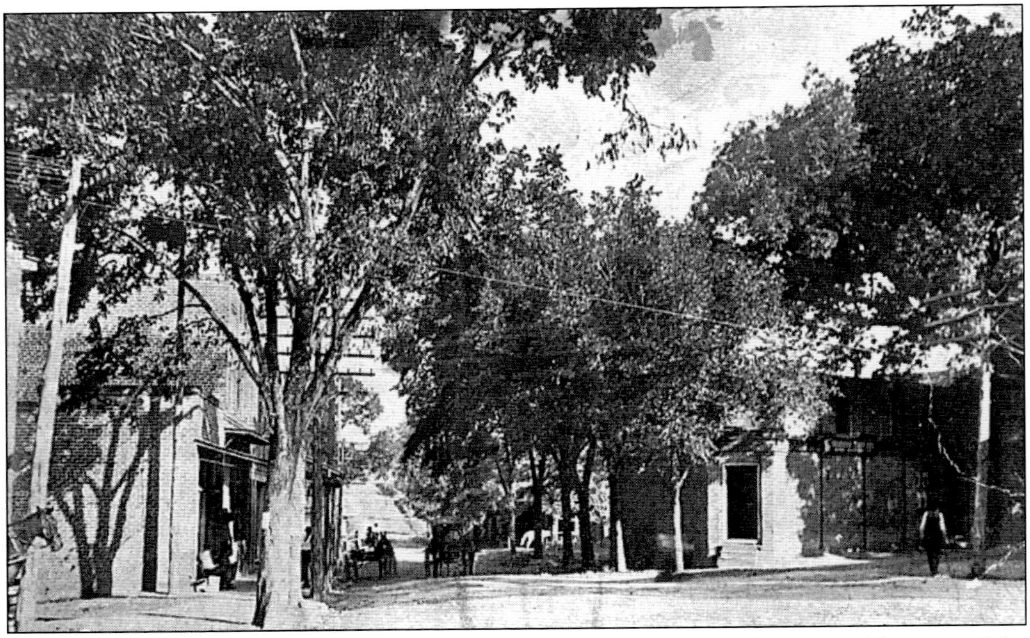

This 1909-postmarked card again shows Franklin Street looking east near the square. (Courtesy of the Eastern Cabarrus Historical Society Museum.)

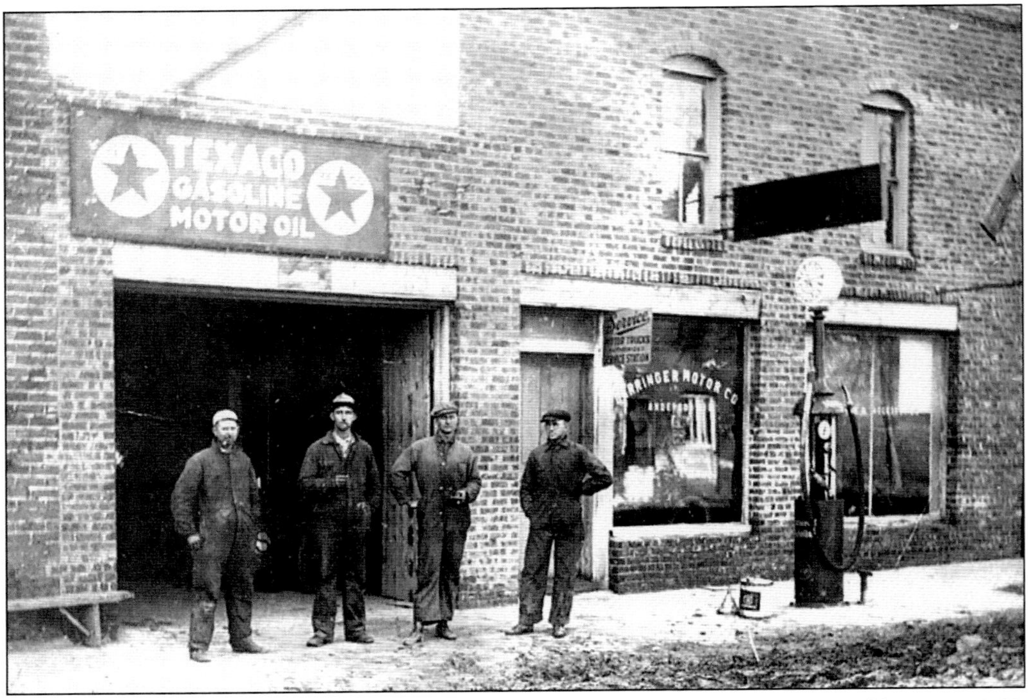

The Barringer Motor Company was located in the old Fisher Livery Stable on West Franklin Street. L.H. Barringer founded this company in 1920. Pictured, from left to right, are ? Cruse, ? Moose, unidentified, and Herman Barringer. (Courtesy of the Eastern Cabarrus Historical Society Museum.)

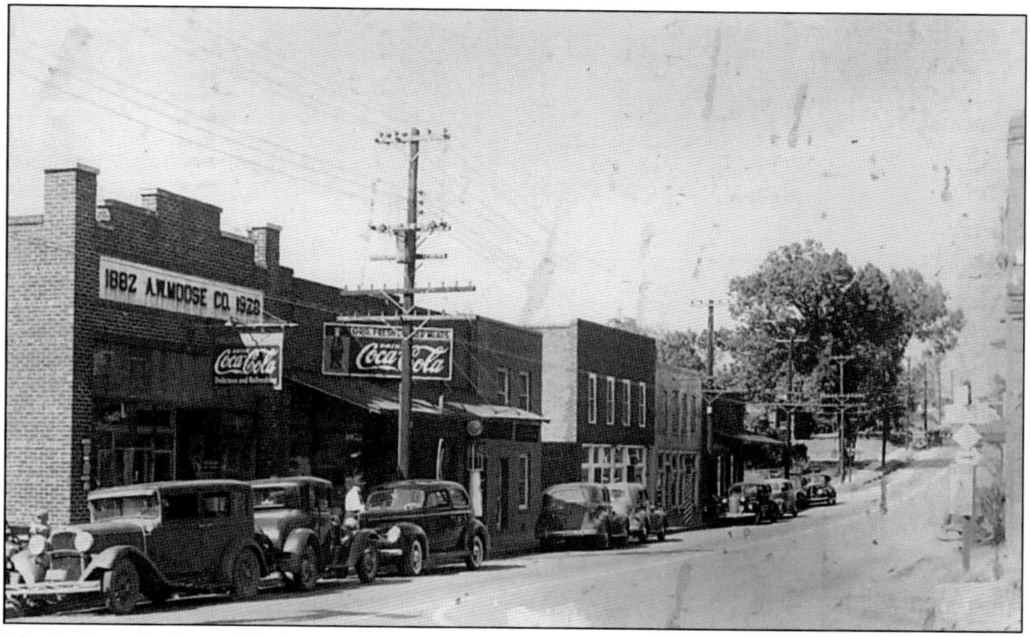

This business district card depicts West Franklin Street and the second A.W. Moose Drug Store, on the left, around 1939. (Courtesy of the Eastern Cabarrus Historical Society Museum.)

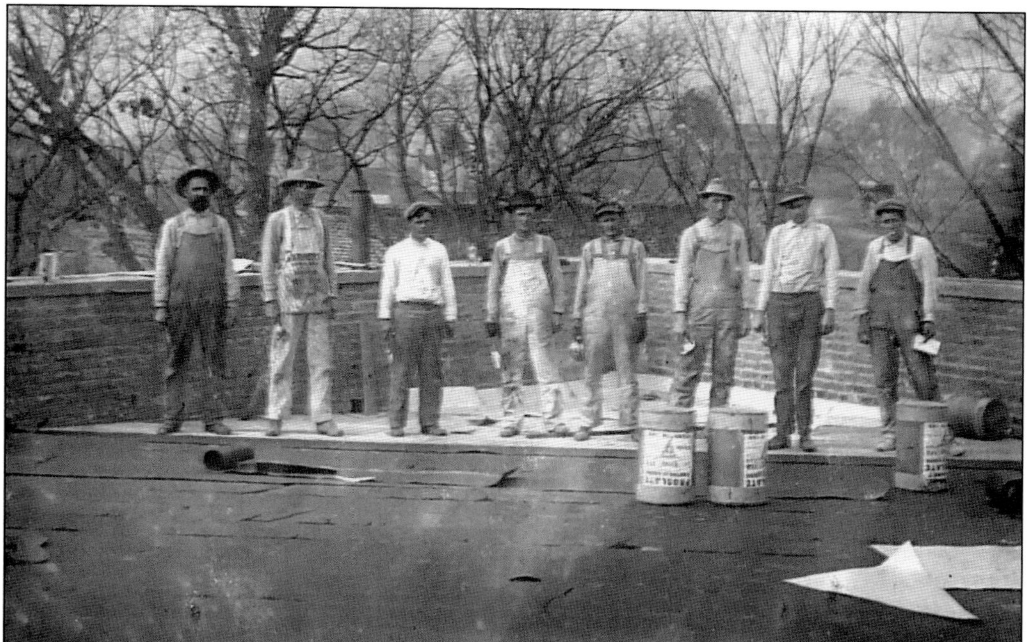

These men are working on reroofing the Moose Drug Store building, the first building destroyed in the fire in 1928. Most of the block of buildings along this stretch of West Franklin Street also burned in the fire. (Courtesy of Robert M. McAllister.)

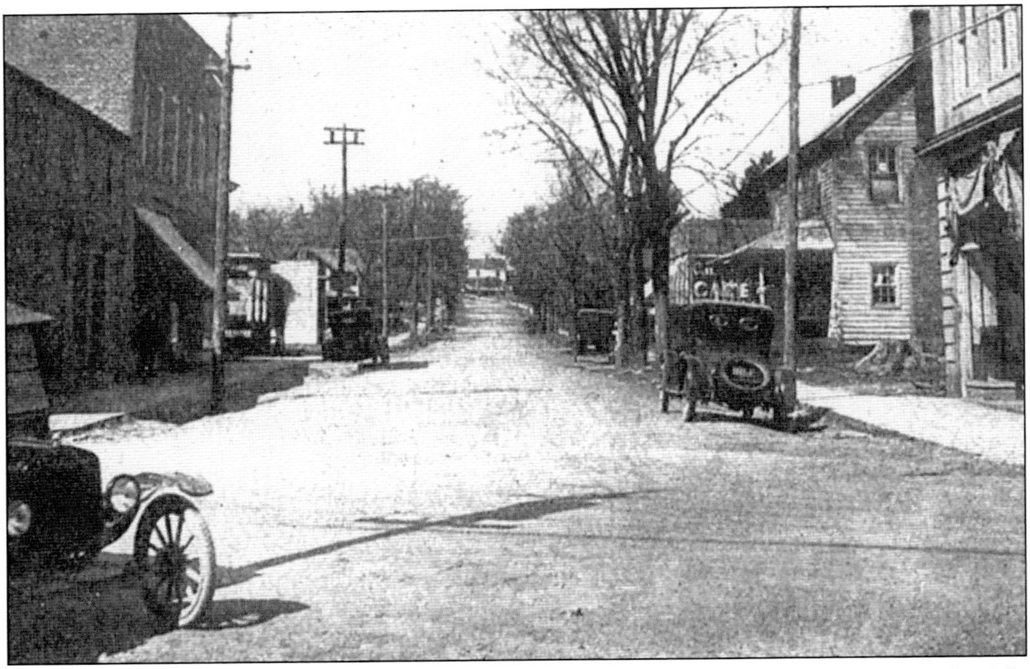

North Main Street near the square is the subject of this image taken in 1904. The first building on the right was The Mercantile, followed by the Bangle Hotel just beyond Lee McAllister's car. On the left side of Main Street is Chulie's Goodie Garden, a favorite hang-out for students, recognized by the steep-pitched awning. (Courtesy of Charles G. Lentz Jr.)

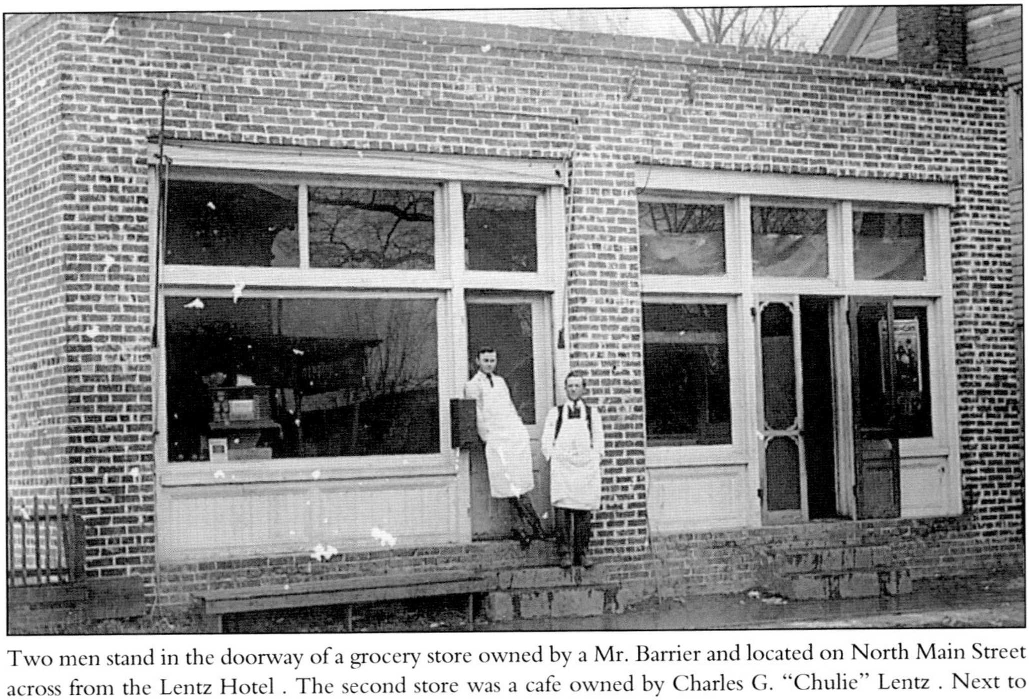

Two men stand in the doorway of a grocery store owned by a Mr. Barrier and located on North Main Street across from the Lentz Hotel . The second store was a cafe owned by Charles G. "Chulie" Lentz . Next to the cafe is the Bangle Hotel, in which Thomas Edison stayed while doing tests at local gold mines. (Courtesy of Robert M. McAllister.)

Four

Residences

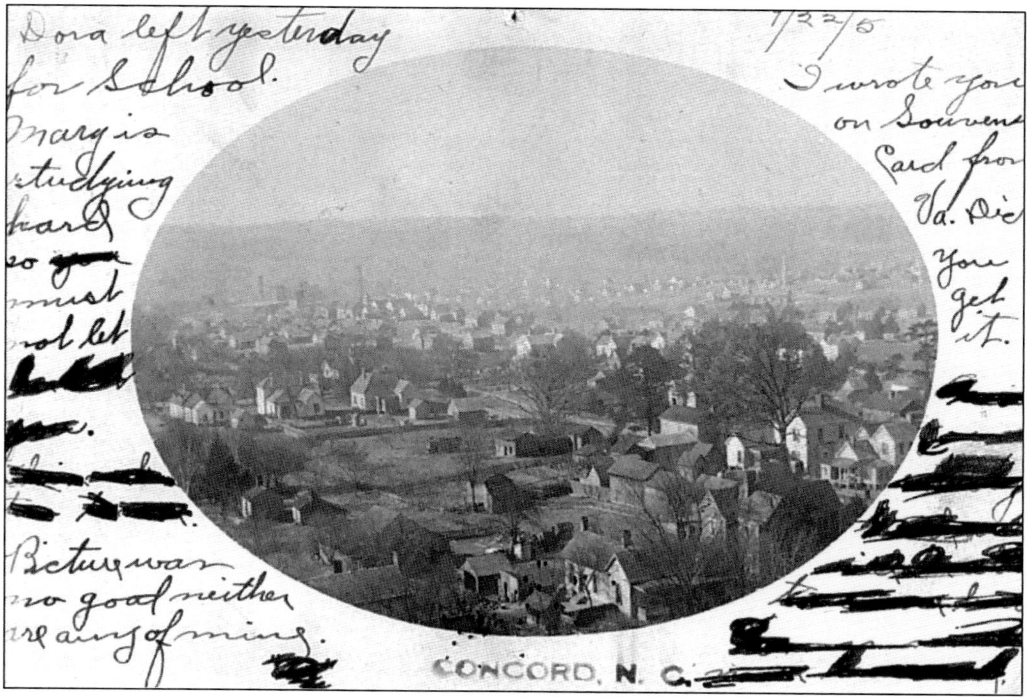

Concord was a good-sized community in the early 1900s when this elevated view was captured. A typical residential area can be observed although the location is uncertain. It is very possible given the time this type of card was published (around 1905) that the mill in the distance could be the Cannon Manufacturing Company or the Odell Manufacturing Company. (Courtesy of the Charles A. Cannon Memorial Library.)

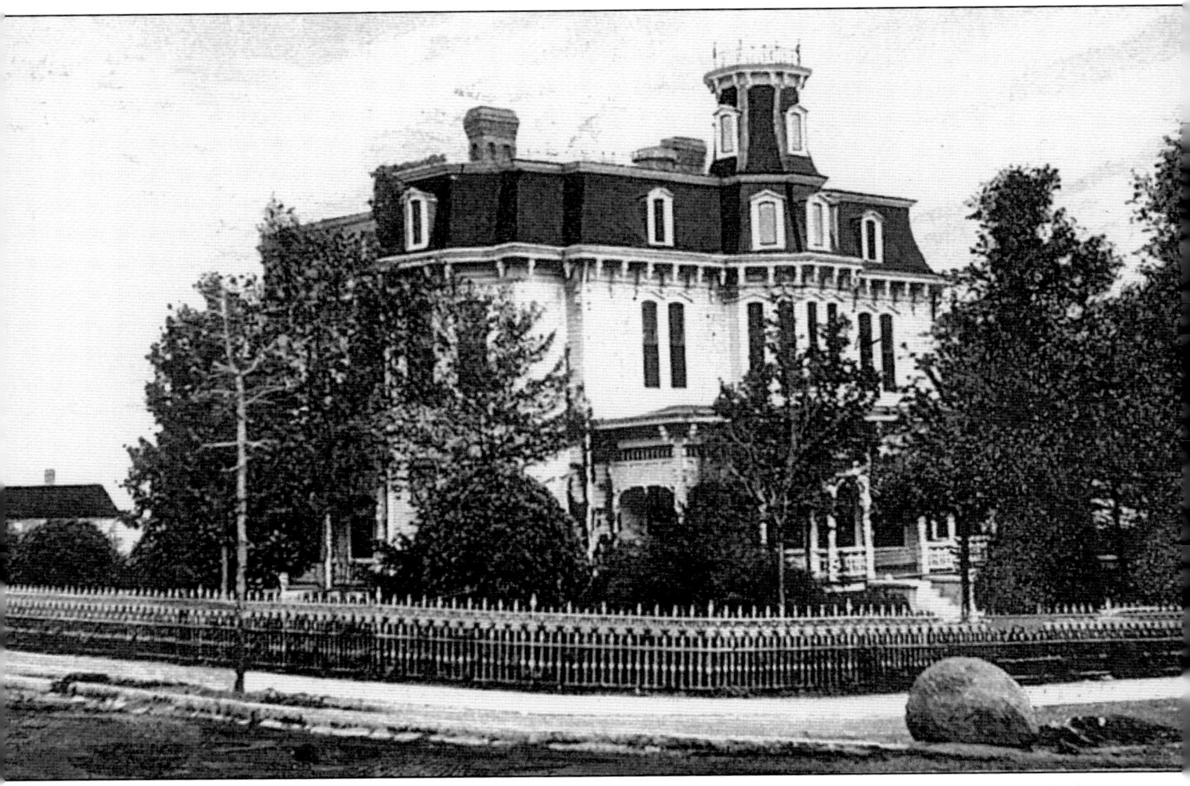

Capt. John Milton Odell, a veteran of the War between the States, erected this dwelling on an ample lot at the beginning of North Union Street about the same time as the 1876 courthouse was being built. Odell was very much the business man, having been part owner of the St. Cloud Hotel, once president of the Concord National Bank, and owner of the Odell Manufacturing Company. He also was president of the Kerr Bleachery Company, the only bleachery in the South with the exception of one located in Atlanta, Georgia. It is of interest that the large rock shown in this image was brought to Concord from a battlefield in Virginia by Captain Odell. It is reported that this boulder saved the young captain's life during the War between the States, so he had it brought to Concord and placed in front of his residence after the war. The rock can be seen today in the front yard under a large magnolia tree. Today this house is used as a bed and breakfast and at this writing is owned by Calvin and Cathie Winfield. (Courtesy of Marian Harter.)

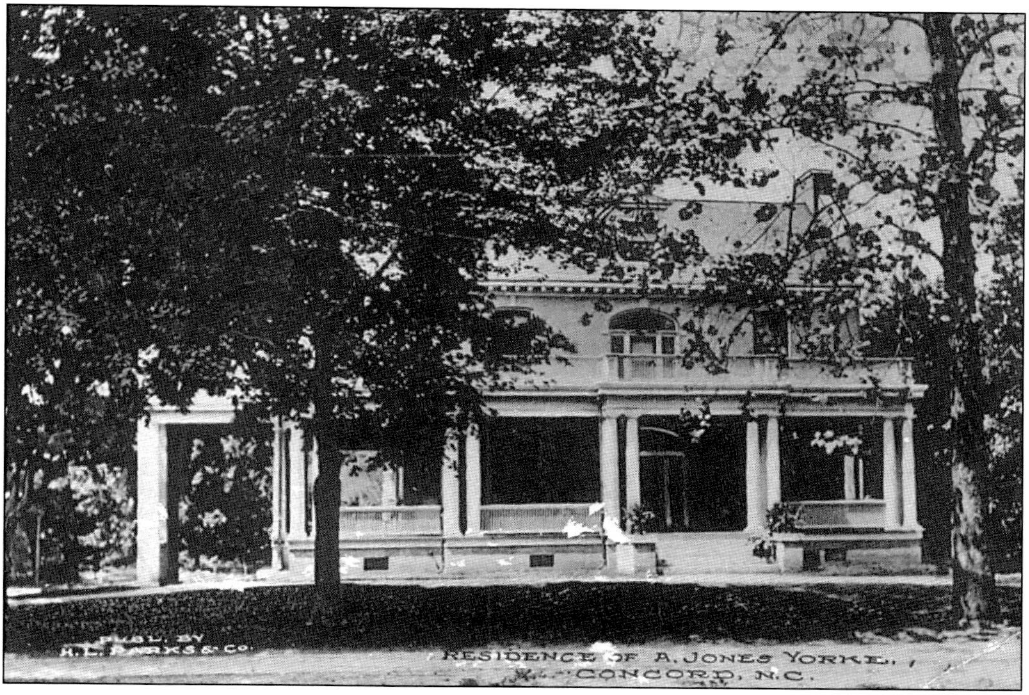

The Aaron Jones Yorke home was built in 1908 from plans prepared by L.L. Hunter, an architect from Charlotte. Yorke, a native of Concord, helped to start local public schools and was the first superintendent of the Cabarrus County Board of Common Schools. His house, located on the northwest corner of North Union Street at Franklin Avenue, is the subject of this 1915-postmarked card published by H.L. Parks and Company. Today David and Anne Mayfield reside in the Yorke Home. (Courtesy of Don and Vickie Cline.)

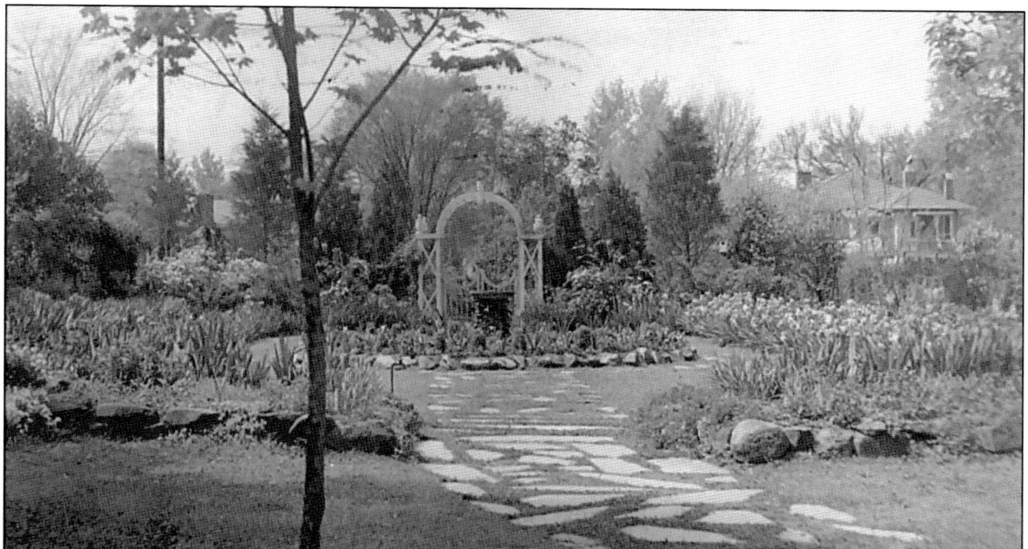

Concord boasted a very active Garden Club and used as its invitations to meetings postcards of the many beautiful gardens around the city. This card shows a beautiful yard in Concord that was the pride of its owner.

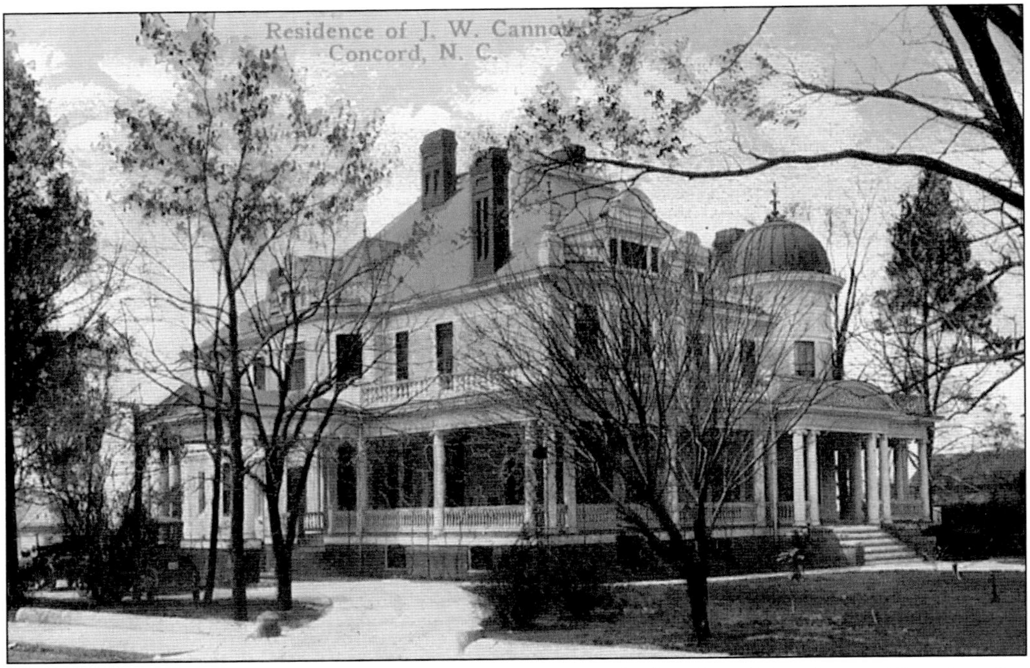

James William Cannon built this home around 1900. He was the founder of the Cannon Manufacturing Company, which became one of the largest textile empires in the world. In 1969 this home was converted into the Cabarrus Academy, but in recent years it has been converted back into a home, owned by Todd Hampton Dickens Sr. and his wife, Mary Margaret Dickens, the great-great granddaughter of J.W. Cannon. (Courtesy of Bub and Jane Craver.)

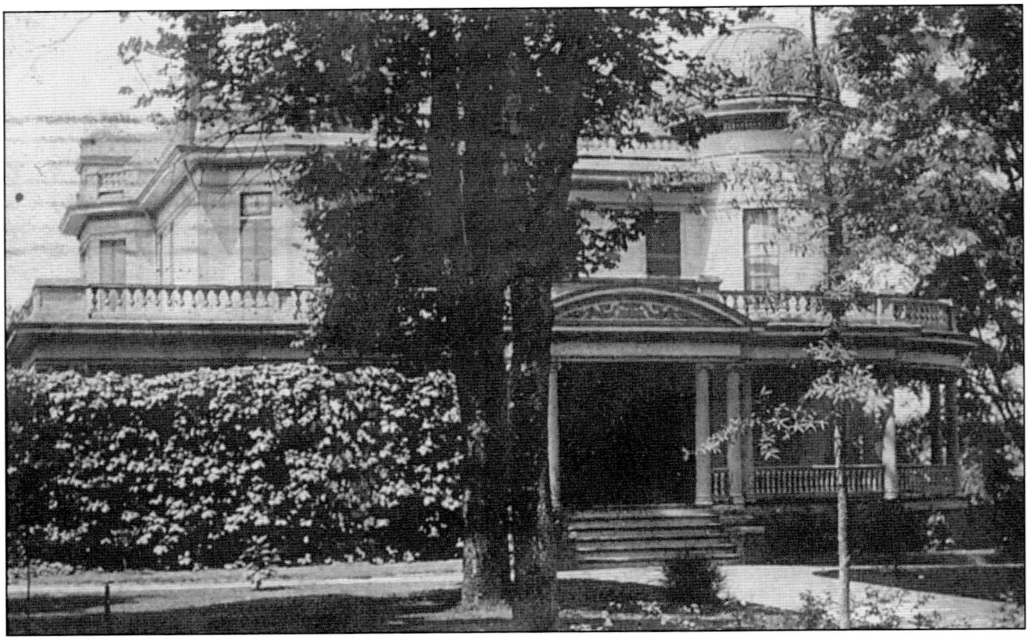

This is another view of the J.W. Cannon home at 65 North Union Street. Noted is the wrap-around porch with its fluted ionic columns. The facade of the Cannon home is a notable Queen Anne composition in which a domed turret is featured. (Courtesy of Marian Harter.)

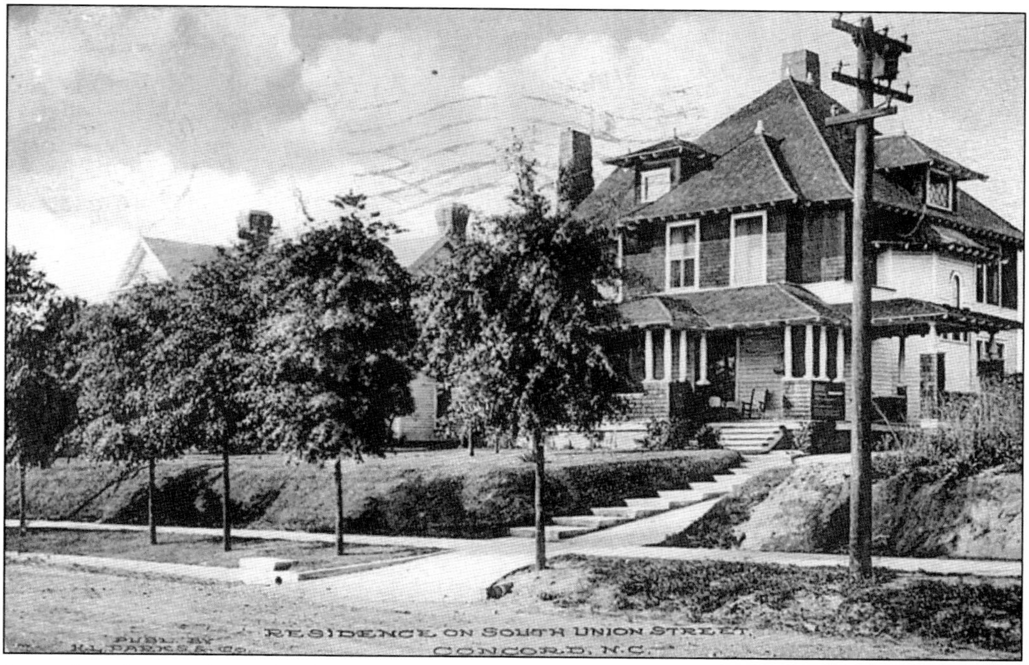

Located on the west side of South Union at the edge of town was the George L. Patterson home. Patterson was at one time the postmaster of Concord, and he later became the owner, following his father, of the G.W. Patterson Grocery business. This card was published by H.L. Parks & Co. (Courtesy of the Charles A. Cannon Memorial Library.)

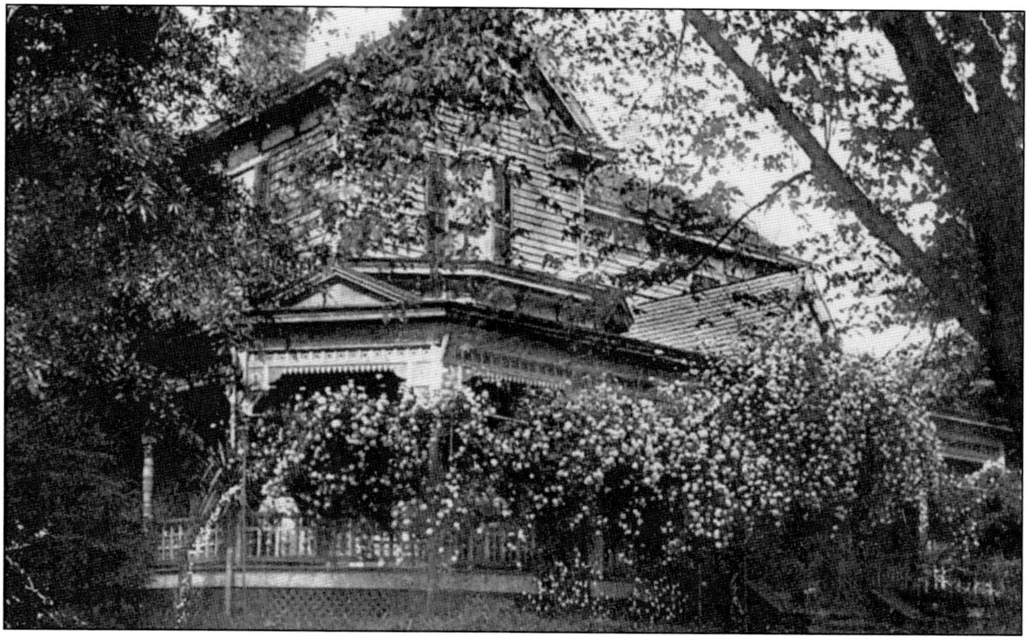

"Brownhurst" is the name given to the home built by Moses L. Brown at 168 South Union Street. The land on which Brown built his home was purchased in 1880 and the house was built by 1882. Brown operated a livery stable on Means Avenue across from the 1876 courthouse. Mark and Pam Novasad are the owners of the Brown home today.

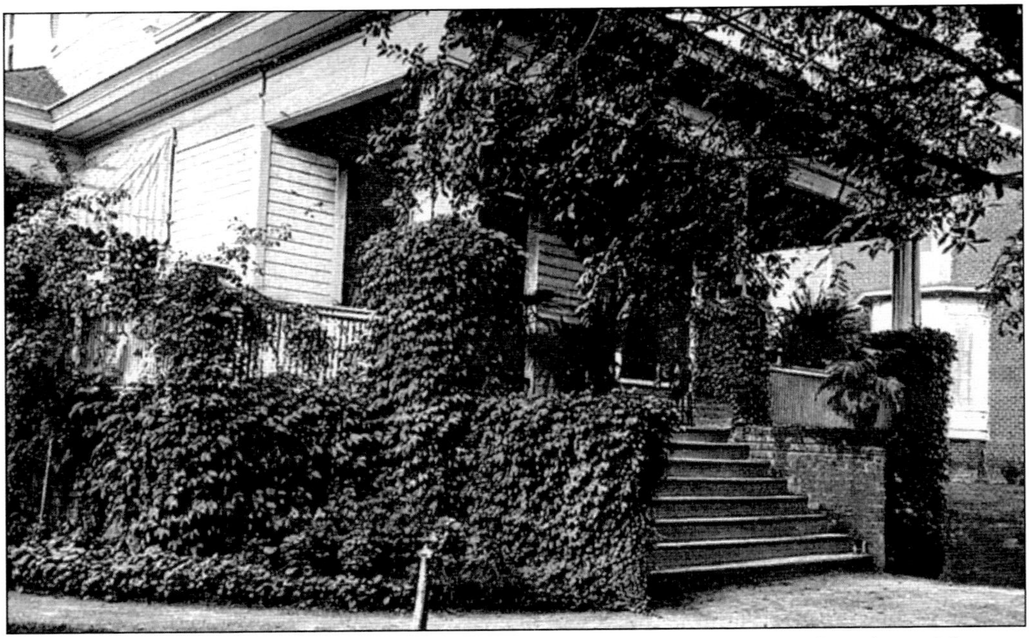

D.L. Bost purchased the land on which this house sits in 1897 and erected this dwelling about eight years later. Bost used the prominent Charlotte architectural firm of Hook and Sawyer to design his South Union Street home. He was a grocer in the firm of Dove and Bost. Today, this is the home of Mr. and Mrs. William F. "Bill" Grist. (Courtesy of the Charles A. Cannon Memorial Library.)

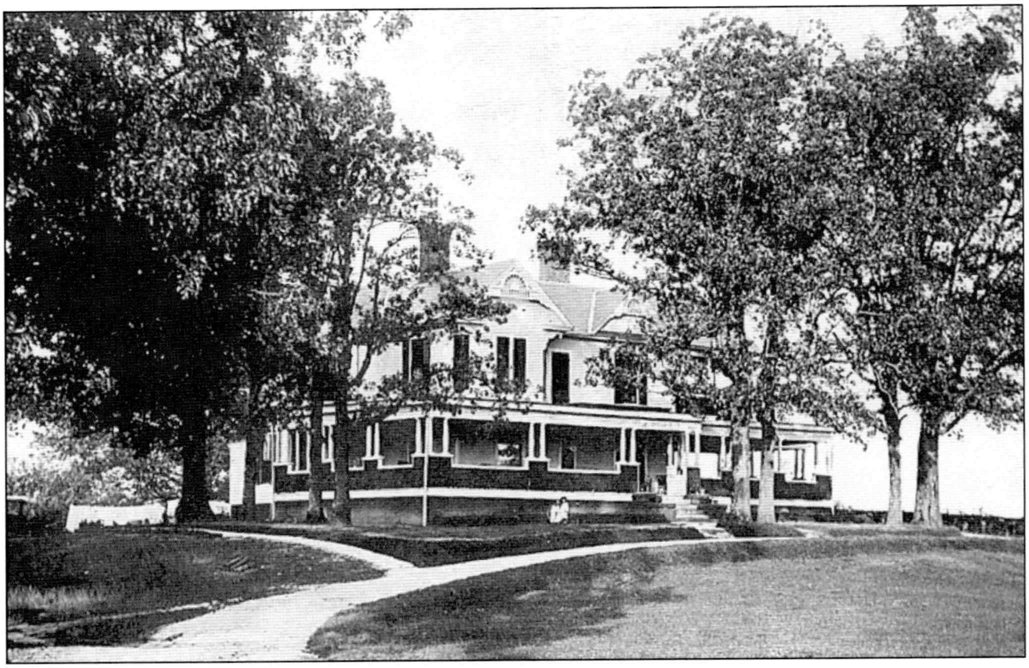

The Charles Franklin Ritchie residence was located at 391 South Union Street. Built around 1903, this house is highlighted with an unusually wide front porch. Ritchie owned Ritchie Hardware, located in the Pythian Building. Heath Ritchie, a grandson to C.F. Ritchie, along with his wife, Carolyn, and their two children Ben and Elizabeth, live here today. (Courtesy of Jimmy and Bonta Kee.)

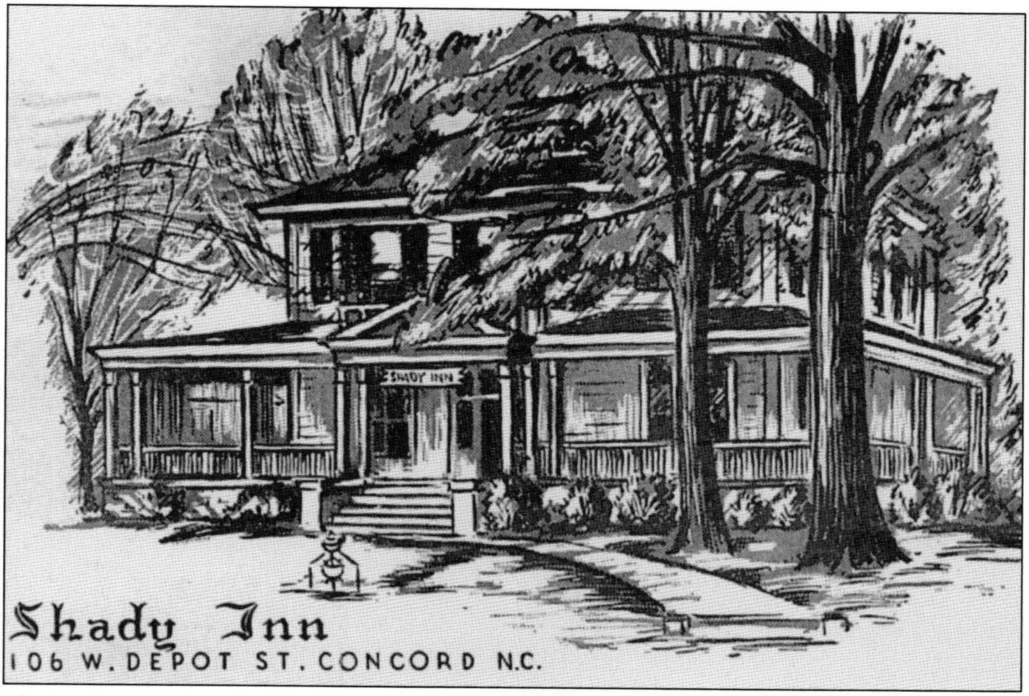

This hand-drawn card with a postmark of 1943 shows the "Shady Inn," located at 106 West Depot Street at the corner of Georgia Avenue. The owner of the inn was John D. Rogers. Today Larry and Susan Hathcock reside at this home. (Courtesy of Susan G. Sides.)

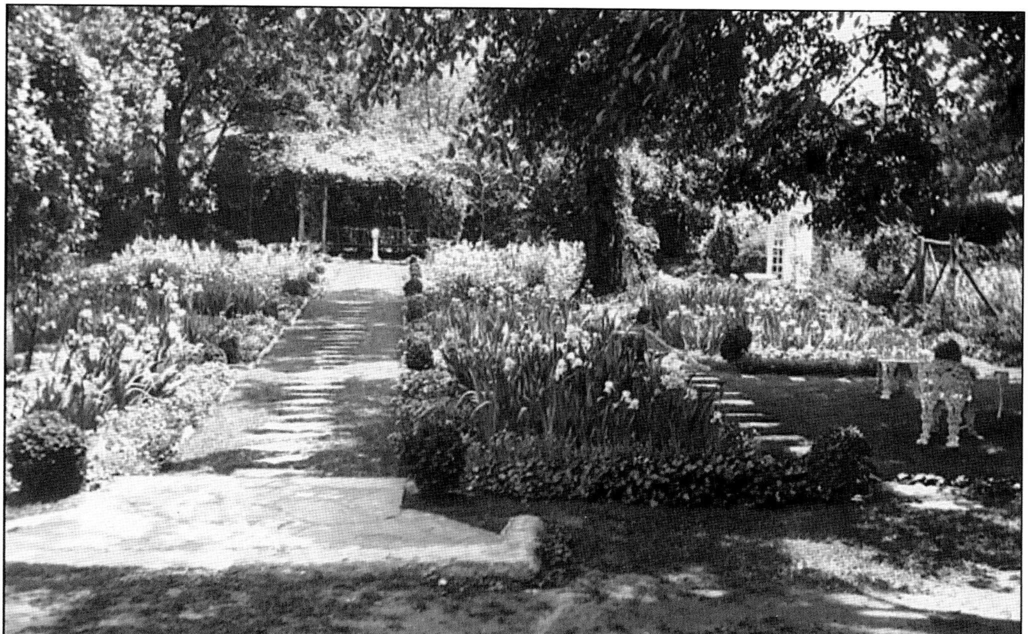

James and Zula Patterson Brown lived in a home on 103 West Depot Street (Cabarrus Avenue), which also had this garden spot. Today Mr. and Mrs. Alfred Brown resides at this residence. (Courtesy of Alex and Jane Patterson.)

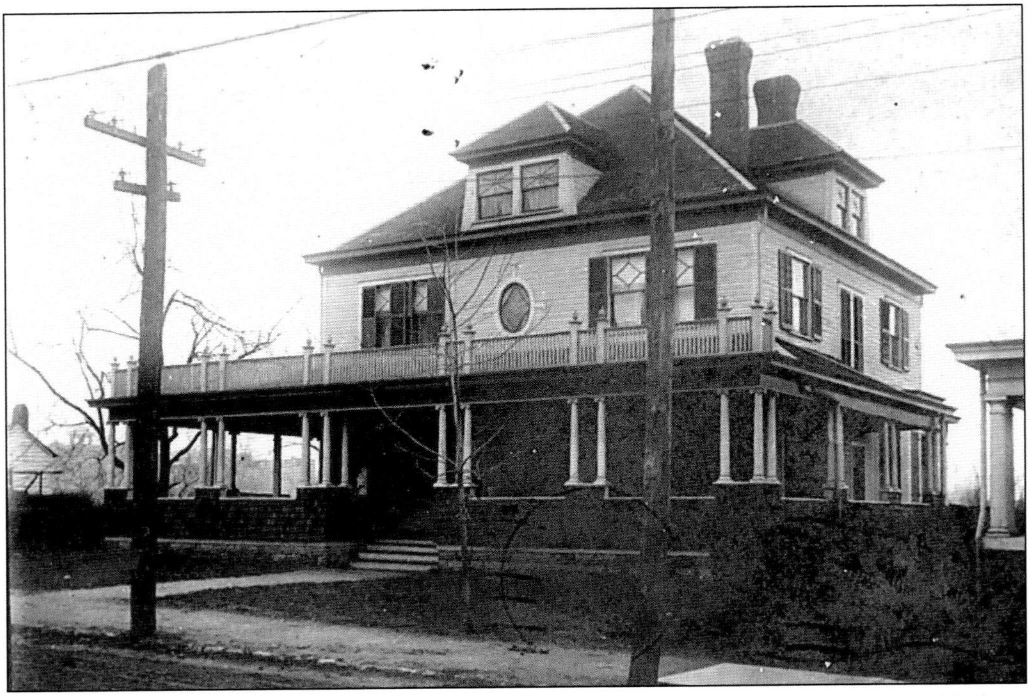

Mr. Robert E. and Fannie Fisher Ridenhour Sr. lived at this home at 63 West Depot Street. Ridenhour was the owner of the Concord Steam Laundry, also located on West Depot Street. (Courtesy of Mike Coltrane.)

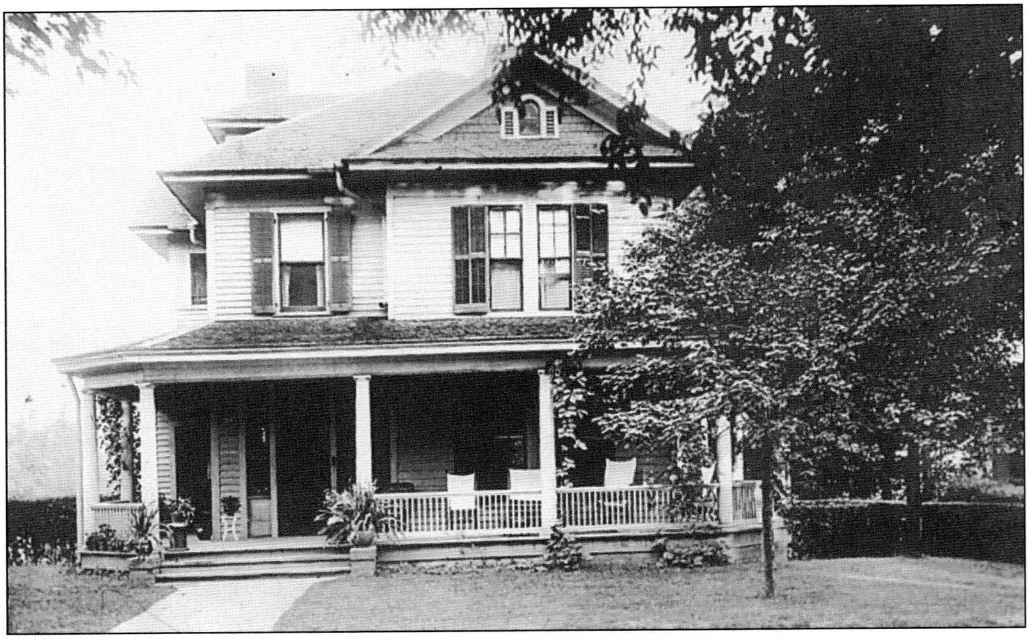

The location of this home, originally belonging to L.A. Weddington, was 59 West Depot Street. When this card was published the home was owned by the K.L. Craven family. Mr. Craven was the owner of Craven and Sons Coal Company, which was established in 1893 on Kerr Street. This card was published by Matthews Studio. (Courtesy of Historic Cabarrus.)

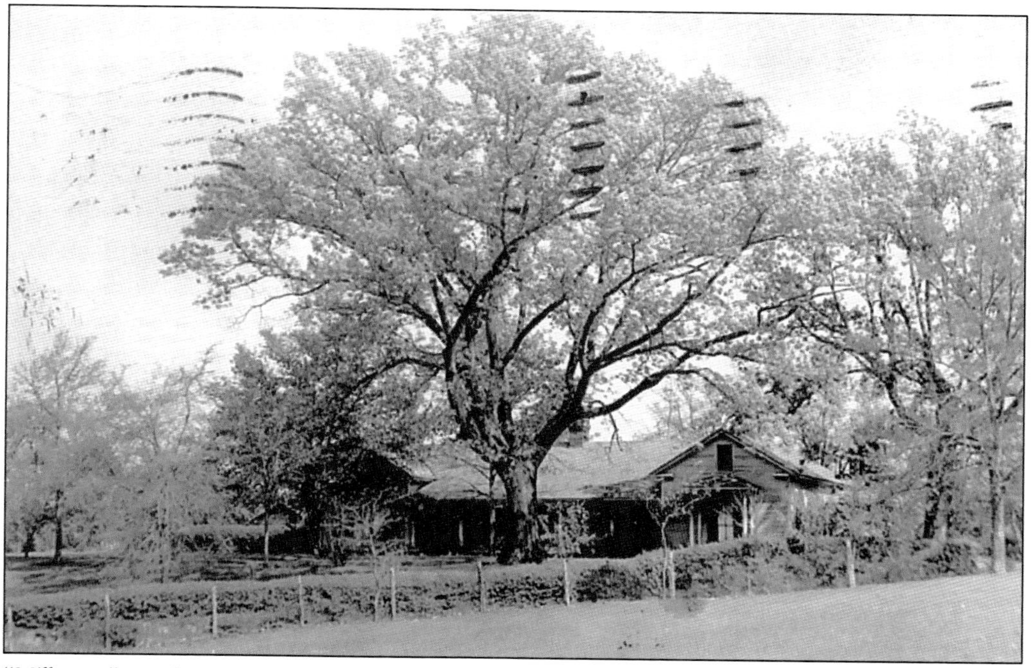

"Millgrove" was the name given to this house located along Rocky River in eastern Cabarrus County. This card was another "invitation" used by the Garden Club of Concord and featured what is today the summer home of the Carl Propst family. (Courtesy of Marian Harter.)

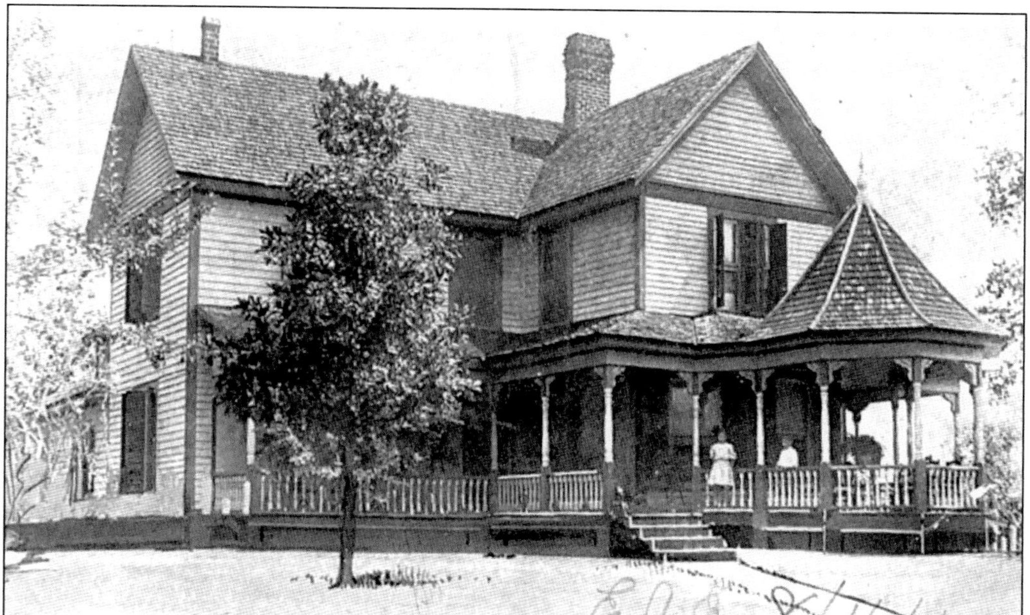

The most notable feature of the A.W. Moose home at 115 East Franklin Street is the octagonal pavilion with a flared witch's cap roof at the center of the front porch. Moose, a doctor and a druggist, bought the land on which this house sits from Lawson G. Heilig in 1885. His pharmacy, still in operation today, is located near the square. (Courtesy of Wayne Chapman.)

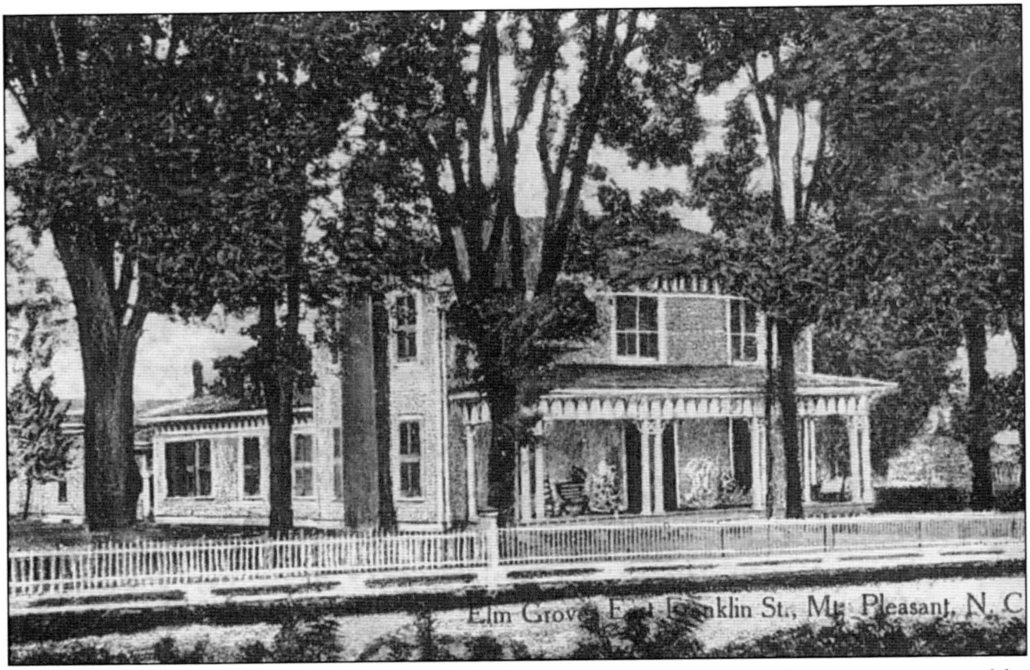

The Heilig Foil house was erected in 1858 and remodeled and enlarged according to plans prepared by Charlotte architect Louis Asbury during the early 1920s. Today Mr. Sam Colerider III makes this his home at 8425 East Franklin Street.

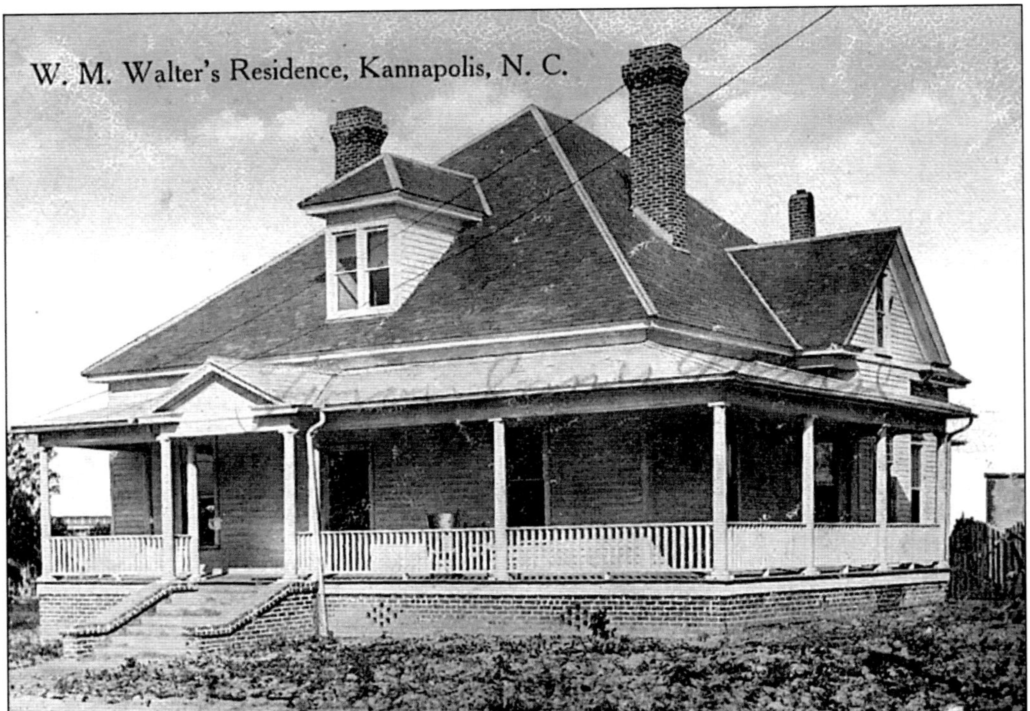

The W.M. "Bill" Walters home was located where Kimball Lutheran Church sits today on South Main Street. Walters owned a grocery store in downtown Kannapolis. (Courtesy of Don and Vickie Cline.)

Five

Churches

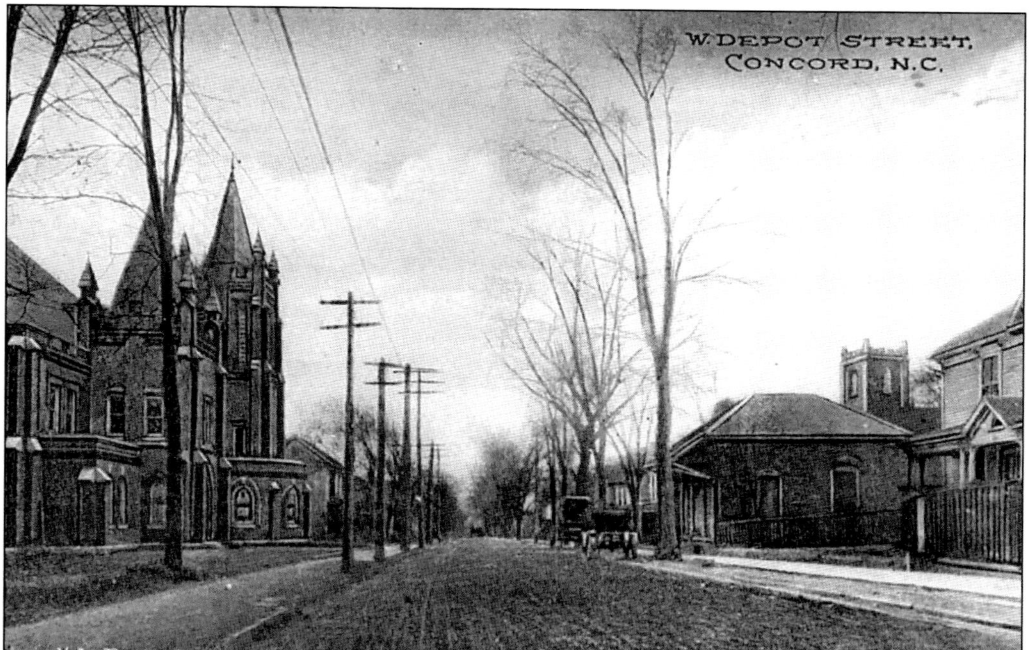

The photographer set his tripod slightly to the south side of West Depot (Cabarrus Avenue) at about Market Street to capture this image. On the left is the fourth building used by the First Presbyterian Church. Directly across the street is All Saints Episcopal Church, whose steeple is seen above the roof tops. (Courtesy of Marian Harter.)

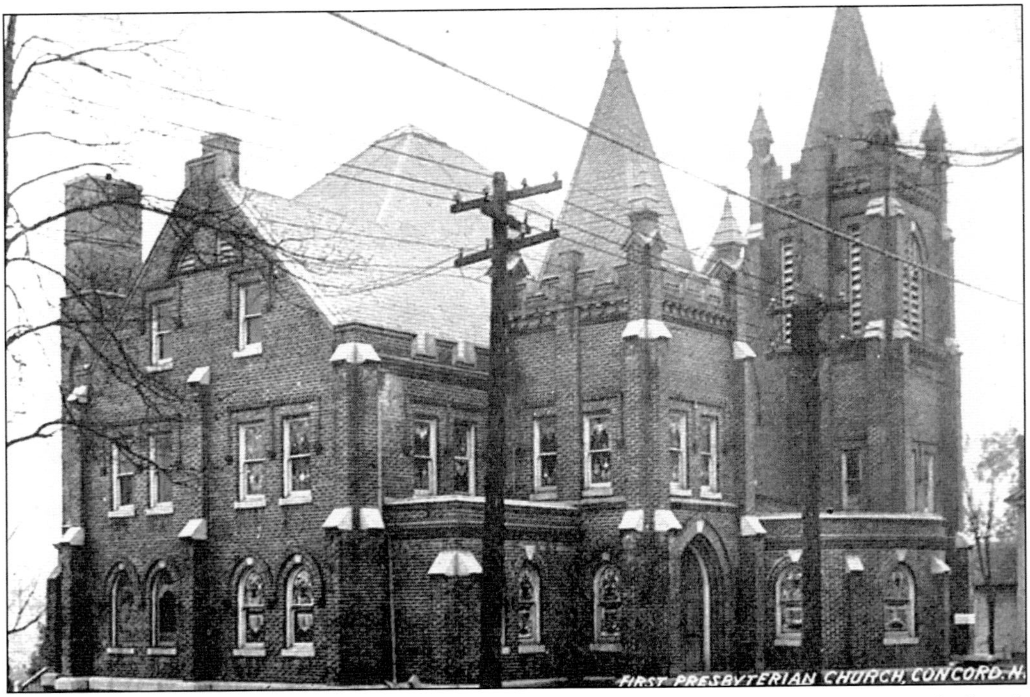

The fourth church building used by First Presbyterian Church can be seen in this 1909-postmarked card. This building was located just west of the third church, which sat where the old Bob's Laundry used to be. This building was first occupied in 1905 and used until their fifth and present church was ready for use in 1927. (Courtesy of Susan G. Sides.)

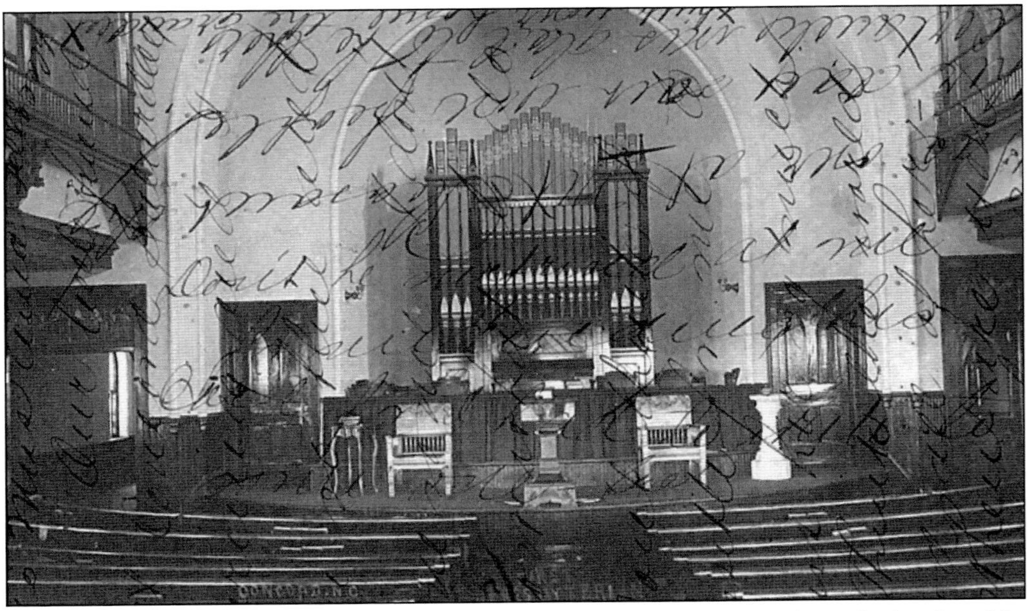

Though the sender used the face of this card to scribble their message, the image shows the interior of the First Presbyterian Church sanctuary. This was the fourth church and shows the grand organ that was the focal point of the sanctuary. The organ is the same one that was in the old Memorial Hall at the Community Center. (Courtesy of Mike Coltrane.)

Shown is yet another image of First Presbyterian Church taken from the west side. Tracks for Concord's streetcar can be seen on Depot Street (Cabarrus Avenue). The first and second buildings of First Presbyterian Church were located a short distance south of (behind) this building.

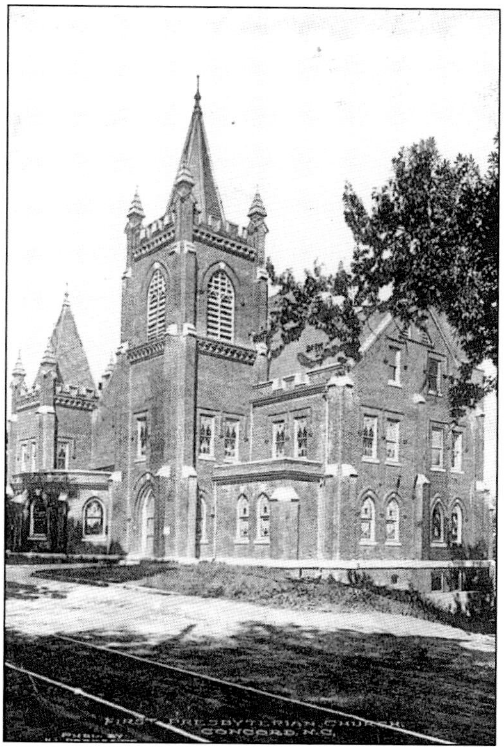

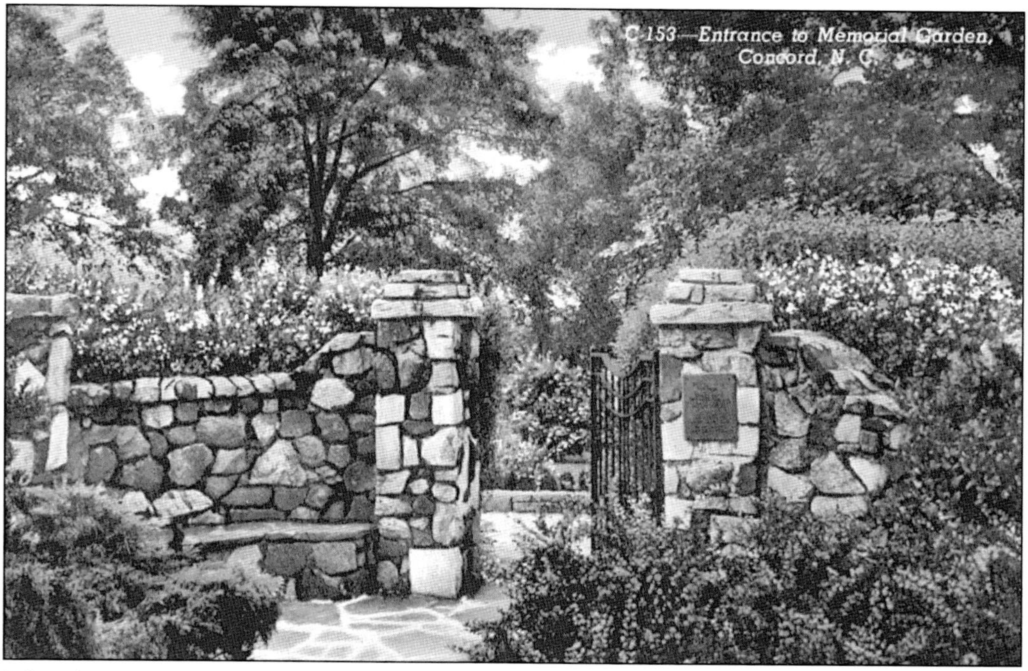

When the First Presbyterian Church's first building was constructed in 1810, land just north of the sanctuary had already been designated for use as a cemetery. The oldest grave in the cemetery is that of Joseph Shinn who died on January 22, 1804. This image shows the beautiful rock entrance from South Spring Street as it looks today.

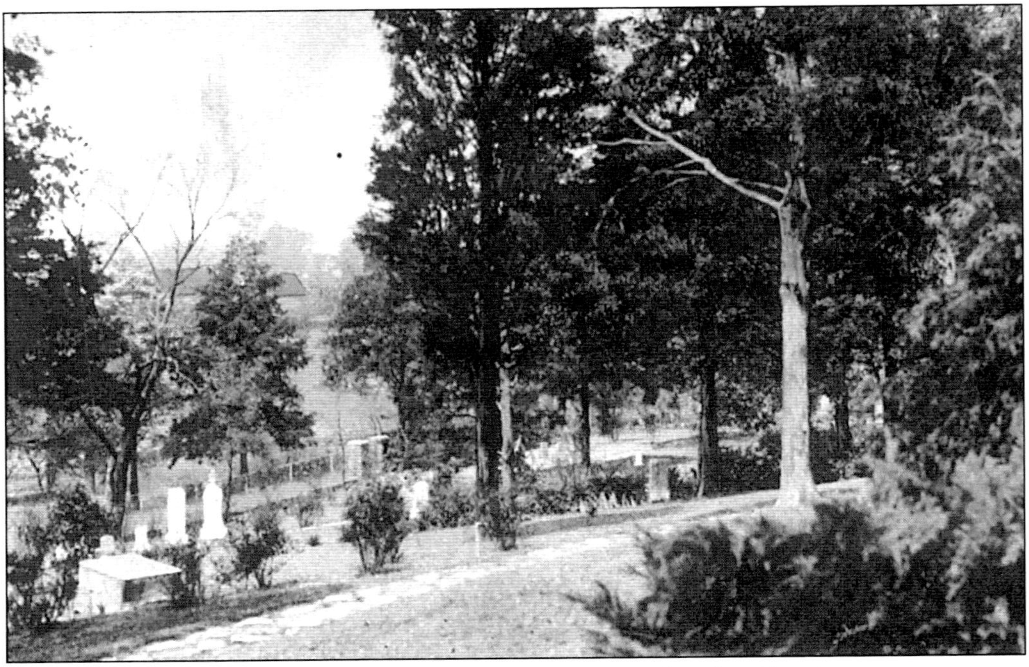

Within the Memorial Gardens, the name given to the First Presbyterian Church cemetery, one can find the graves of some of the earliest settlers of Concord. This image was taken from the hill where the first and second church buildings were located, looking down into the cemetery. (Courtesy of Marian Harter.)

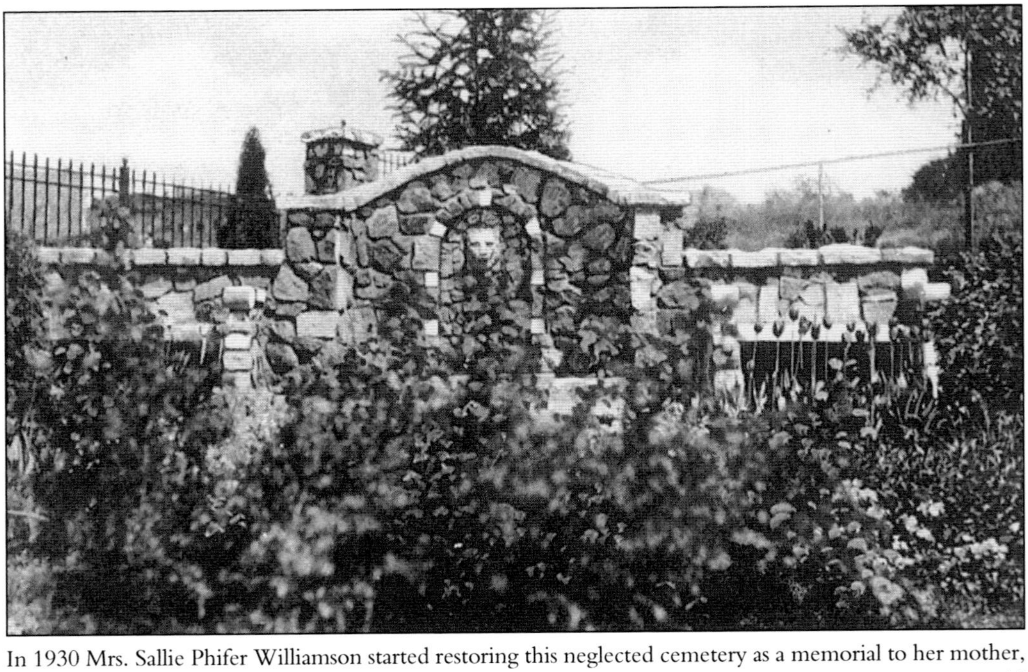

In 1930 Mrs. Sallie Phifer Williamson started restoring this neglected cemetery as a memorial to her mother, Mrs. Adeline Ramseur Phifer. Aaron Jones Yorke and his wife, Martha Best Yorke, also deserve special mention for their help in the development of the garden we see today. This image is of the Lion's Head fountain located there. (Courtesy of Marian Harter.)

The congregation of First Presbyterian Church commissioned New York architect Hobart Upjohn to design a new house of worship to be located at 70 North Union Street. This was their fifth and present church building. This is another Dexter Press Company postcard. (Courtesy of Alex and Jane Patterson.)

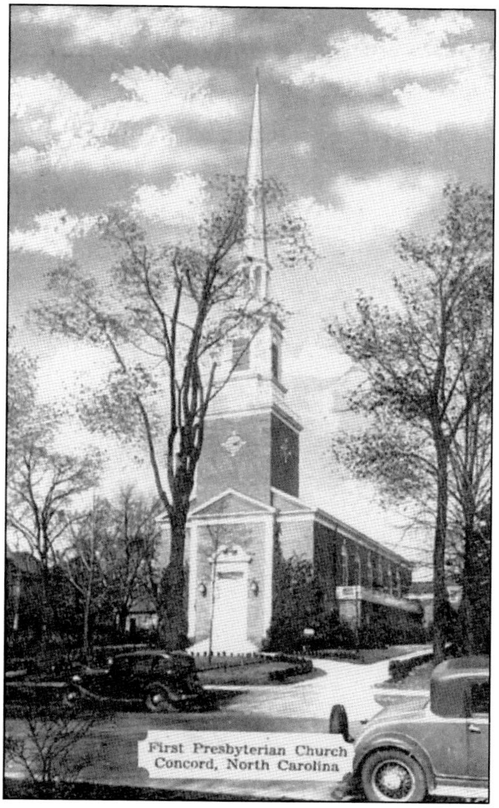

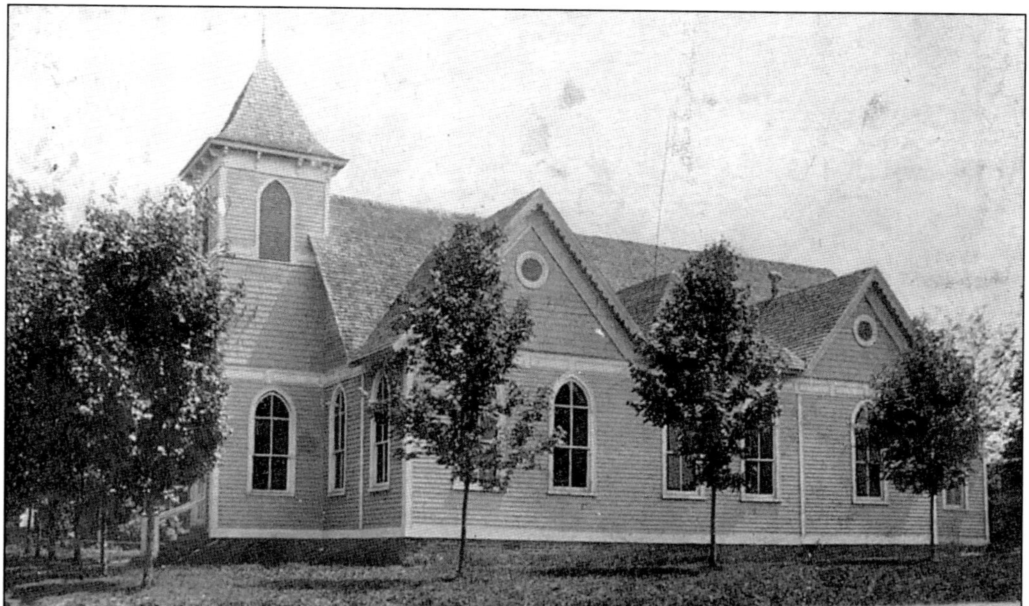

Built in 1888, First Baptist Church was located at the intersection of Spring Street and Grove Avenue. The building was replaced at this same location in 1924 by a modern place of worship. Today First Baptist Church overlooks the city at 200 Branchview Drive.

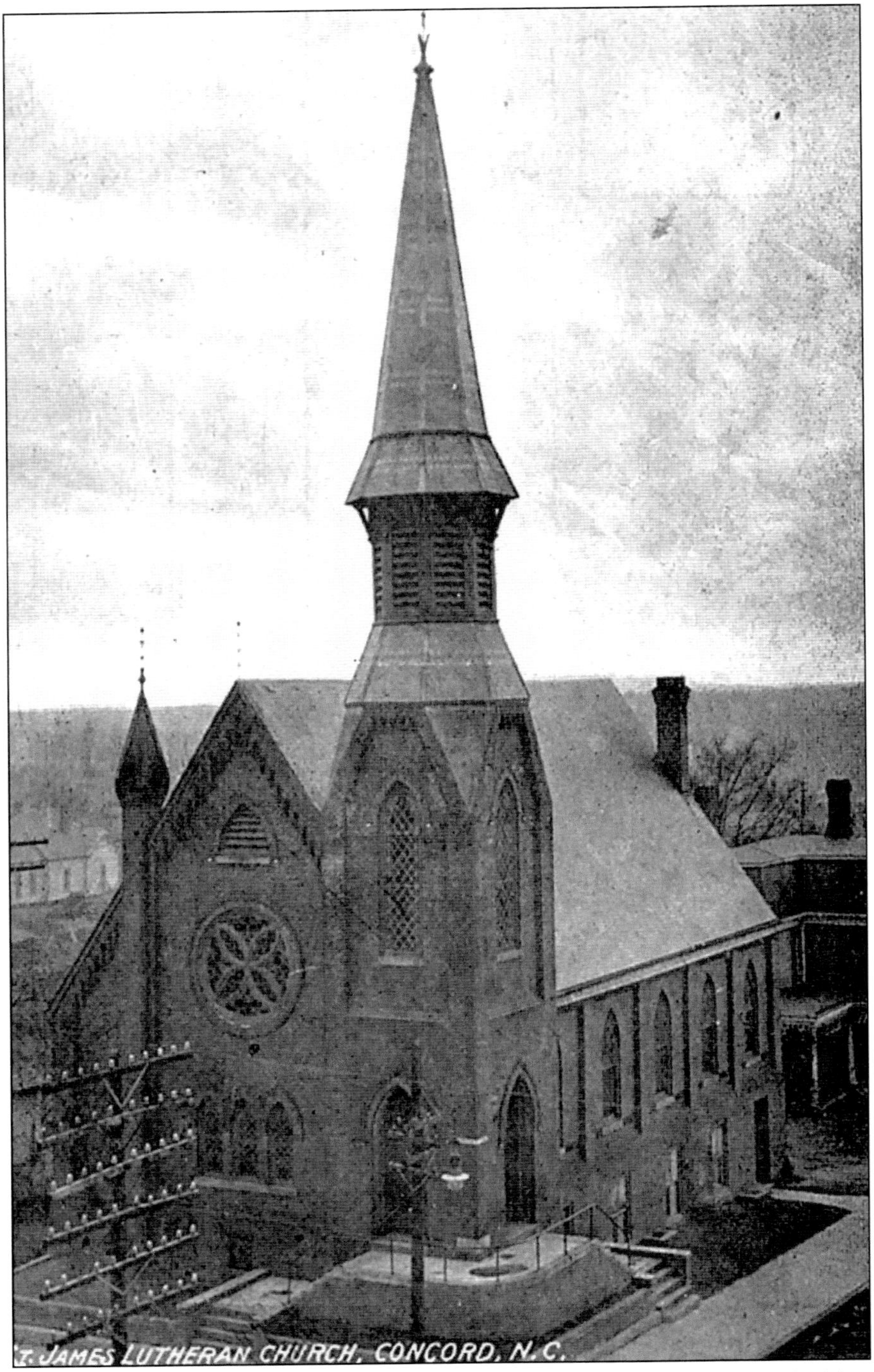

St. James Lutheran Church was a focal point to Concord's downtown. This second church building, located on the southwest corner of South Union and Corban Street, was erected in 1882 on property owned by Robert W. Foard and known as "Foard's Corner." The building served the congregation for 45 years but was razed in 1927 to make room for the third St. James Evangelical Lutheran Church. This card was produced by the White, Morris, Flowe Company, and the photographer placed his camera on the Allison Building to capture this image.

With its 115-foot lofty spiral, St. James Lutheran Church's steeple seemed to pierce the clouds and could be seen from many hill tops in Cabarrus County, making it one of the best landmarks in town. The symmetrical beauty of the exterior commands admiration and the worshipful interior makes people feel they are on hallowed ground.

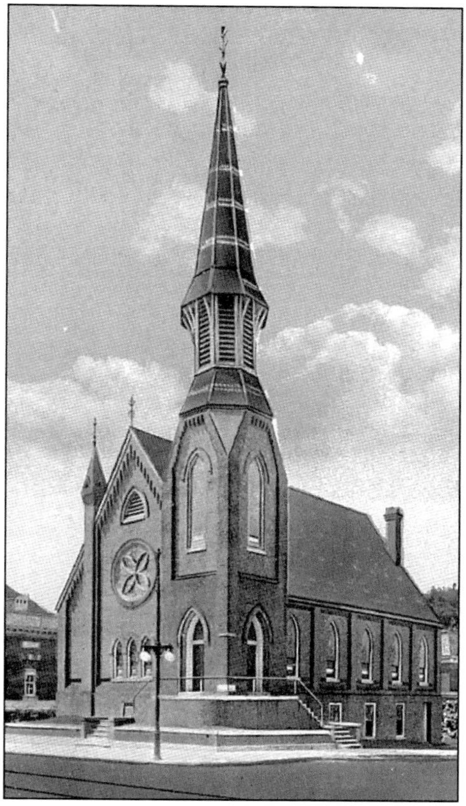

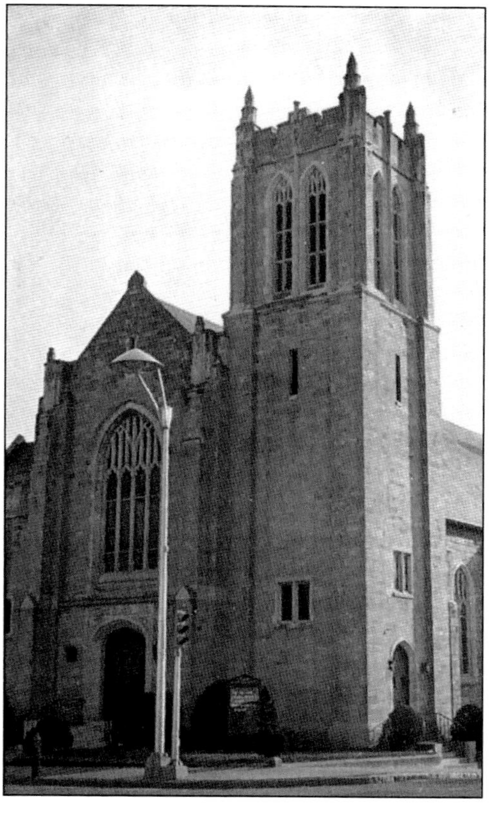

This present structure is the third house of worship of Concord's oldest Lutheran congregation, which was founded in 1843. The first church building was a simple frame structure erected in 1845 and stood at a site on Corban Avenue just southeast of Church Street. The second building was a imposing brick Gothic Revival building that stood on the site of the present church. Concord's most sophisticated Gothic sanctuary, St. James Lutheran Church's third building was constructed in 1928.

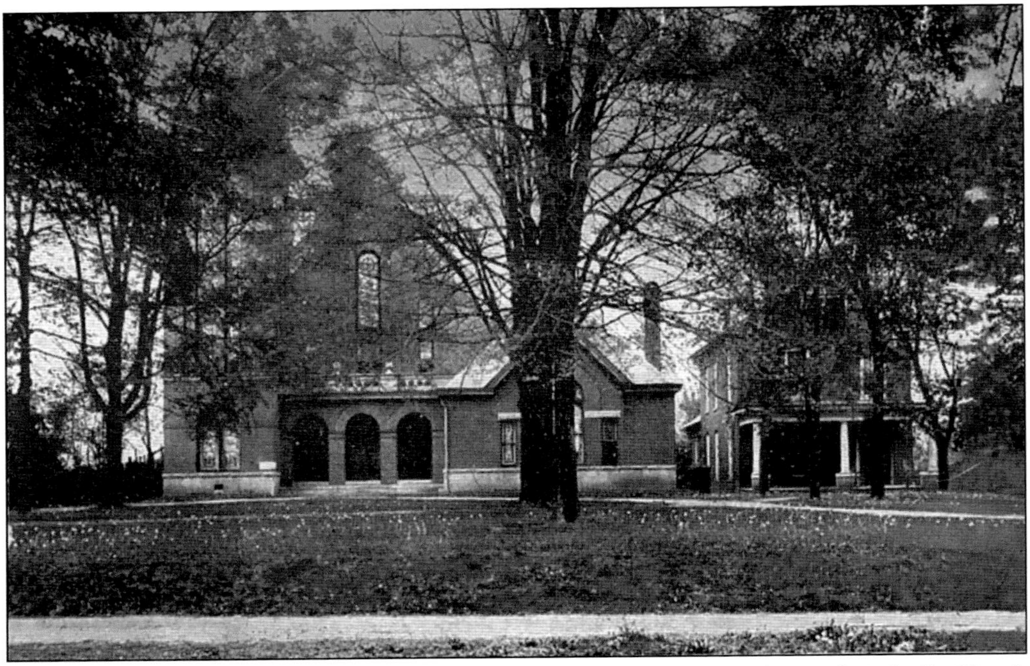

Prominent members of the Concord community challenged the move of Central United Methodist Church from its first location at the corner of Church Street and East Depot to North Union Street at the very edge of town simply because the Methodist were "too noisy in their worship and shouted too much." This move took place around 1860. (Courtesy of Susan G. Sides.)

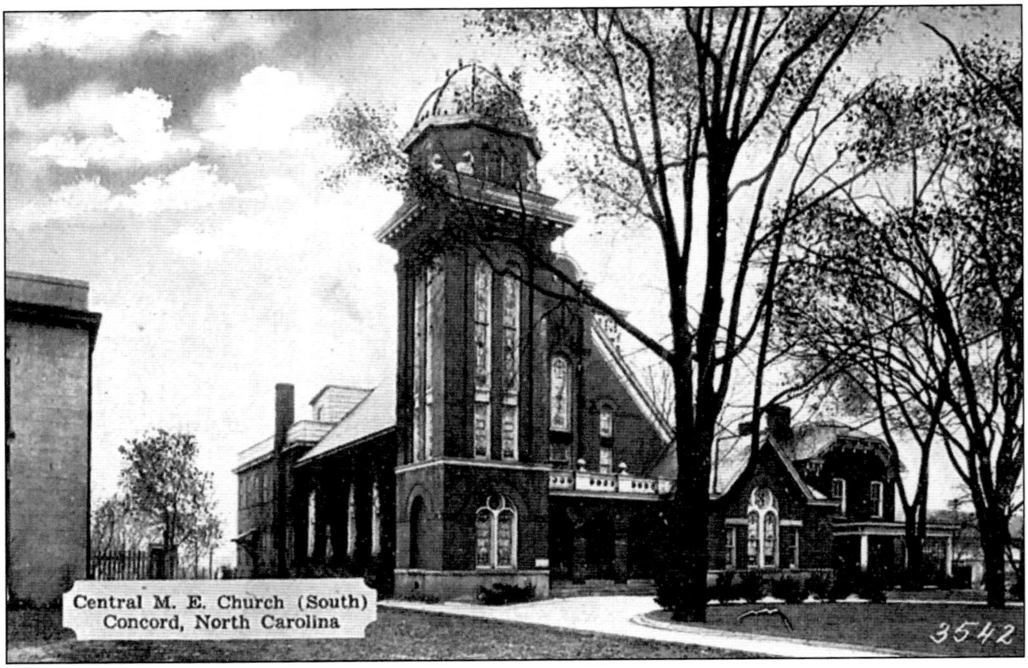

Another view of Central United Methodist Church made by the Dexter Press Company shows the north side of the church. Just to the left is the Sandy Smith residence, which later became the YMCA. The church parsonage can be seen to the right of the church.

Located on Gold Hill Road northeast of Concord, this was the first building used by St. James Catholic Church. The card shows Father Cowan who, according to the sender of this card, was "the best man in the world." This first church building was constructed in 1869 and this image was made after the 1925 renovation of the front porch was completed.

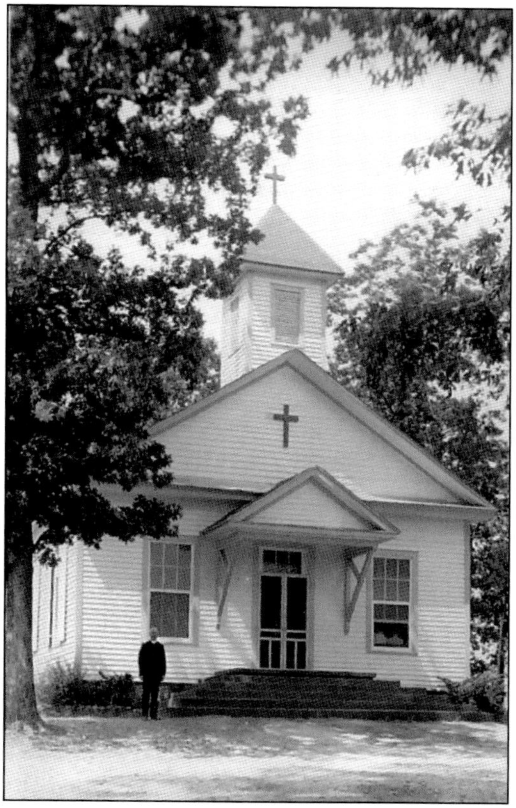

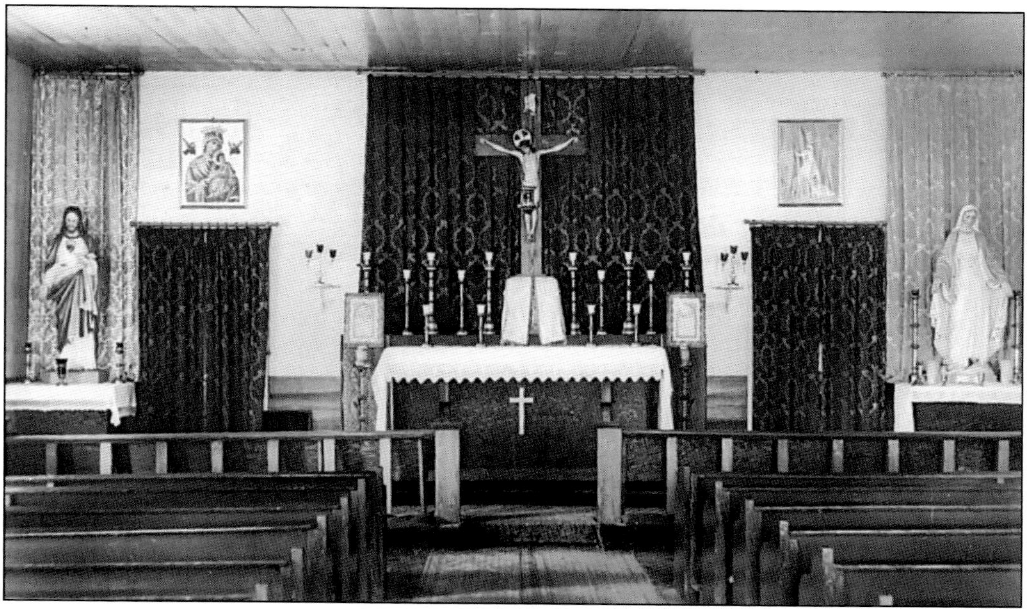

In February 1954, Mrs. Guy Cress observed dense, black smoke coming from St. James Catholic Church and before long the entire building was engulfed in flames. Very little could be salvaged. That same year work began on North Union Street for St. James's new and present sanctuary. This card shows the interior of the Gold Hill Road sanctuary.

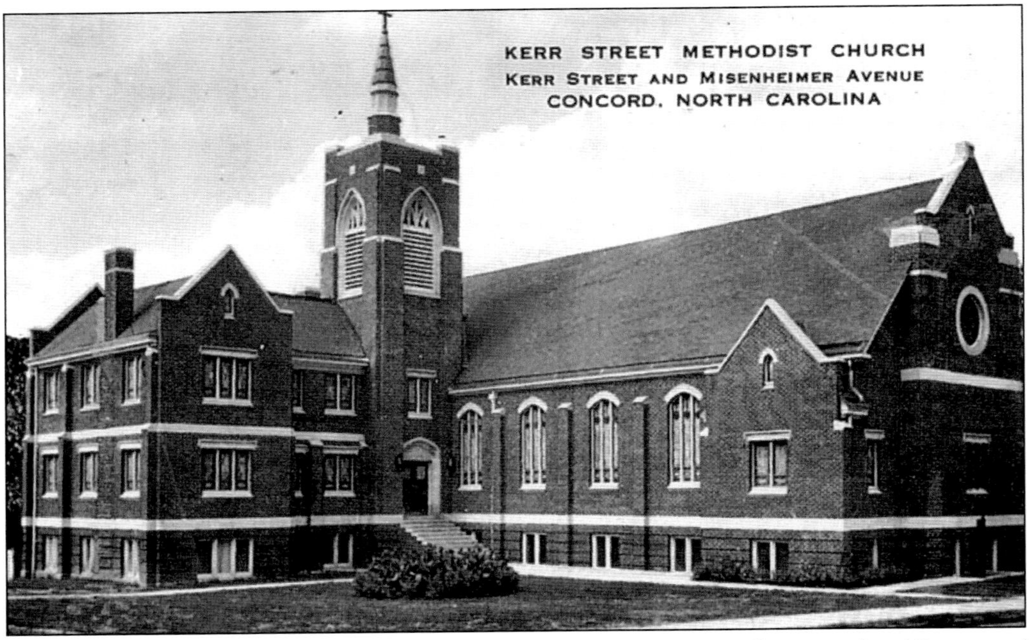

Pictured here is Kerr Street Methodist Church, located in the Gibson Mill community. (Courtesy of Marian Harter.)

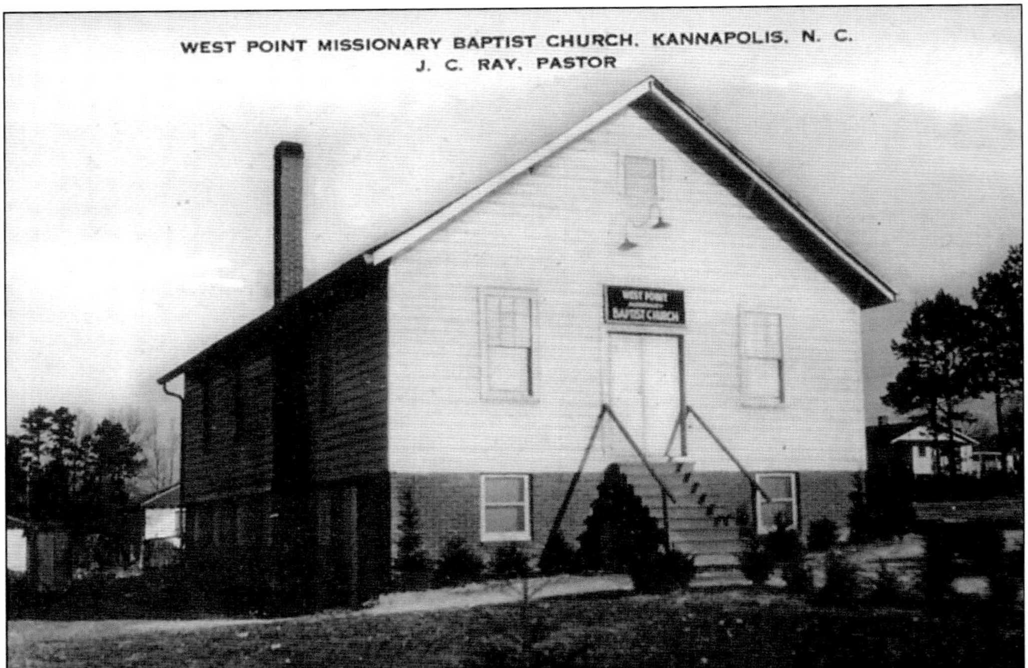

West Point Missionary Baptist Church had the Reverend J.C. Ray as its minister when this postcard was made. Rev. Ray preached here from 1937 to 1943. This was the church's first building and it was located on Pine Street in the existing West Point Baptist Church parking lot. (Courtesy of Marian Harter.)

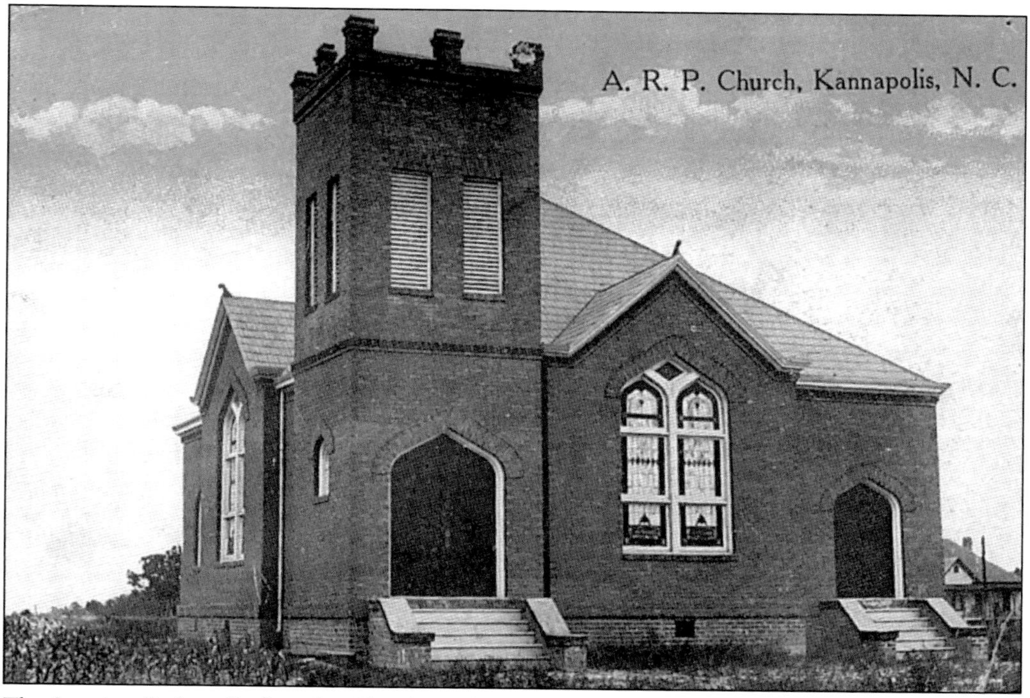

The Associate Reform Presbyterian Church was located across the street from Kimball Lutheran on South Main Street. (Courtesy of Marian Harter.)

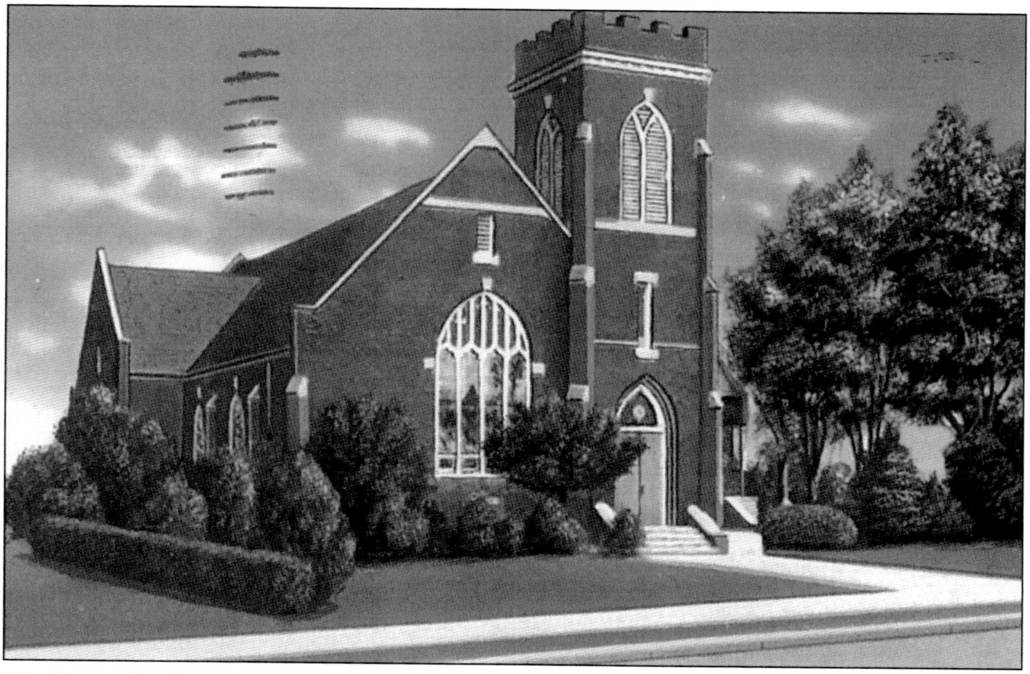

Worship services began on December 14, 1913 in the Cannon YMCA for a group of Lutherans from the area. The cornerstone was laid for Kimball Memorial Evangelical Lutheran Church March 29, 1917, and on February 17, 1918, the first services were held. This sanctuary was razed to allow for a second church building to be built, and on December 22, 1963, the first service was held in the present-day sanctuary.

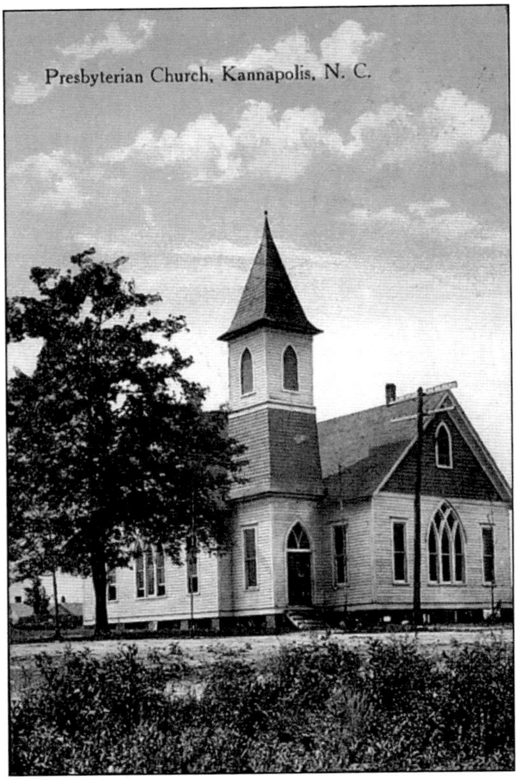

The Presbyterian Church was organized on June 27, 1909 with 25 charter members. This building was on Main Street right up in the heart of town. Records show that services were first held here in January 1911. (Courtesy of Marian Harter.)

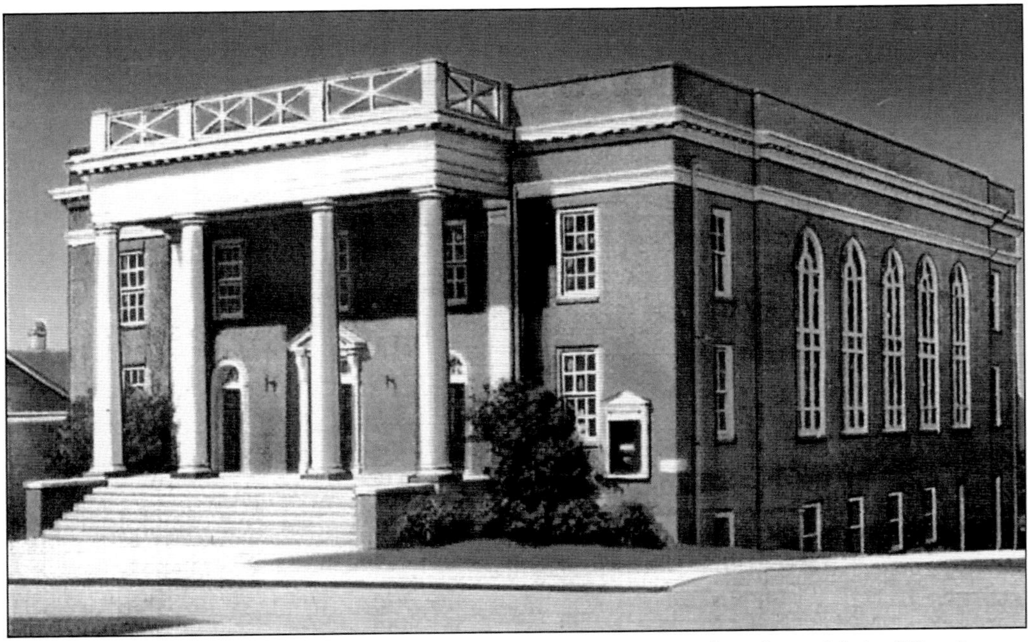

The second building of the First Presbyterian Church was built in 1924 and was located facing West Avenue with Vance Street on the north side. On March 18, 1925, the congregation held the first worship service in its main auditorium. In 1974 First Presbyterian's congregation began services in their third and present church building. (Courtesy of Marian Harter.)

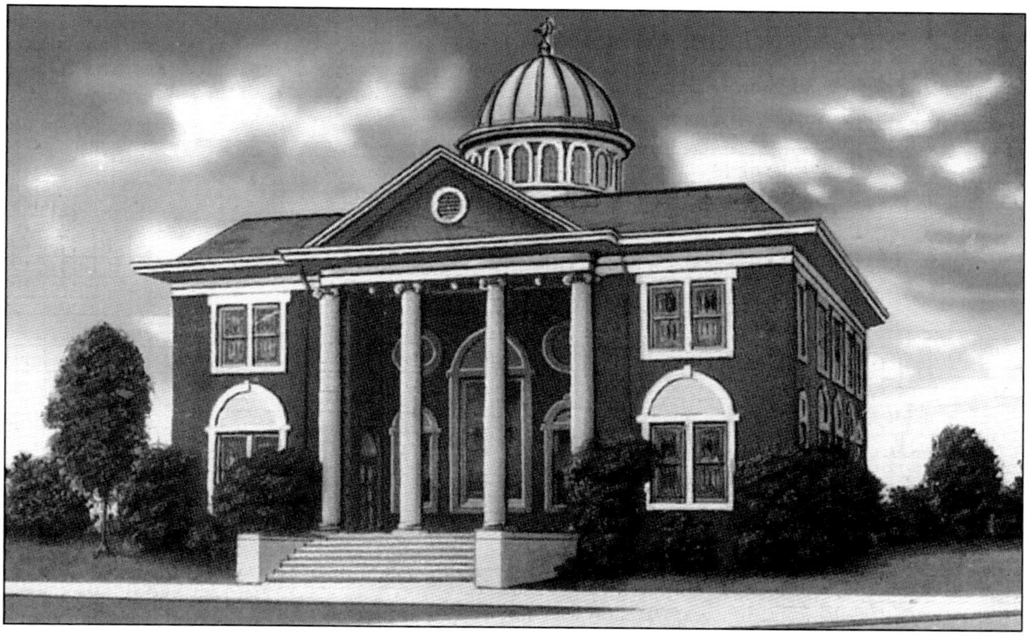

On the night of October 11, 1908, at 8 p.m., the First Baptist Church of Kannapolis was formed. The very first service was held on Thanksgiving night in 1912 with snow lying on the ground. This postcard shows the church with its new sanctuary located on North Main Street at First Street and today's Lake Circle Drive. (Courtesy of Jim Ramseur.)

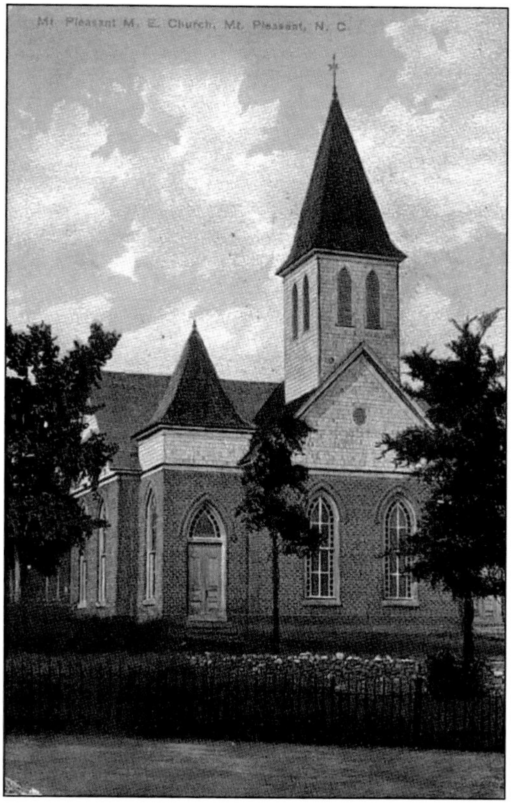

Land was purchased from Jacob Ludwig to build the Methodist Church in Mt. Pleasant with the oldest known deed of land, dating back to September 17, 1847. Three church buildings were used before this fourth church was built in 1885. The fifth and present church was built in 1949. (Courtesy of Wayne Chapman.)

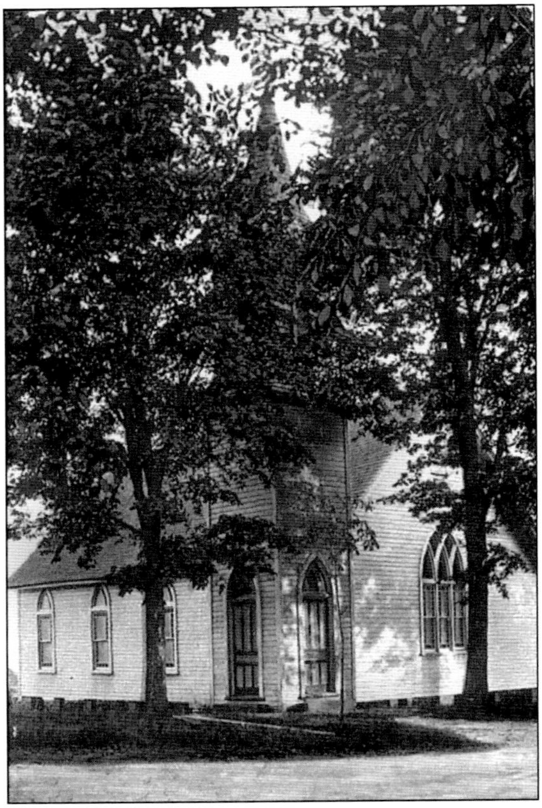

St. James United Church of Christ was organized on December 3, 1884, in the home of Mrs. Edmund Foil. The organizing pastor was Rev. Dr. Paul Barringer. The original building was begun in September 1895 on land donated by W.J. Heilig. The present structure of St. James Reformed United Church of Christ, as this church is known today, was completed in 1924 and is located on Walnut Street. (Courtesy of Wayne Chapman.)

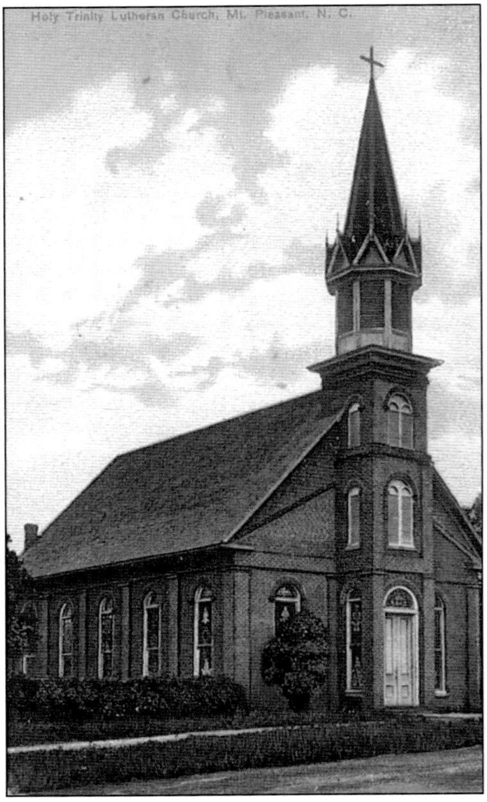

Holy Trinity Lutheran Church was located on South Main Street across from Mont Amoena Seminary. The congregation first used the chapel in the old North Carolina College in 1868 as a place to worship. Their minister was Rev. C. Groseclose, and they held services there for five years. On March 18, 1871, a lot was secured and the following year this building was constructed. (Courtesy of Wayne Chapman.)

Six

TRANSPORTATION

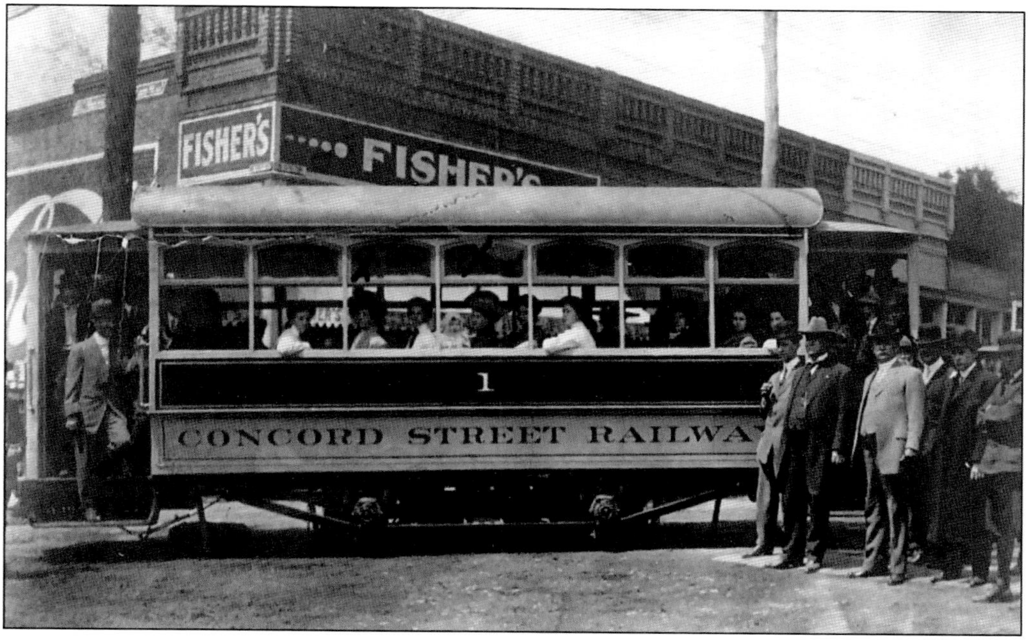

This postcard shows the inaugural run of Concord's streetcar in the fall of 1910. Only ladies are sitting at the car windows. Sam, a streetcar official from Salisbury, stands covering the "Y" in "RAILWAY." The first woman in the third window from the left is Mother Wadsworth and in the center of the fourth window is Mary Va. This streetcar proved unsatisfactory and was replaced with a conventional trolley about 1912. Approximately 10 years later, the trolley was discontinued. (Courtesy of the North Carolina Collection, University of North Carolina Library at Chapel Hill.)

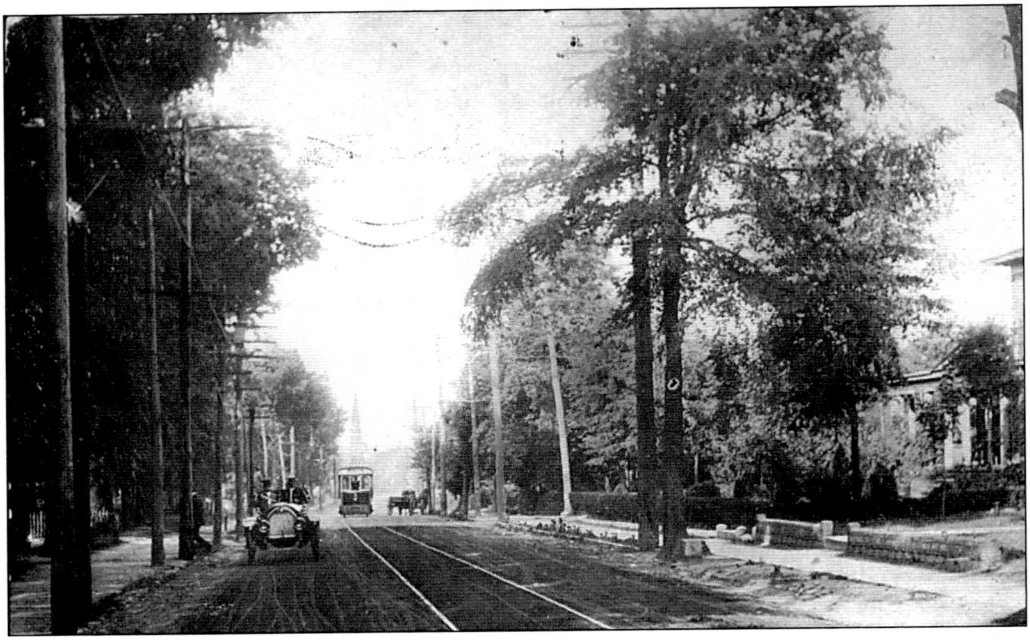

Davis Drug Company published this card of West Depot Street that shows quite a variety in transportation. An automobile, a horse-drawn wagon, the trolley, and a pedestrian are all shown on this 1914-postmarked image, taken just east of Georgia Avenue looking west.

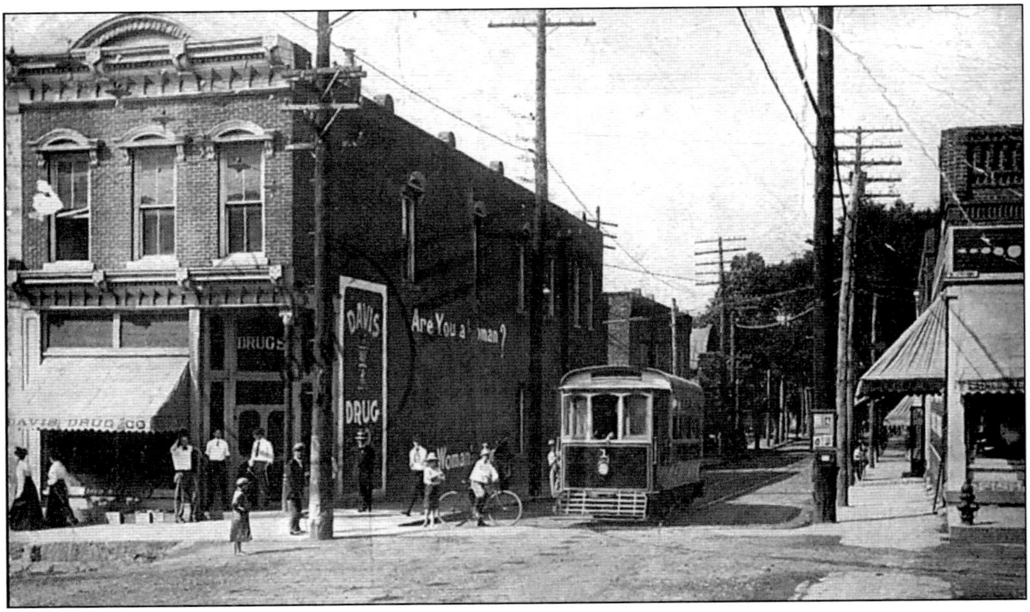

Dr. I.I. Davis was the proprietor of the Davis Drug Company (formerly Fetzer's Drug Store) located on the southwest corner of the square. This image was taken around 1910 and shows the streetcar approaching the square from West Depot Street. Dr. Davis is reported to be the gentleman with his hand on the awning near the front door. (Courtesy of Wayne Chapman.)

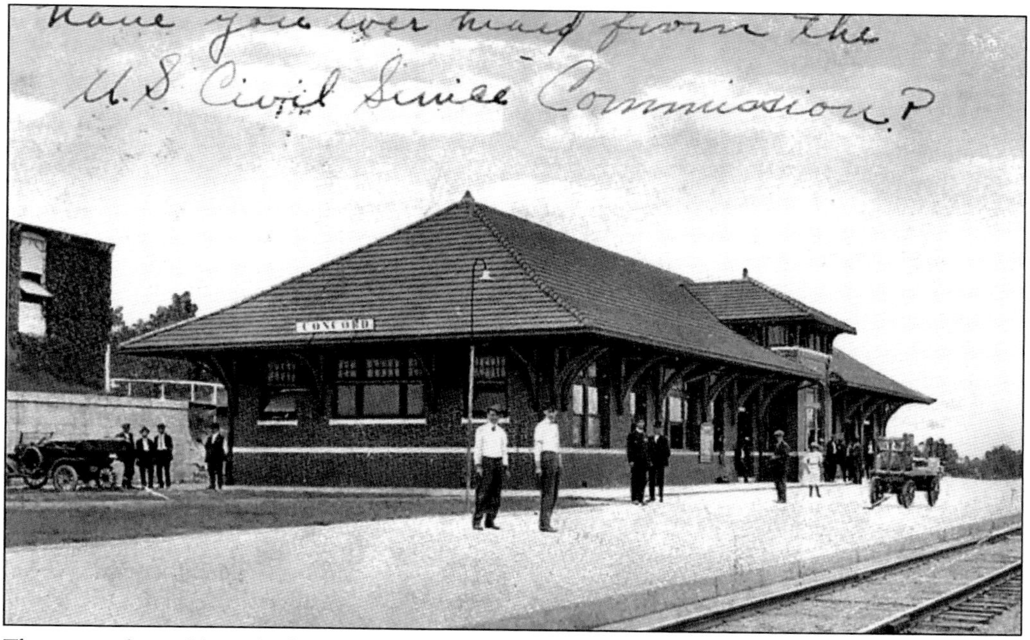

The postmark on this card of the Passenger Station of Southern Railway is 1917. The railroad was one reason for the many postcards depicting Cabarrus County scenes. The train depot was located on West Corban Street and was built in 1913.

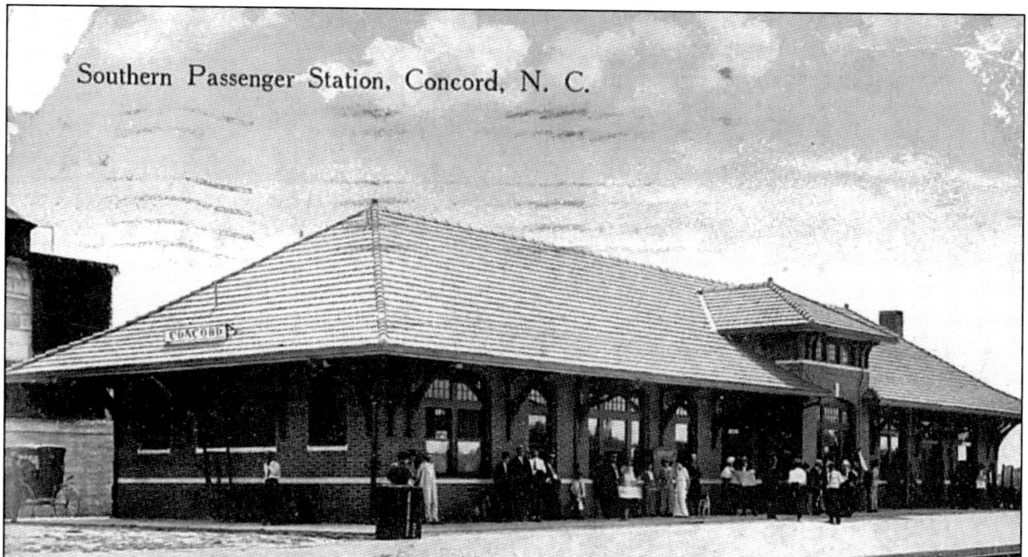

Another view of the Southern Railway Passenger Station, which was adjacent to the Cabarrus Cotton Mill, was produced around the mid-1920s. (Courtesy of Historic Cabarrus.)

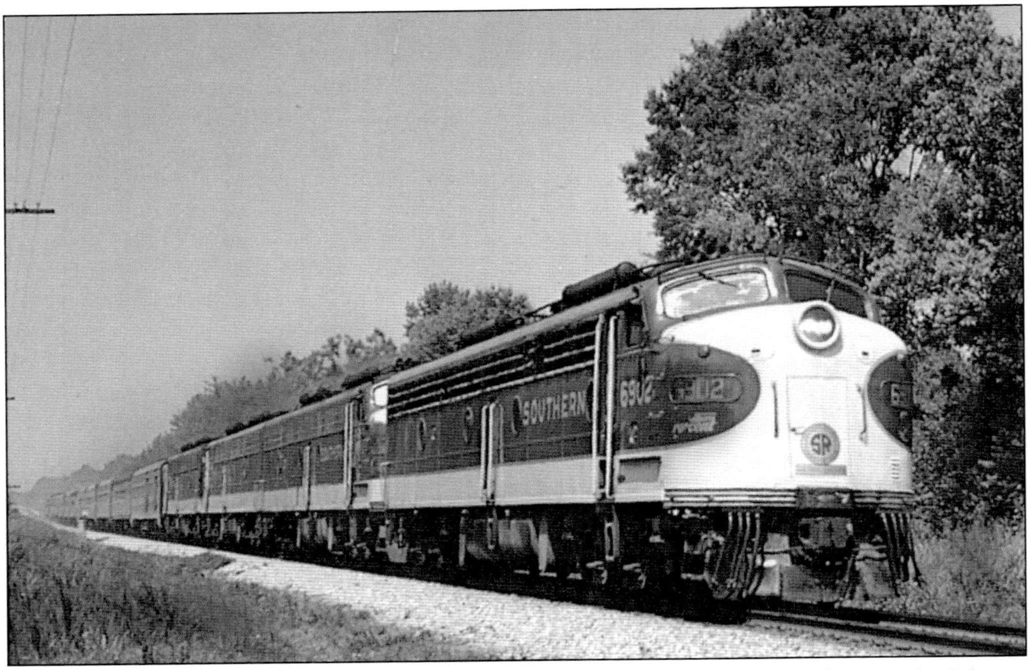

Southern Railway's "The Southern Crescent," powered by three E-8 Units, was often seen in Cabarrus County. Many passengers utilized this train at the Kannapolis and Concord depot. It was the main passenger line from Washington, D.C., through the heart of Dixie to New Orleans, Louisiana. (Courtesy of Marian Harter.)

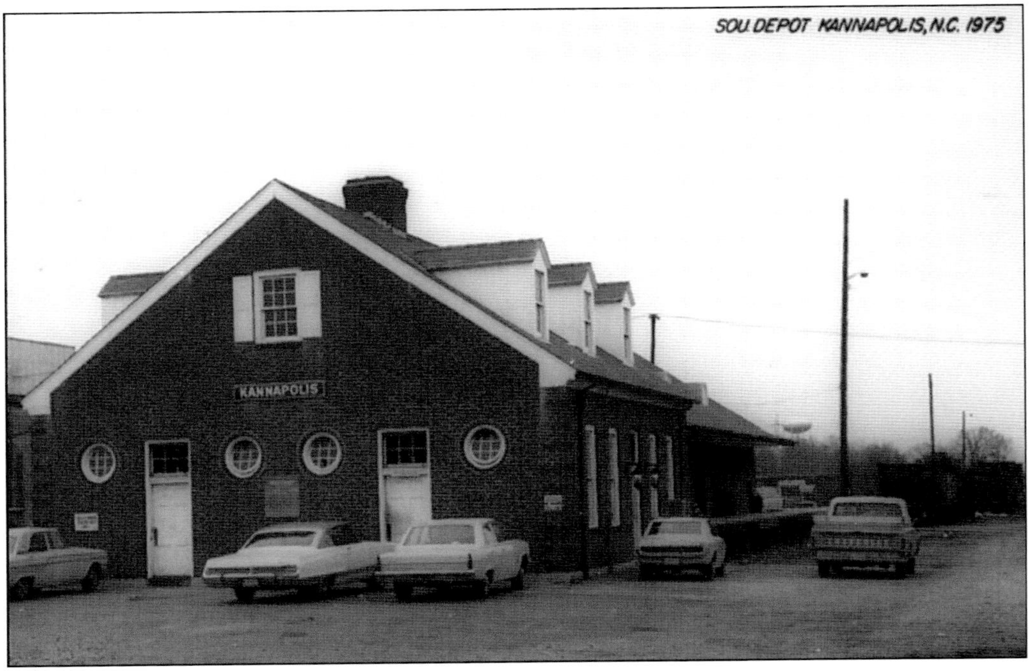

Kannapolis was just a hop and a skip north of Concord, but their train station was still a very active place due mostly to Cannon Mill. It is believed that the depot was built around 1937–1939 in the colonial tradition that was quite popular with Mr. Cannon. (Courtesy of Susan G. Sides.)

Seven

Cotton and Textiles

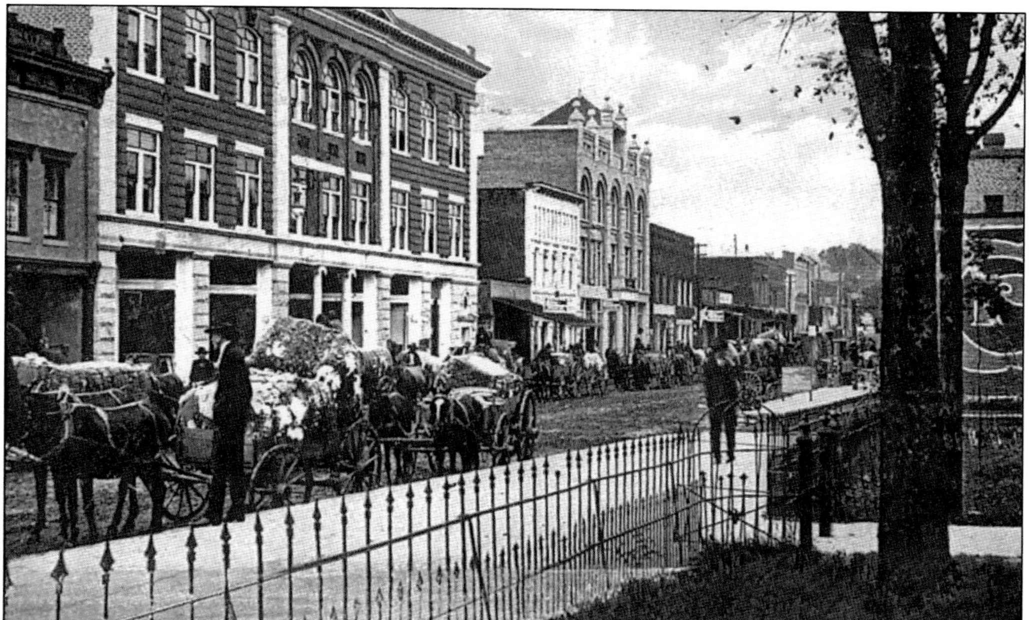

This card, postmarked 1909, was taken by the photographer O.V. Foust standing on the lawn of the 1876 courthouse. The wagons that are lined up on both sides of Union Street are filled with cotton waiting to be weighed and sold at the Cotton Platform, located behind city hall. Cotton was a tremendous boost to the economy in Concord, generating a sudden cash flow.

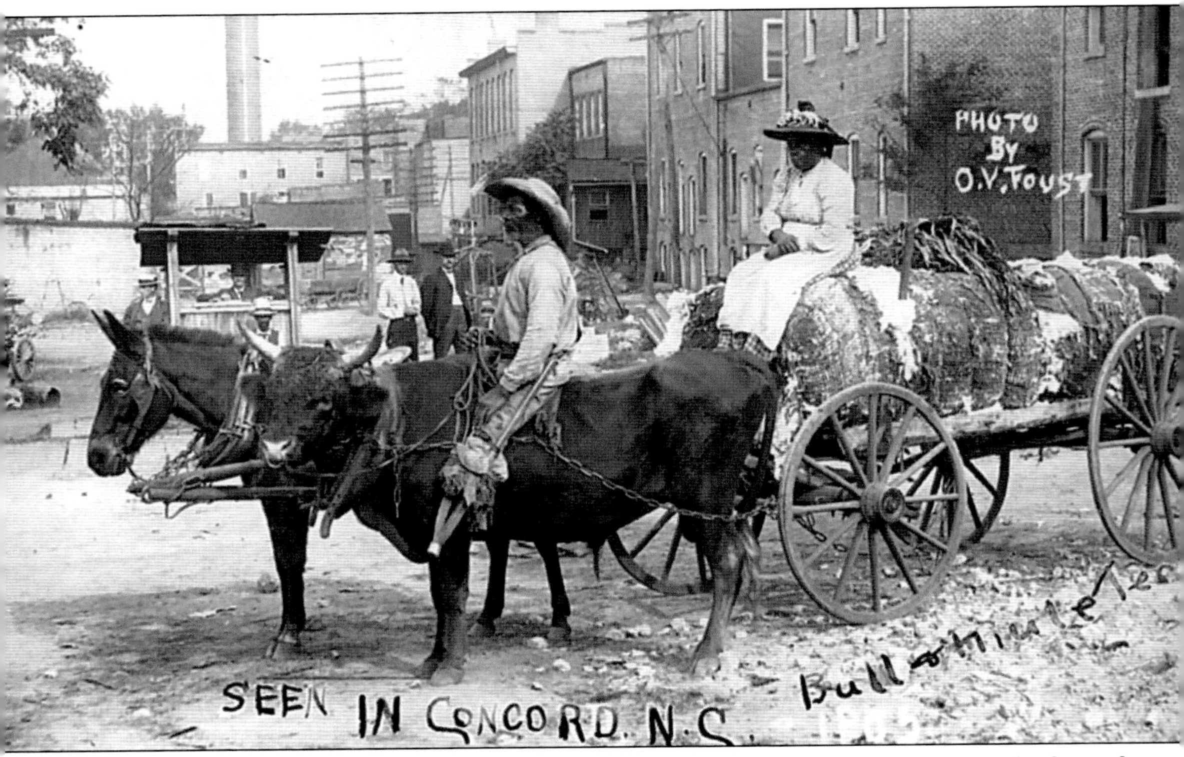

On Cotton Day farmers came from many miles away, including neighboring counties, to sell the fruits of their labor. This was due to the fact that buyers paid more for cotton in Concord than almost any other town. Shown here is an African-American farmer waiting his turn to deal with the buyers. The gentleman is Harvey Alexander, and his wife sits on top of a bale of cotton on their wagon. It is reported that Alexander was the owner of 30 acres of land located on Zion Church Road, and one can only imagine the hardships he and his family must have endured to have reaped such a large bounty of cotton even with his disability (notice his left leg). The man sitting in the small covered building beyond the mule's head is John K. Patterson. He oversaw the sellers as they entered the cotton platform. O.V. Foust was the photographer who captured this image around 1905. (Courtesy of Wayne Chapman.)

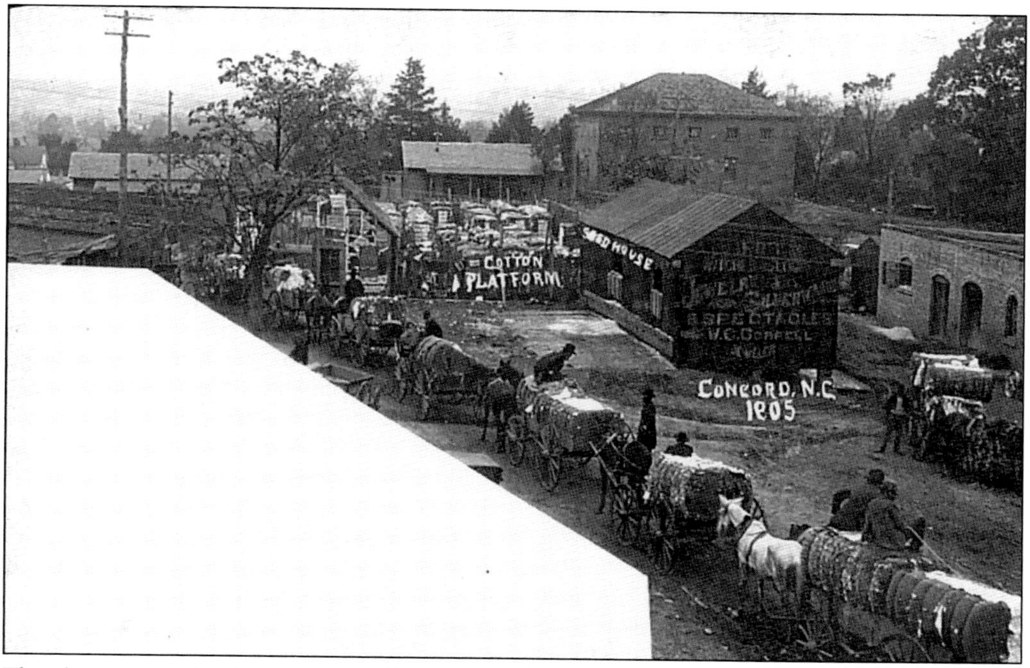

The photographer dated his image 1905 and captured wagon after wagon lined-up to enter the cotton platform. Wagons line what is today's Barbrick Street and appear to be at a standstill. Notice the "seed house" with its advertisement for W.C. Correll's Jewelry Company. Also seen in this picture is the large two-story brick building that was the "second" First Presbyterian Church building. (Courtesy of Durwood Barbour.)

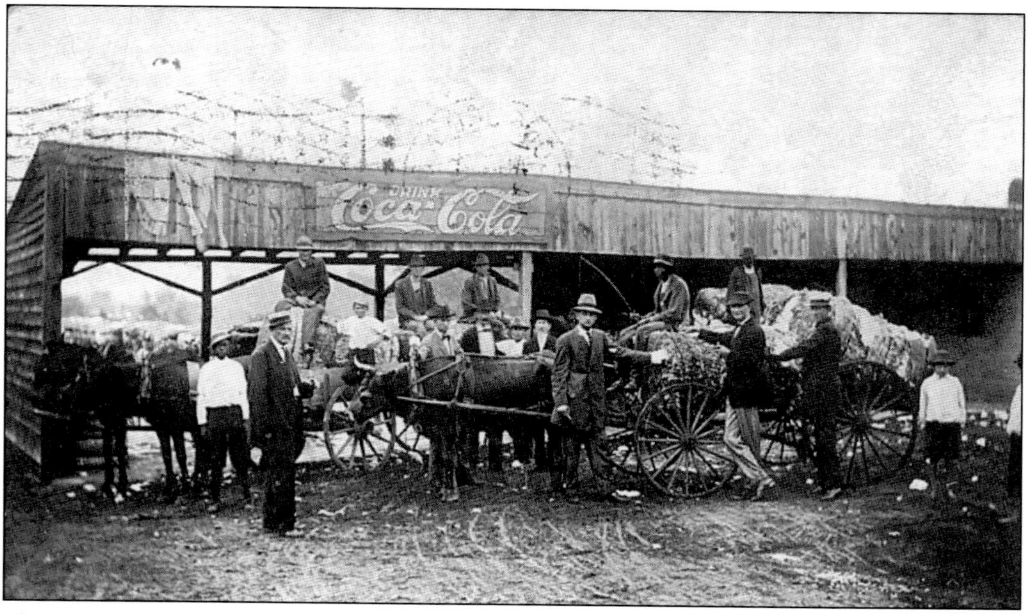

The Cotton Platform was where farmers came to sell their cotton. This card was made around 1905 and is a special card to the author in that his great-great grandfather William Propst stands in the center just behind the oxen's hip wearing a black hat and sporting a white beard. Propst, a Confederate veteran, was a banker, farmer, and owner of a cotton gin.

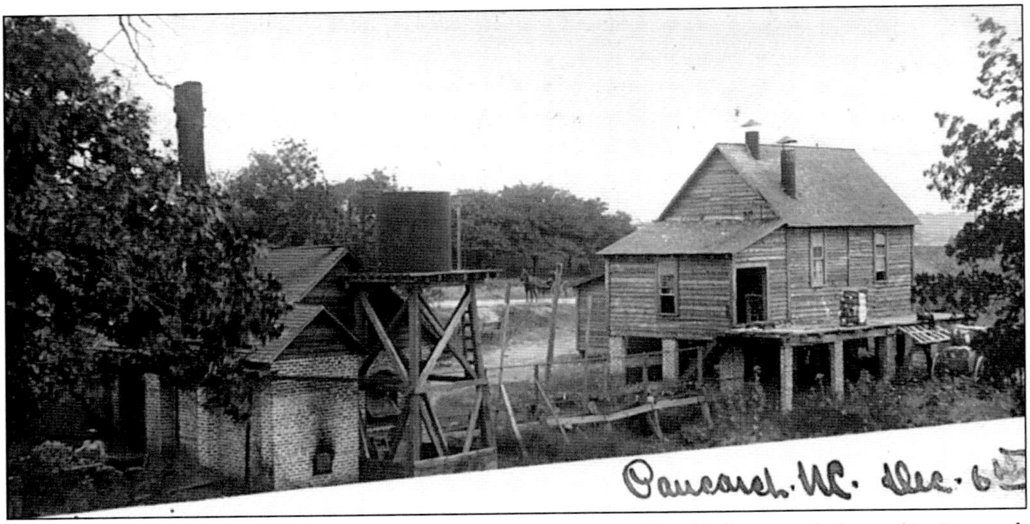

December 6, 1905 is the postmark for this card, which depicts an unidentified cotton gin located in Concord. It is not certain, but the tall cylindrical object on the left could quite possibly be the standpipe, making the location of this operation near the downtown area. (Courtesy of Marian Harter.)

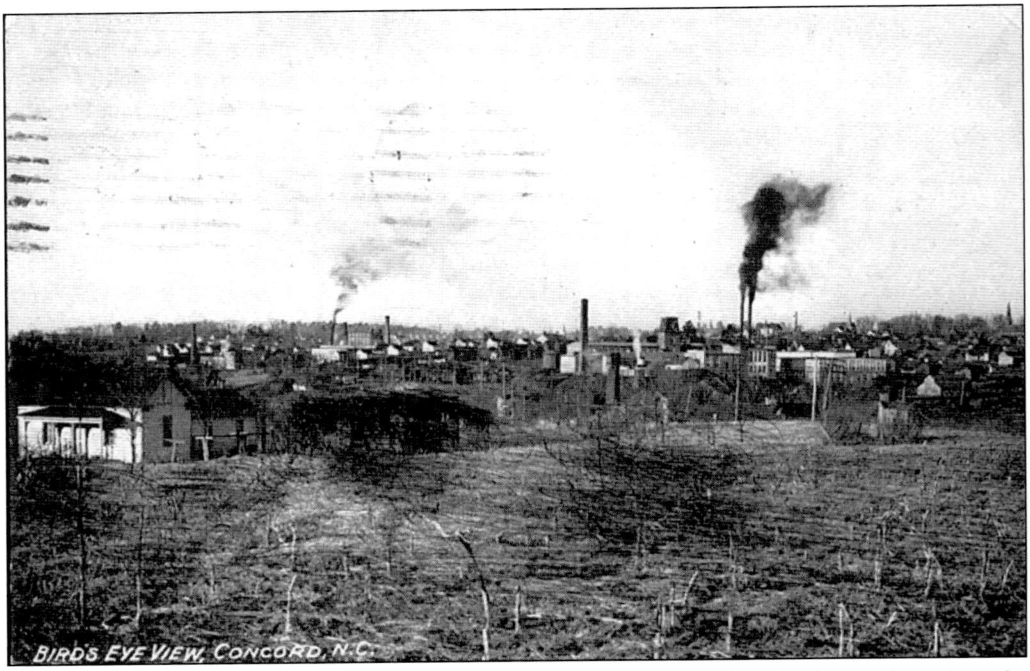

A "Bird's Eye View of Concord" is the scene of this 1911-postmarked card. Its hard to say just where the photographer set his tripod to capture this image, but it is the feeling of many that it was near the Old Charlotte Road and shows the Cabarrus Cotton Mill in the center with heavy, black smoke coming from its smokestack and the Cannon Manufacturing Company and Kerr Bleachery both to the left.

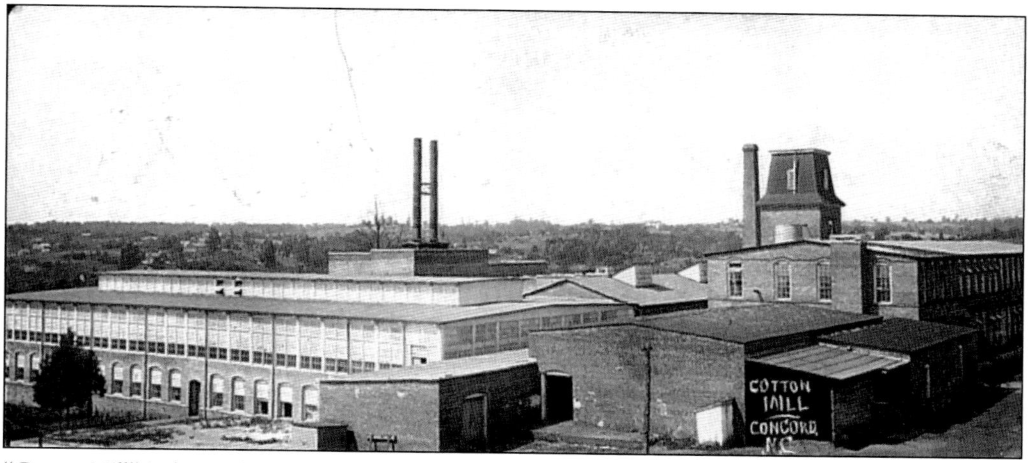

"Cotton Mill" is the caption on this card sent by "Fred," who lived at the St. Cloud Hotel and spent a good bit of time in Concord around 1906. He had relatives in Ohio and the author has seen at least four cards of Concord sent by this person. (Courtesy of Durwood Barbour.)

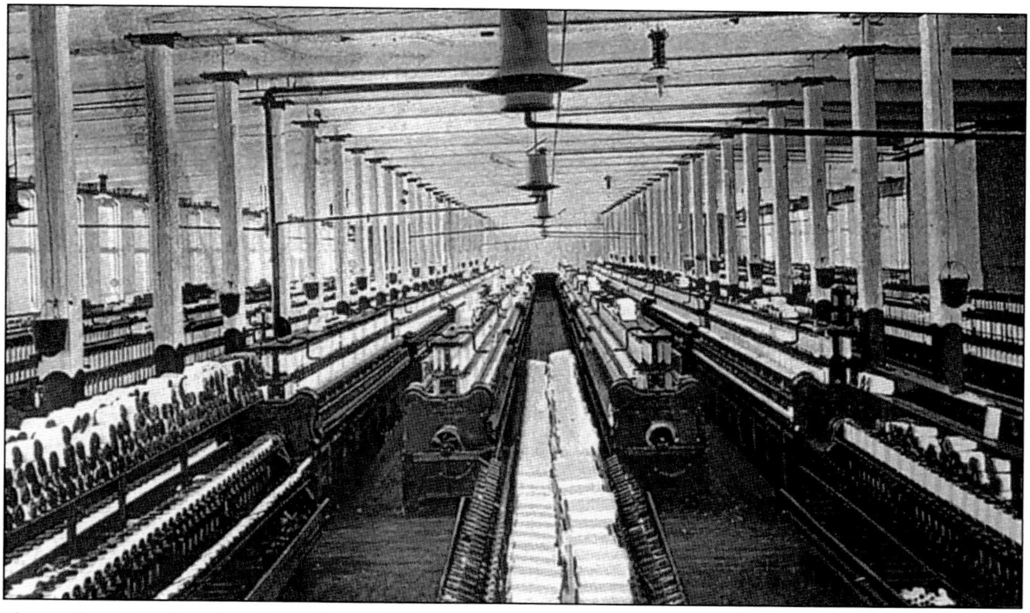
Shown here is an interior view of one of the many cotton mills located in Concord. There is a postmark of 1909 on this colored card. (Courtesy of Durwood Barbour.)

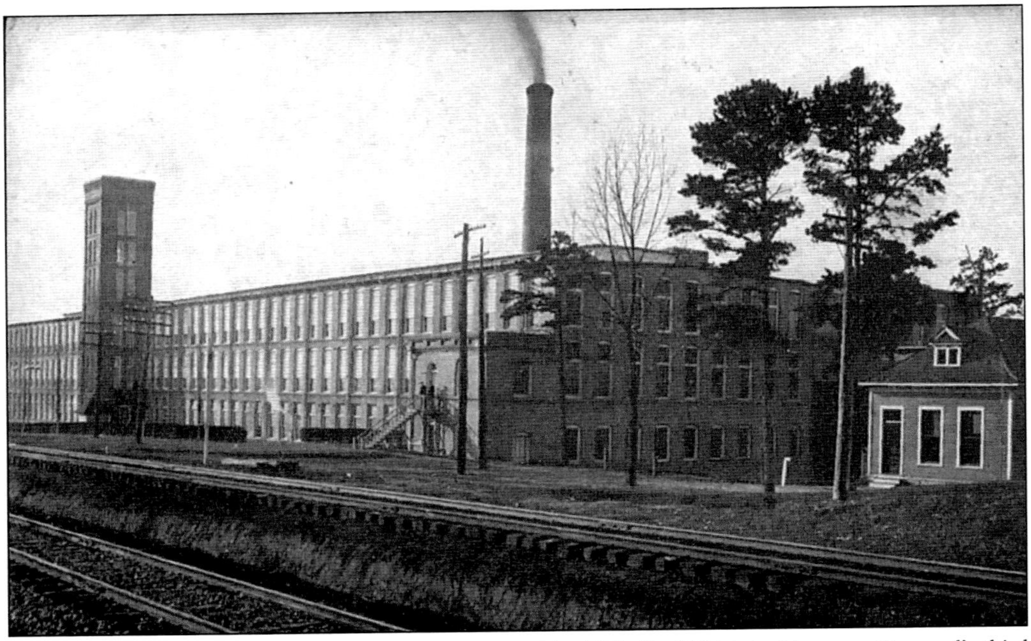

The Gibson Manufacturing Company was incorporated in 1899. By 1904 it had become Concord's third largest textile facility. Gibson Mill became part of the consolidated Cannon Mills Company in 1928 and became known as plant 6. Today a vacant lot remains where this building once stood.

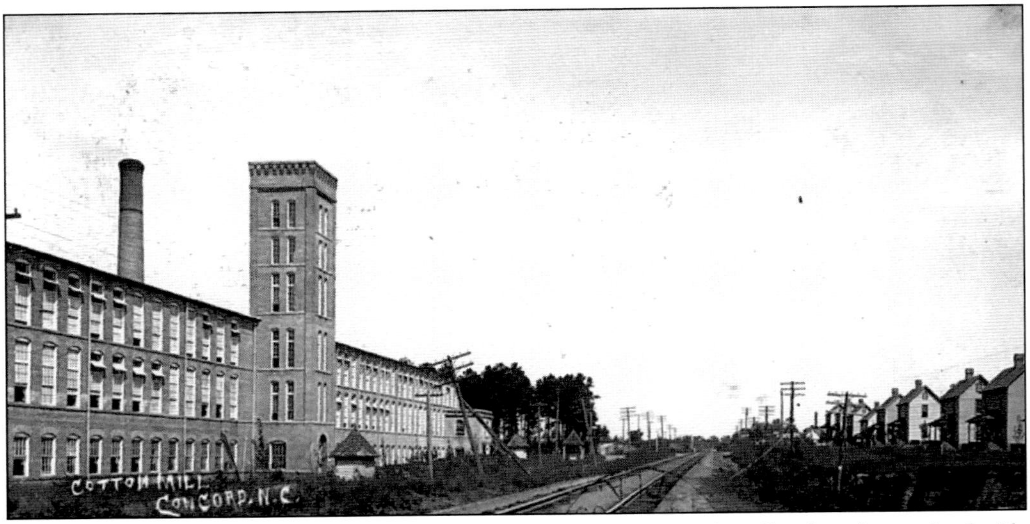

Looking north at the Gibson Manufacturing Company, this view shows the railroad tracks running beside the mill and a line of homes that were used for the workers. Construction began in 1900 on 90 dwellings, and by 1920, a rather large neighborhood had developed with its own churches, barber shops, grocery stores, and cafe. Gibson village was given additional impetus by the construction of an electric streetcar line, connecting this village with downtown Concord. (Courtesy of Marian Harter.)

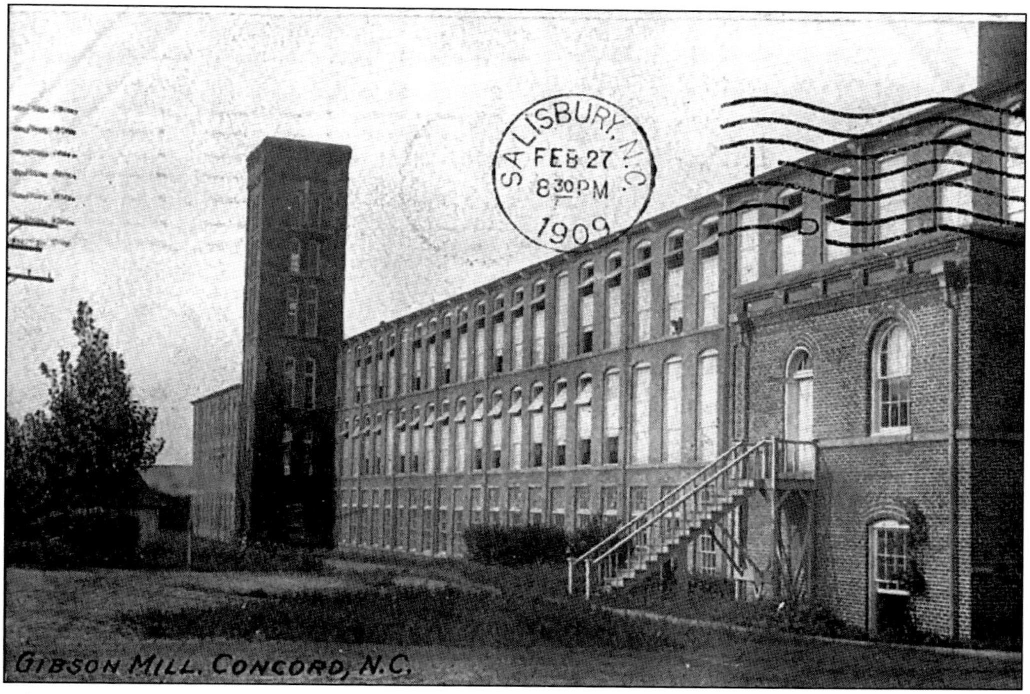

February 27, 1909 is the postmark on this card, which shows the Gibson Manufacturing Company from McGill Avenue.

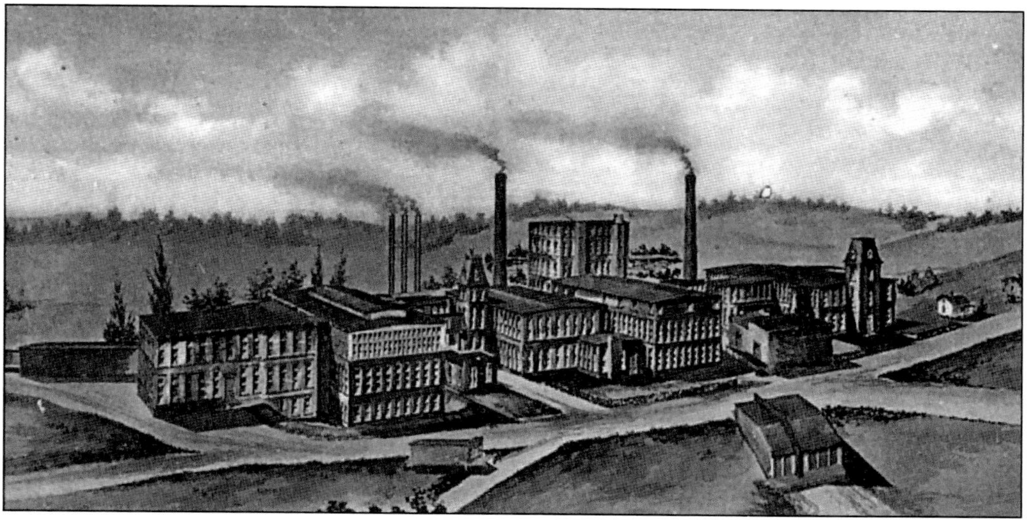

In 1887 James W. Cannon started his first textile operation, the Cannon Manufacturing Company. H.L. Parks Company captured Mr. Cannon's mill in this image, which has a postmark of 1910. The buildings represent three phases that made up the plant in Concord. (Courtesy of Susan G. Sides.)

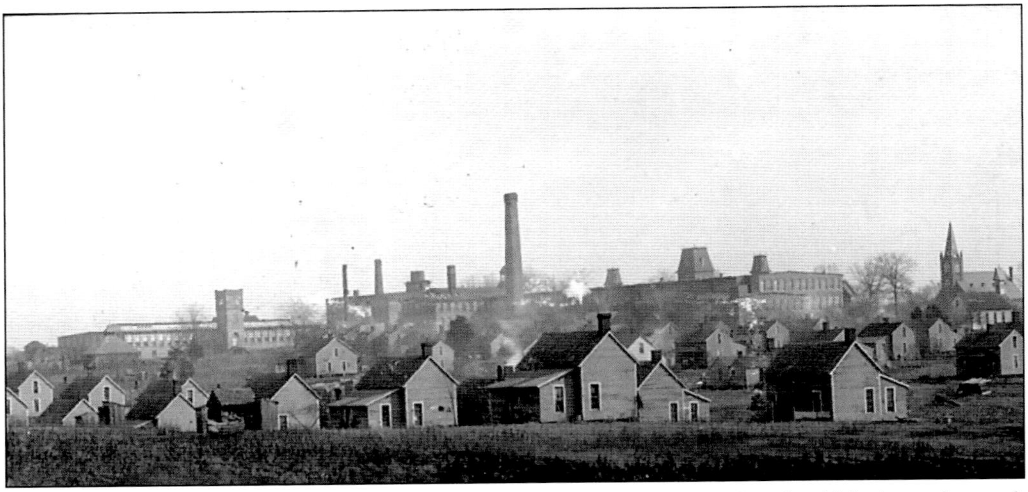

"One of the large cotton mills in town" is written on this December 6, 1905 card, which shows the north side of the Odell Manufacturing Company. This mill was located in the northern part of Union Street known as "Forest Hills." The church steeple of Forest Hill United Methodist Church can be seen to the right side of the mill. Note also the many "mill houses" that were scattered near the Odell Plant. (Courtesy of Marian Harter.)

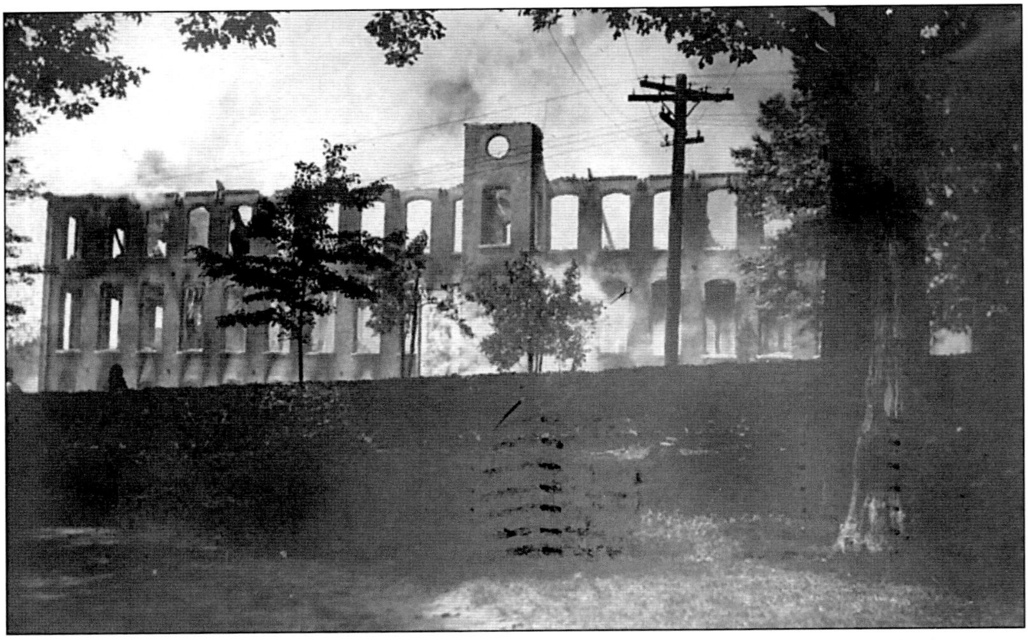

At 11:50 p.m. on August 15, 1908, the largest fire in Concord's history occurred. Odell Mill Plant 4 was completely destroyed. The fire burned all night Saturday, though continuous streams of water were kept on it. Efforts were successful in retaining the fire to just this one plant, although the church steeple at Forest Hills Methodist sustained damage and firefighters had to be called to prevent further damage. (Courtesy of the Charles A. Cannon Memorial Library.)

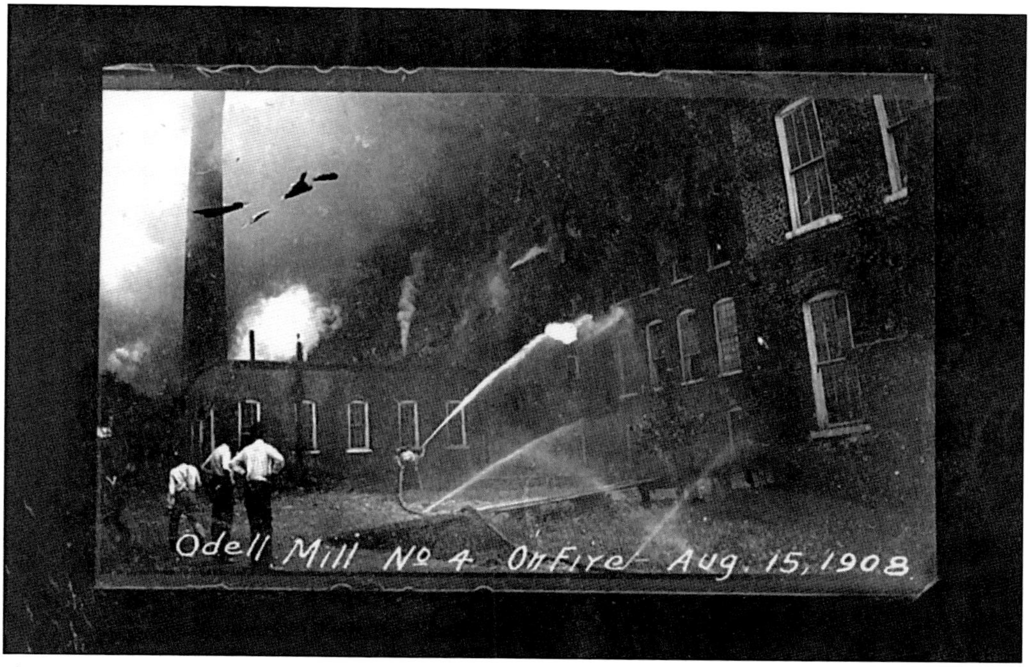

Shown is another postcard of the fire at Odell Mill plant # 4. It is reported that within a few moments after the alarm was sounded, Main Street was alive with spectators. The dense smoke was seen from all over the county. It is also reported that in an astounding show of care for their fellow men, a number of single men of Concord who worked at other mills offered their jobs to the married men of plant 4. (Courtesy of Jim Ramseur.)

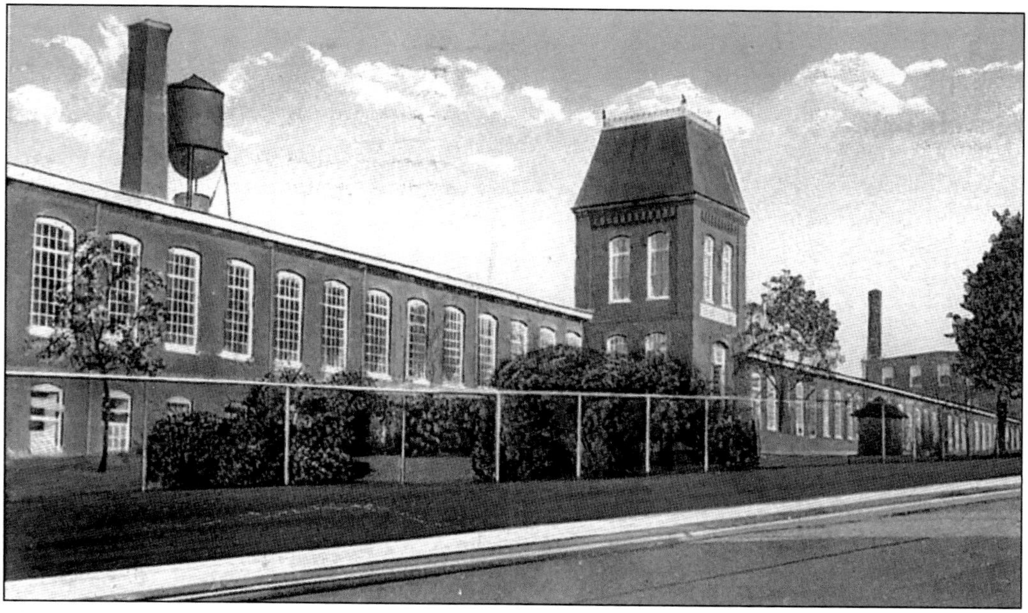

The Concord Cotton Factory was built in 1839 and later became known as the McDonald Cotton Mill. In 1877 John M. Odell purchased this property and changed the name to Odell Manufacturing Company. Then came the Locke Cotton Mill followed by the Randolph Mill. Today this building is known as the Locke Mill Plaza and houses a cafe, a number of offices, and condominiums.

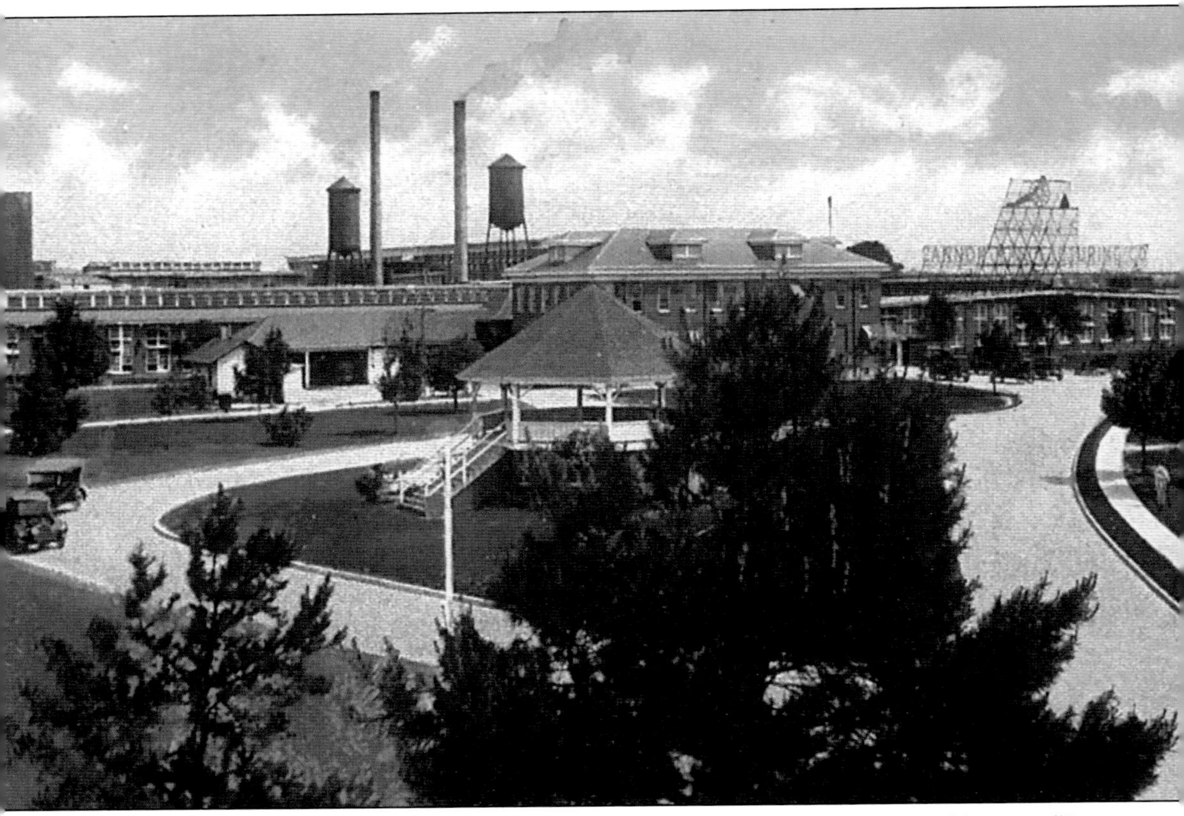

Kannapolis was the name James W. Cannon gave to this area of Cabarrus County, and it means "Loom City." Cannon was born in Mecklenburg County, North Carolina in 1852 and was just 16 years old when he came to Concord to work for his brother D.F. Cannon at the Cannon-Fetzer general store. In 1887 he opened a small mill that was to grow into a rather large manufacturing plant. In 1898 the mill began to make "huck" towels and "terry" towels, the first mill in the South to do this type of production. As towels became popular, Cannon bought 600 acres of farmland seven miles north of his original location and, in 1907, built the first plant in Kannapolis. Fourteen years later, James W. Cannon died. His youngest son, Charles Albert Cannon, became president of all of his father's enterprises. Shown in this image is the gazebo located in front of the main office of Cannon Mills used for speakers, musical concerts, and city functions. (Courtesy of Whitley's Funeral Home.)

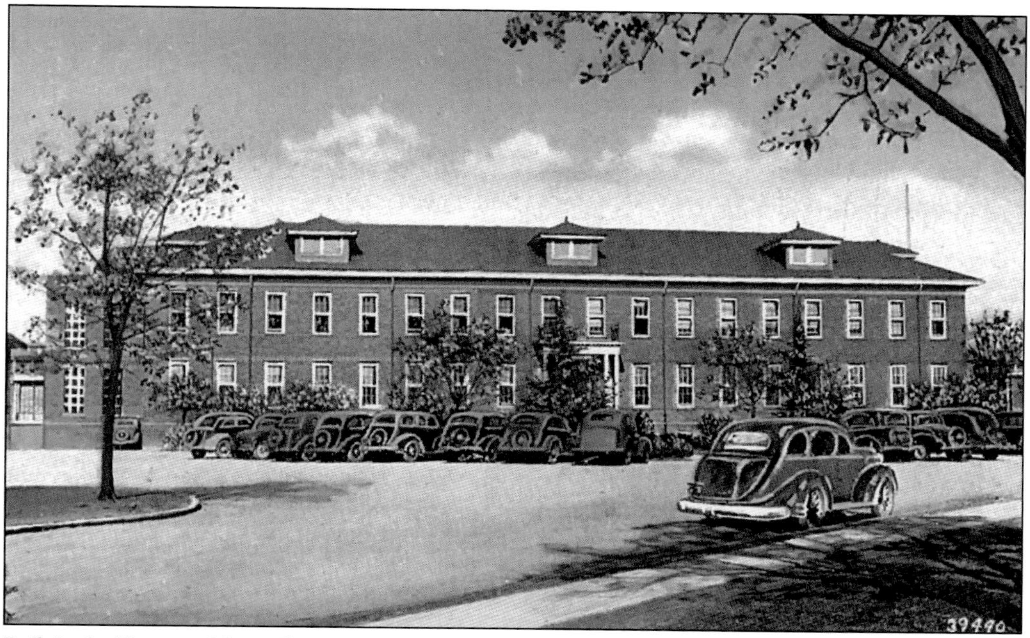

Built in the likeness of the Williamsburg, Virginia village, the Cannon corporate office was located at the site of the city park and lake. This image was published in the 1940s. (Courtesy of Susan G. Sides.)

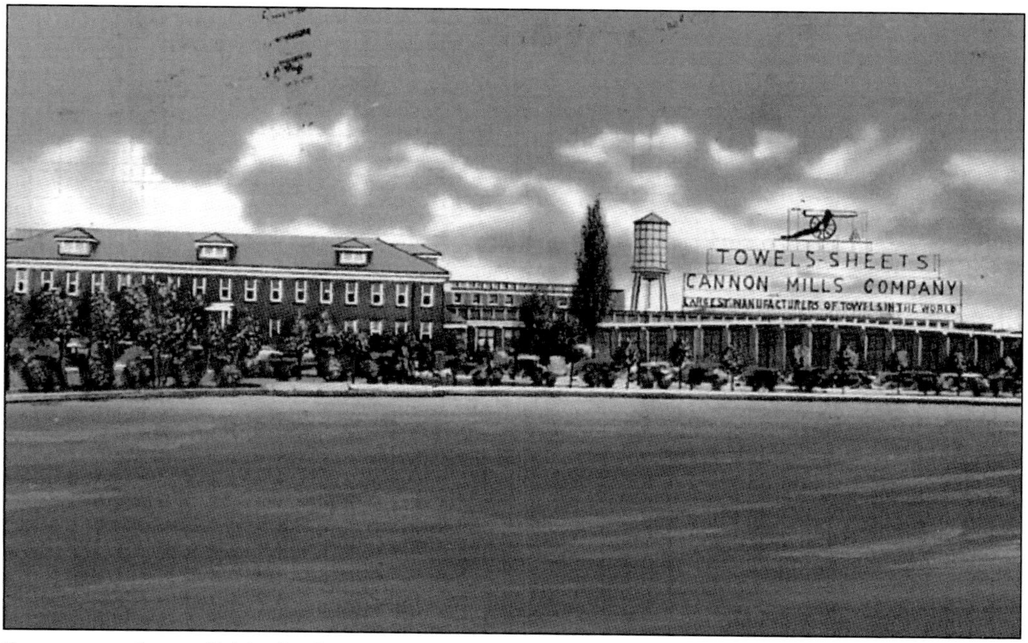

From across the small lake in the center of town a large neon sign announces that this is the home of those husky Cannon towels and soft white Cannon percale sheets. The lower half of the sign describes the Cannon Mills company as the "Largest Manufacturers of Towels in the World." (Courtesy of Susan G. Sides.)

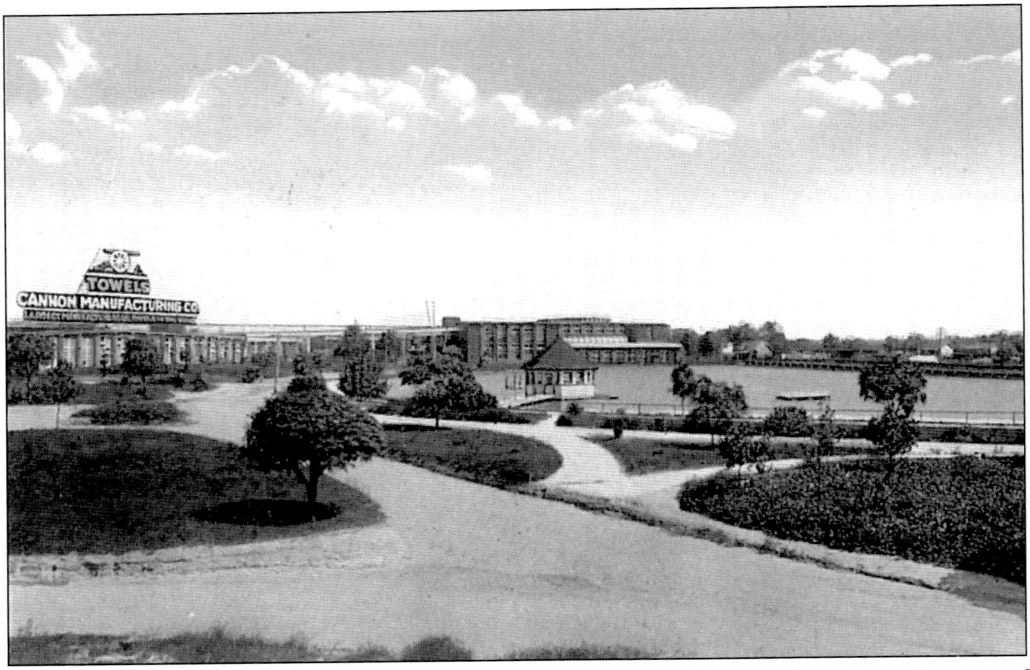

Sitting out on the city lake is the gazebo or "music stand" that was used for special occasions. (Courtesy of Whitley's Funeral Home.)

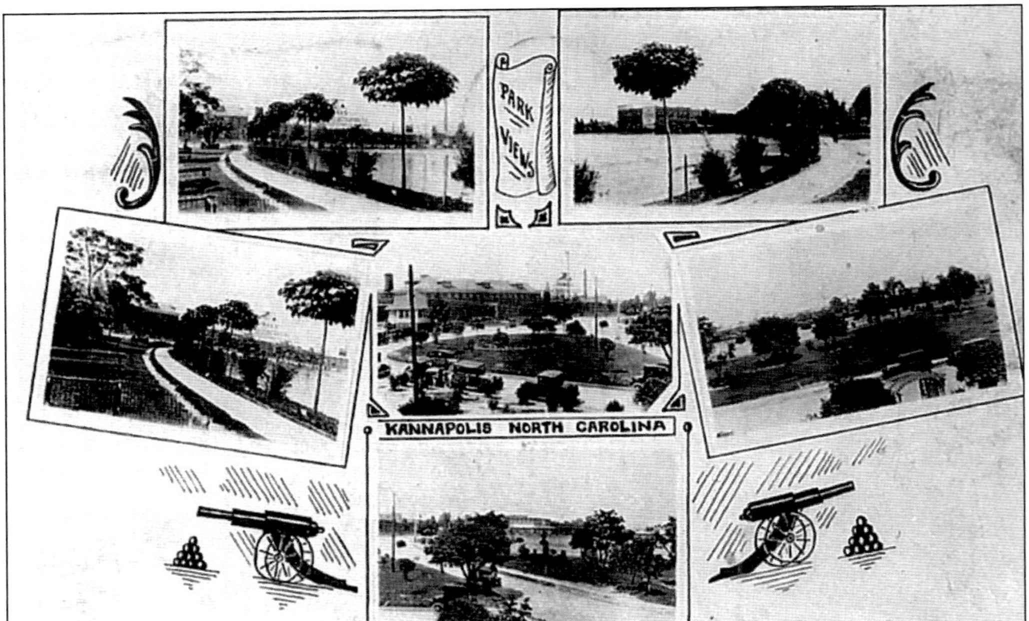

"Park Views" of different scenes around the lake at the main Cannon Mills plant in Kannapolis are found on this card made during the 1930s . (Courtesy of Durwood Barbour.)

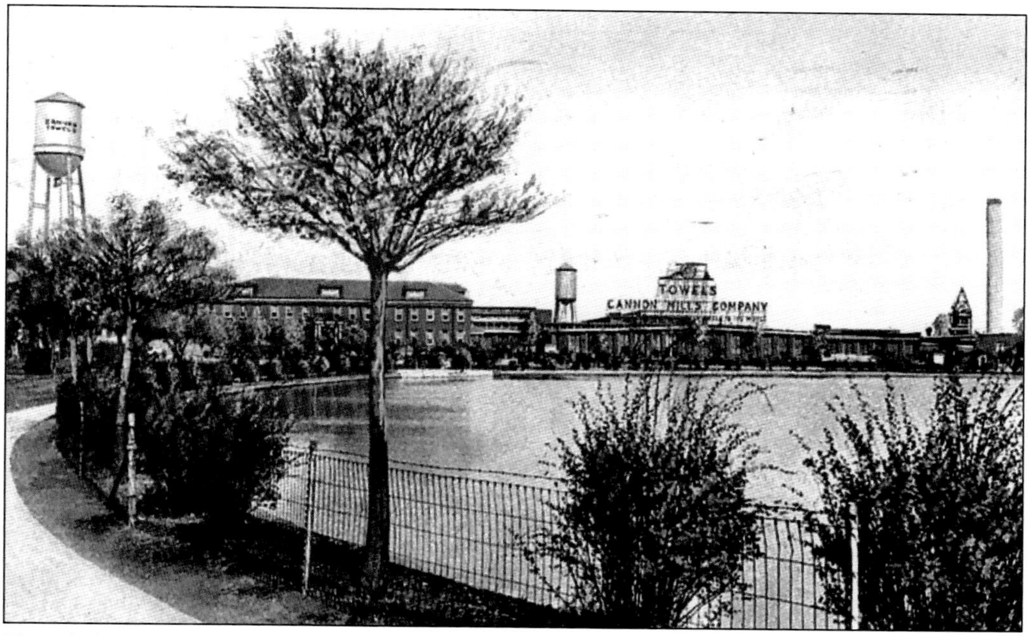

Though this postcard states that this plant is located in Concord, it is a mistake. The structures are part of the main plant in Kannapolis. (Courtesy of Susan G. Sides.)

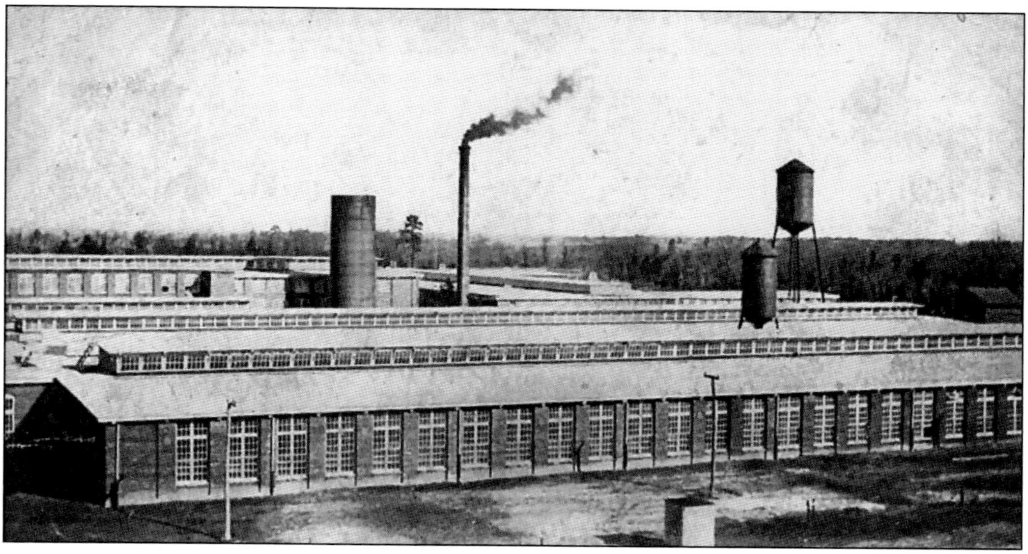

F.L. Smith Drug Store was the publisher of this card that has a postmark of 1911. This was just one small part of the Cannon Mills Manufacturing Company. (Courtesy of Mike Coltrane.)

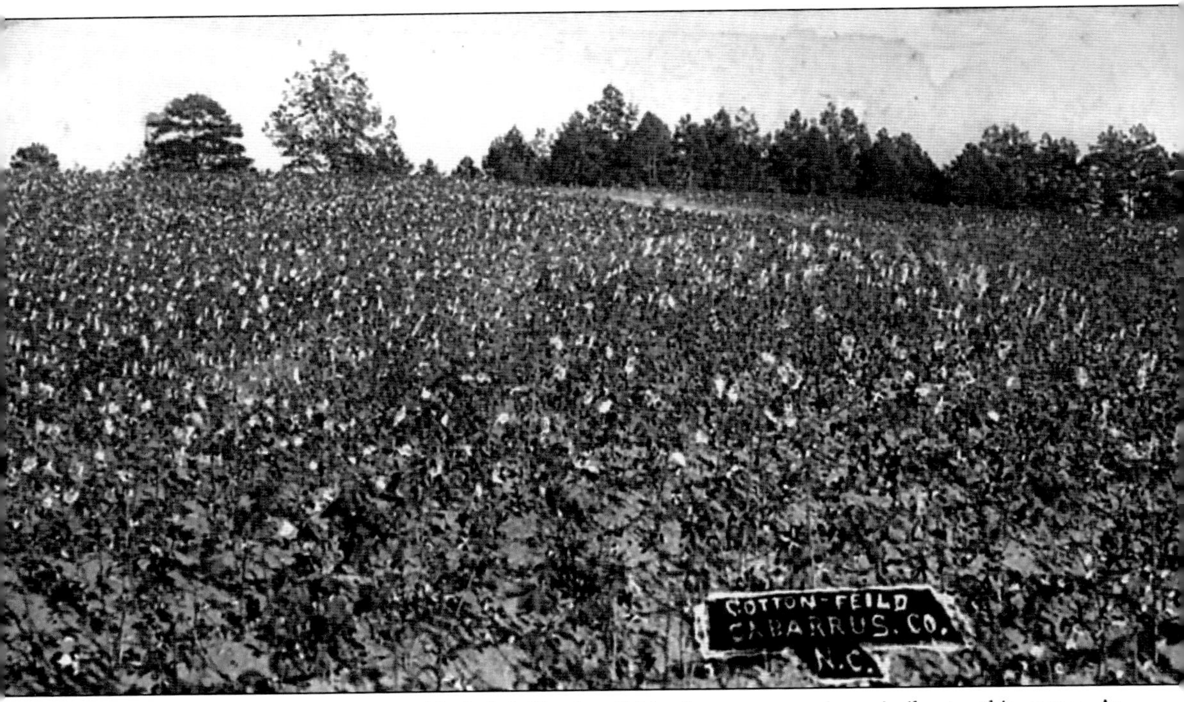

Throughout the South one could find field after field of cotton growing, similar to this scene. At first sight, many people may find cards like this one to be a most unusual subject for a postcard. However, it is after all, here in the South that "cotton was king," especially in Cabarrus County. (Courtesy of Marian Harter.)

Eight

Education

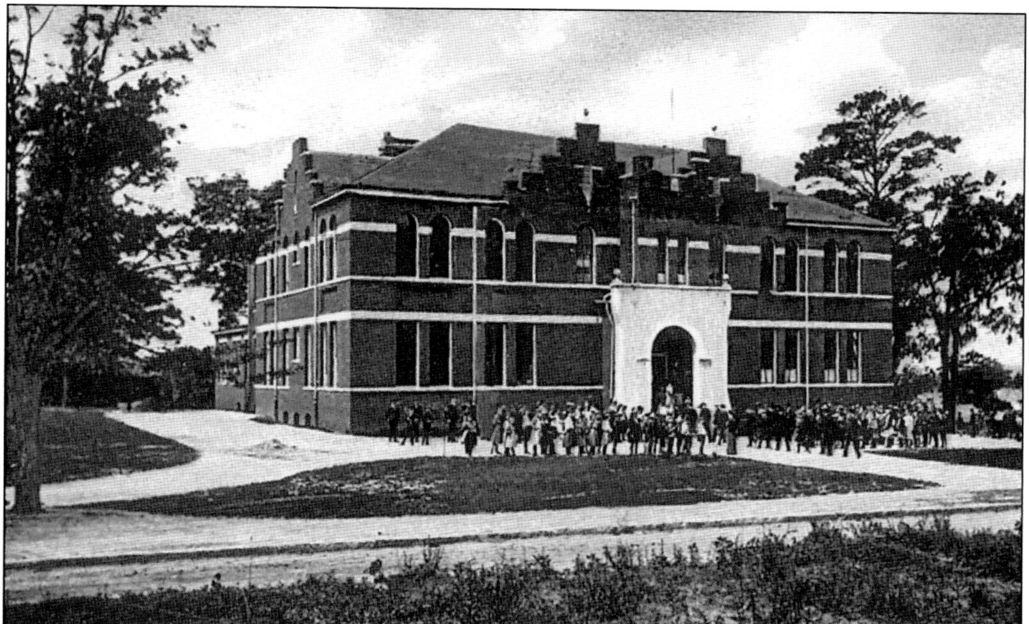

Published by the Fetzer Drug Company, this 1909 postmarked card is of Central Graded School. The postcard shows children playing in the schoolyard. This was originally the site of the Concord Female Academy. (Courtesy of Mike Coltrane.)

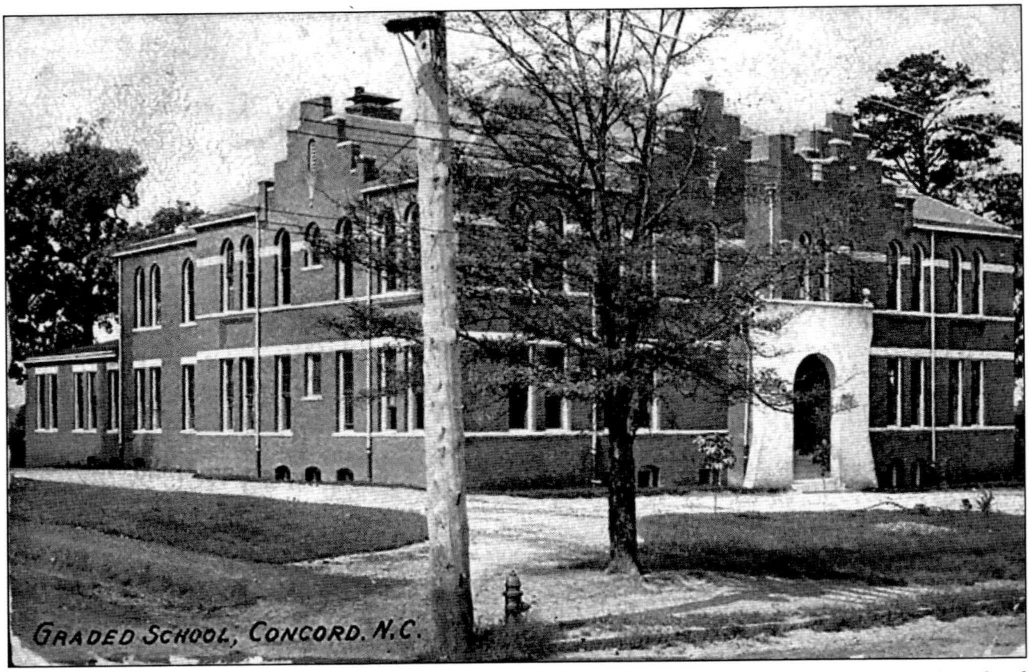

The Concord Graded School was built in 1901 on the west side of Spring Street at Grove Street. The school stood here until 5:40 a.m. on Sunday, March 3, 1946, when fire destroyed the building. The next day school resumed in the Webb building with only eight pupils absent. Students continued classes in the Webb building until the new Coltrane School could be occupied on September 3, 1947.

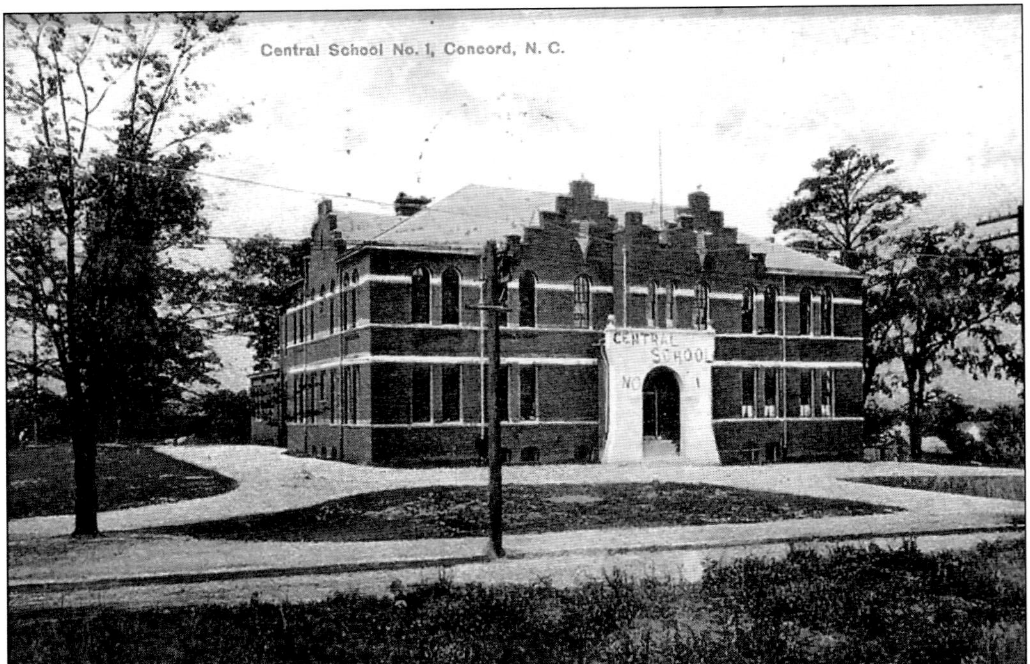

Another card of the Central School #1 has a postmark of 1908. Just to the left of this school was the First Baptist Church.

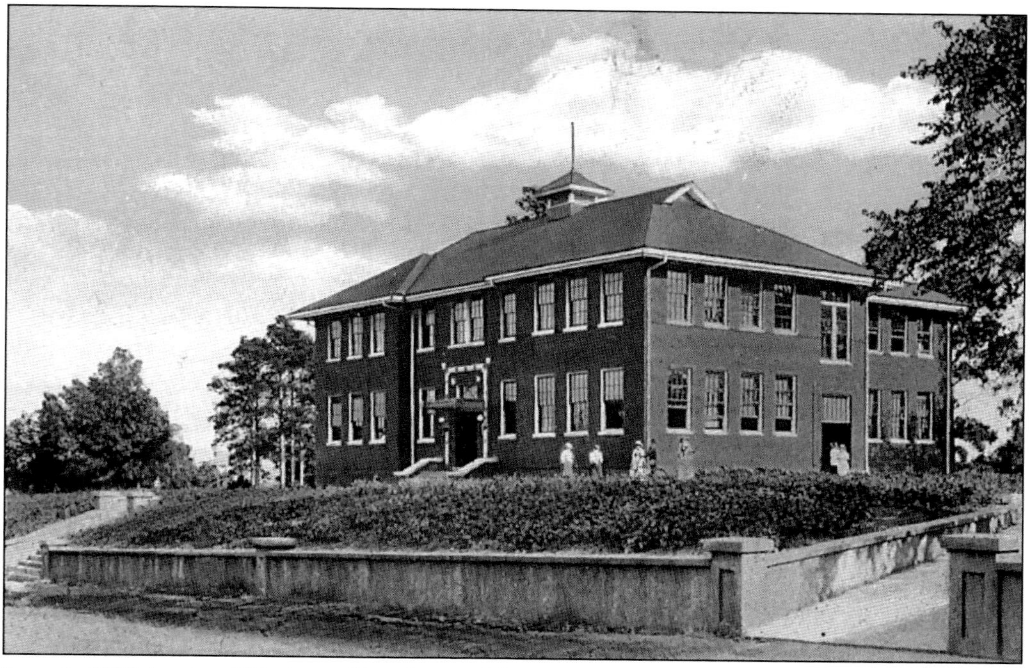

It was in 1908 that the old Lutheran Church was sold and moved away to be replaced six years later with the Concord High School. The site was on East Corban Street (the Fayetteville Road) just a block from town. This building was later used as an elementary school and named for Miss Clara Harris, a beloved Concord teacher and principal.

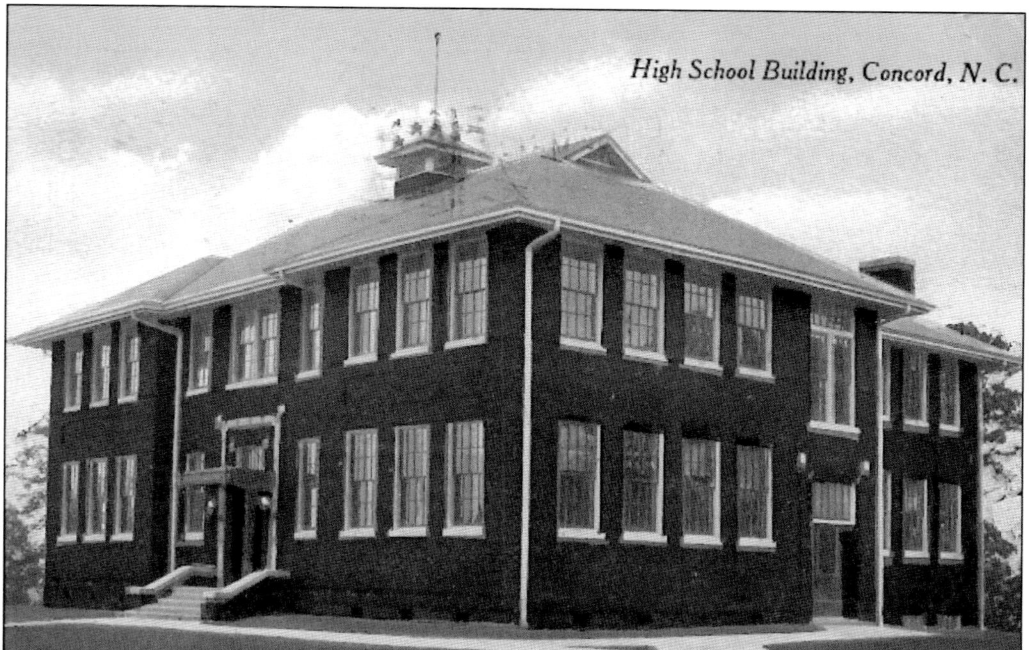

An earlier card of Concord High School dates to 1918. It is of interest that the exercise field was located on the east side of the school where the Lutheran Church had its cemetery. Students were often seen chasing "home run balls" into the cemetery. (Courtesy of Marian Harter.)

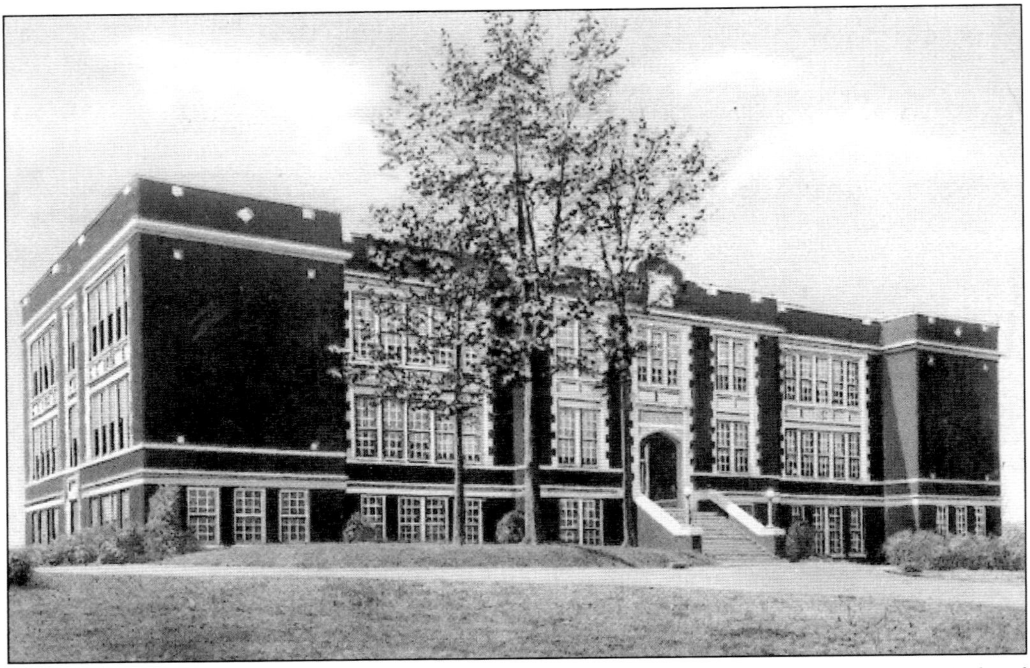

The Concord Board of Education erected this handsome school following the passage of a $225,000 bond issued in 1924. The building replaced the Corban Street School as Concord's high school. This card has a postmark of 1941.

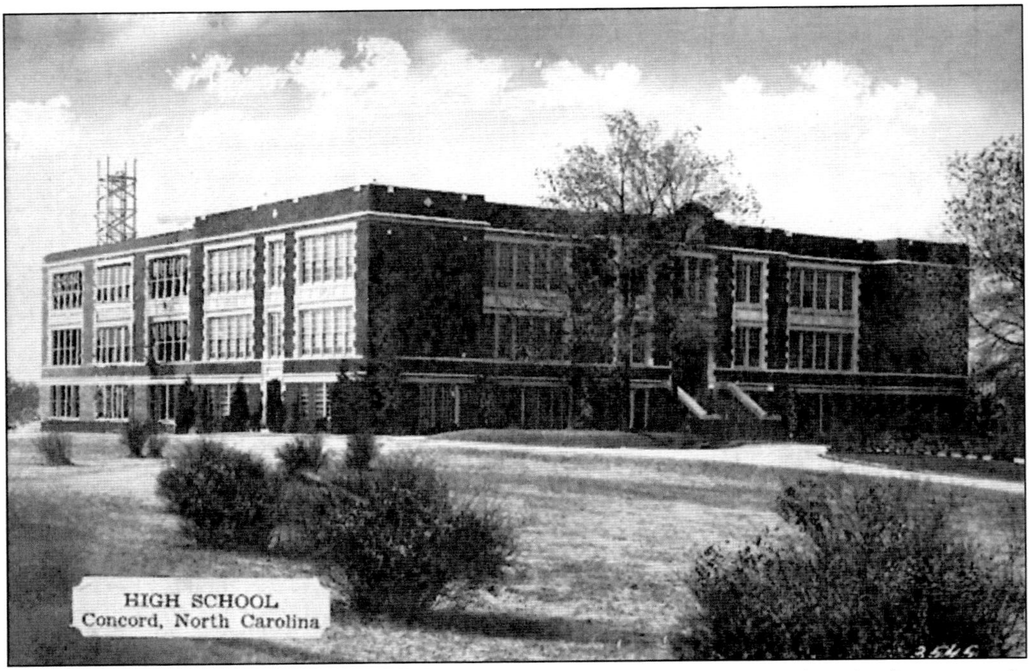

The location of this high school was 120 Marsh Avenue, Northwest. In 1937 the school was severely damaged by fire but was back in full operation by 1939. This building became the Concord Junior High in 1970, and in 1999, the middle school moved to its present location off Neisler Road, east of Concord. (Courtesy of Alex and Jane Patterson.)

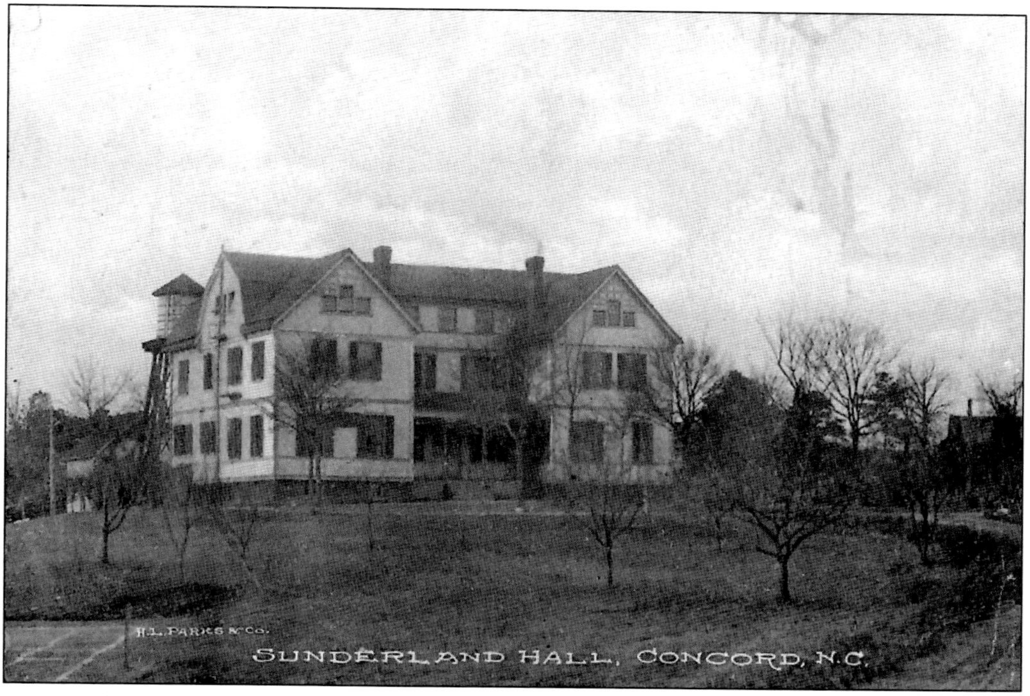

Laura Sunderland Hall, a school for young ladies built by the Northern Presbyterian Church, offered a home economics course and advanced education including eighth, ninth, and tenth grades. This building replaced "White Hall," which was destroyed by fire during the 1890s. H.L. Parks produced this card, which has a postmark of 1910.

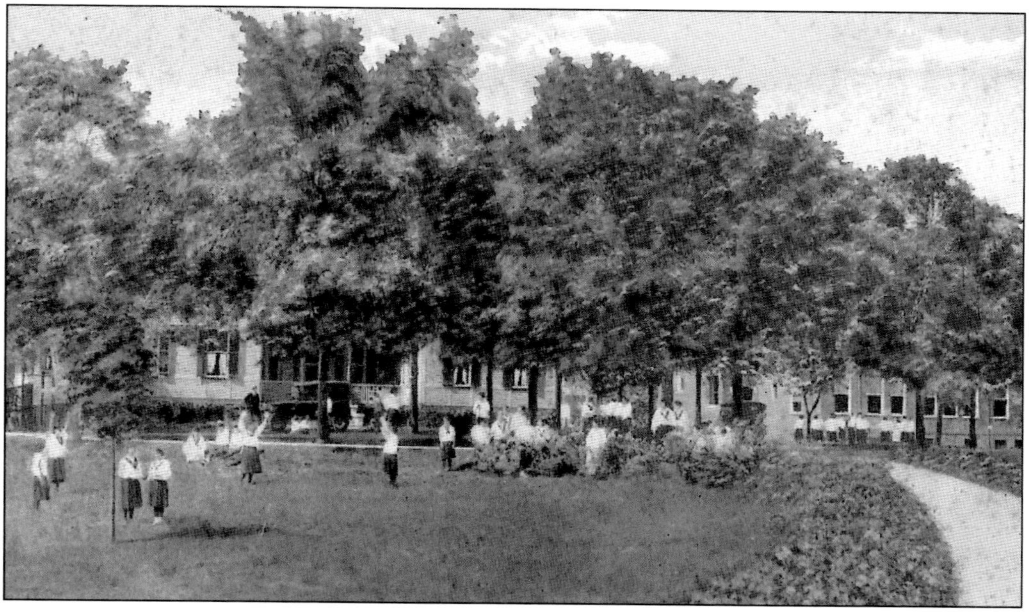

Sunderland Hall was built on land owned by Esquire George M. Lore, a Confederate soldier and prominent Concord business man. The card features students enjoying the front lawn of the school. White, Morrison, Flowe Company published this 1909-postmarked card. The building still stands today, except for the top two stories which were lost due to a fire.

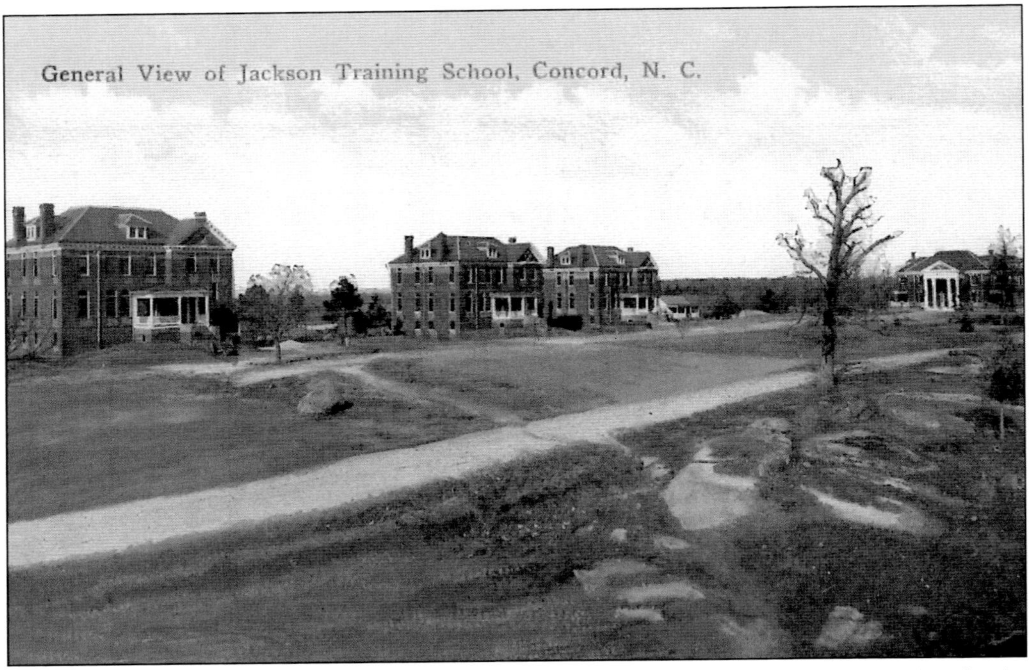

The next four images are of the Stonewall Jackson Training School, founded in 1909 by J.P. Cook who served as chairman of the board of trustees. This school was a reformatory for young wayward boys. (Courtesy of Bub and Jane Craver.)

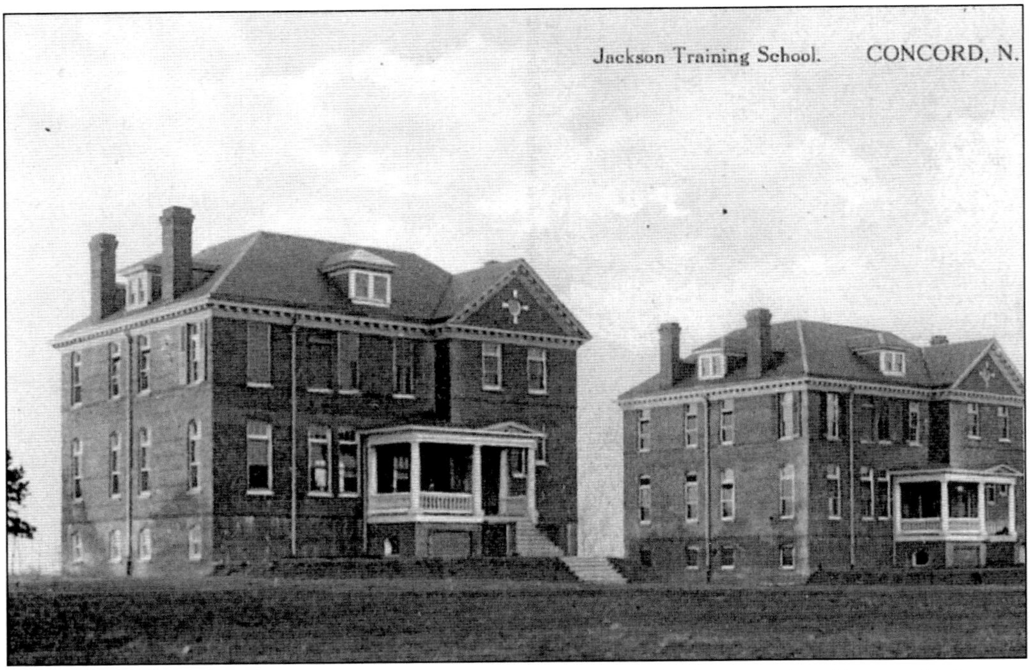

This training school, still in operation today, is located on the Old Charlotte Road at Highway 49. It was a little city within itself and is dedicated to the reclamation of wayward boys. From its portals every year go scores of youths reclaimed for a useful place in society. The postcard has a postmark of 1910. (Courtesy of Mike Coltrane.)

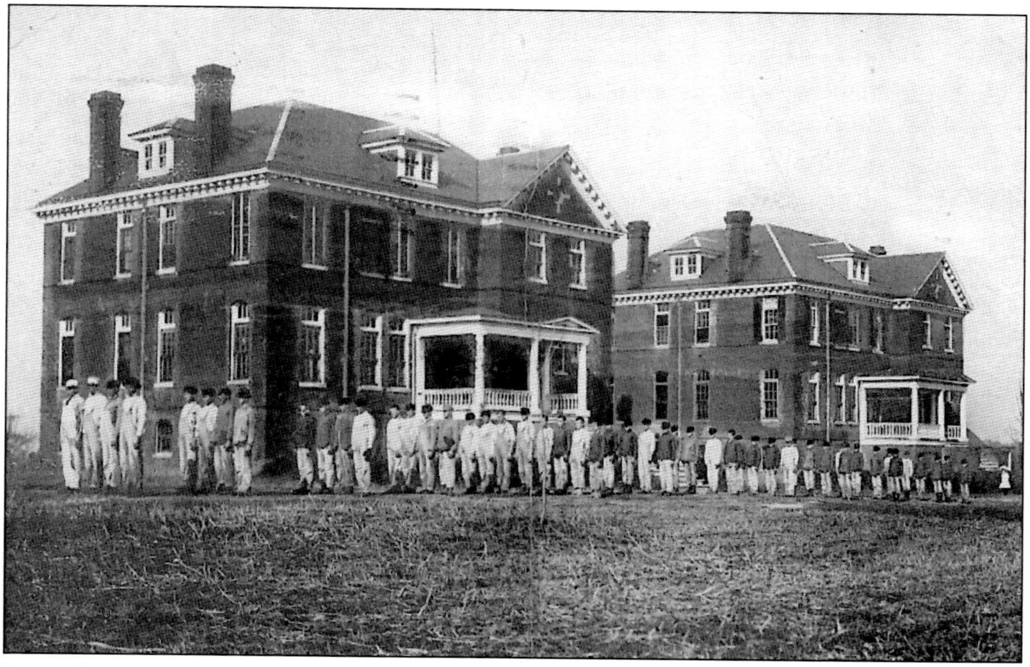

Postmarked July 9, 1911 and published by White, Morrison, Flowe Company, this postcard shows two of the many cottages with young boys standing in the yard. The population of the school was around 550 and included people who were housed in 16 cottage homes. The school was maintained with a course of study running through the eighth grade. The boys were taught agriculture, dairying, wood-working, printing, banking, shoe repairing, as well as other trades. (Courtesy of Mike Coltrane.)

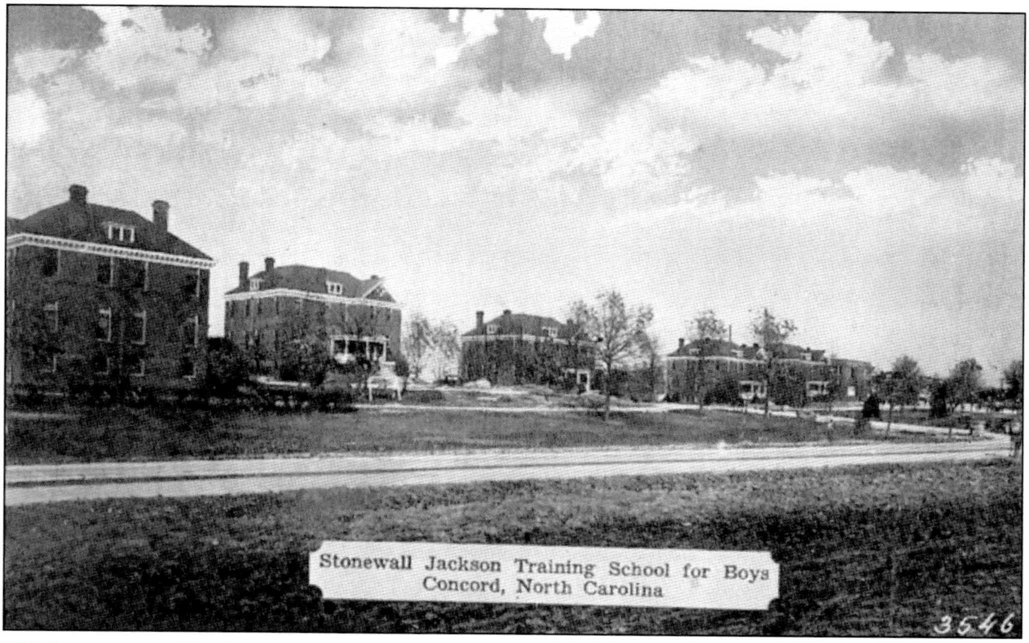

This is not a typical high school but a state-run training school. Many of the young men in attendance here were being punished for something they had done. This 1936-postmarked card was made by the Dexter Press Company in Pearl River, New York. (Courtesy of Jim Ramseur.)

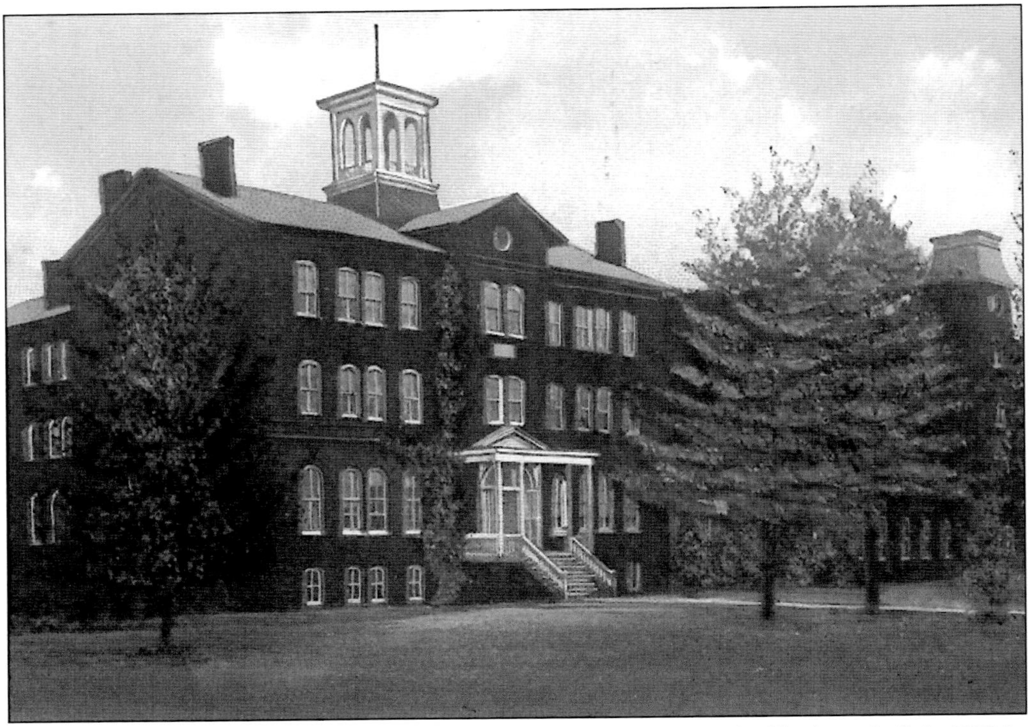

Originally a school for "colored girls," Scotia Seminary's Faith Hall (distant building) was built in 1876 by Capt. F.W. Ahrens of Charlotte, who also built the 1876 Cabarrus County Courthouse. Graves Hall (closer to the camera) was built in 1891. This school (Barber-Scotia College) is still in operation today and is located on West Depot Street (Cabarrus Avenue.)

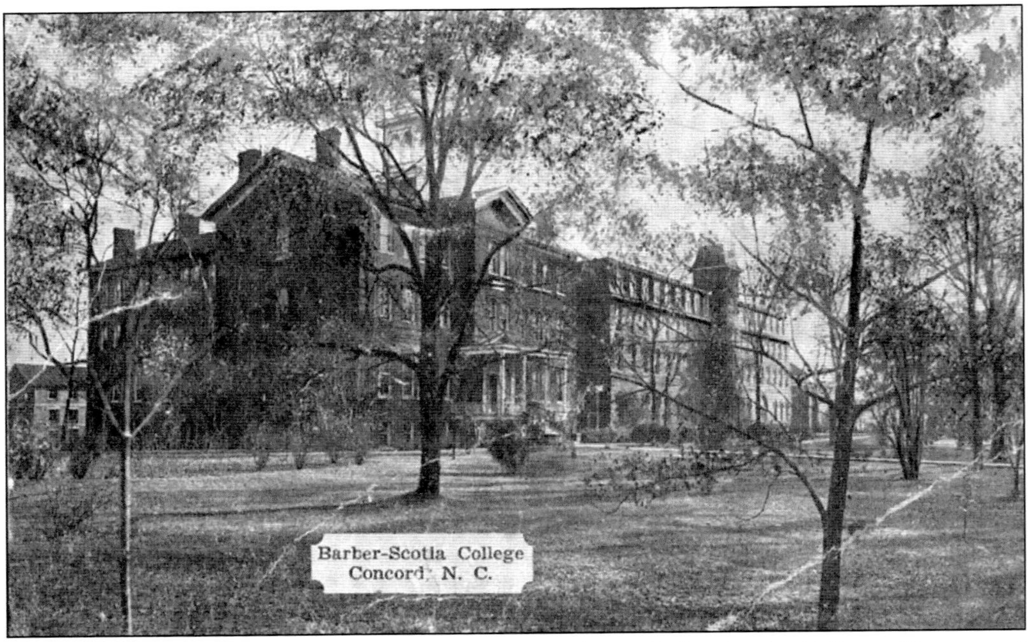

Another card made by the Dexter Press Company shows Barber-Scotia College. (Courtesy of Marian Harter.)

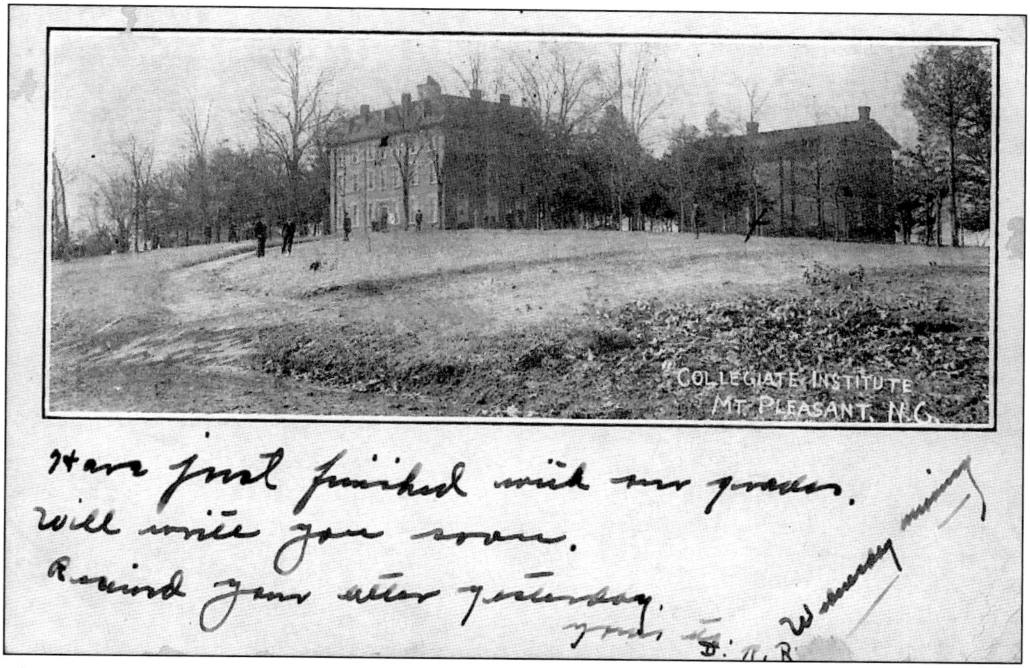

The postmark on this card of the Mt. Pleasant Collegiate Institute is 1909. This was a male academy sponsored by the North Carolina Synod of the Evangelical Lutheran Church in America, which was designed to educate young boys of the faith. (Courtesy of Marian Harter.)

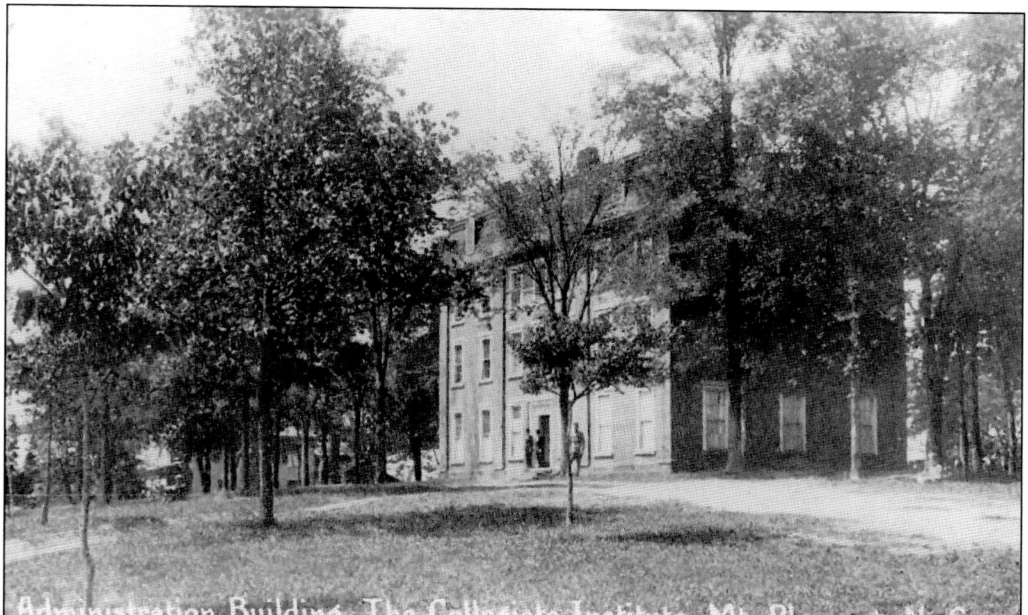

Set on the crest of the hilltop campus overlooking the town of Mt. Pleasant, this handsome three-story main building was completed in 1855 and served as the administration building to the Collegiate Institute. (Courtesy of the Eastern Cabarrus Historical Society Museum.)

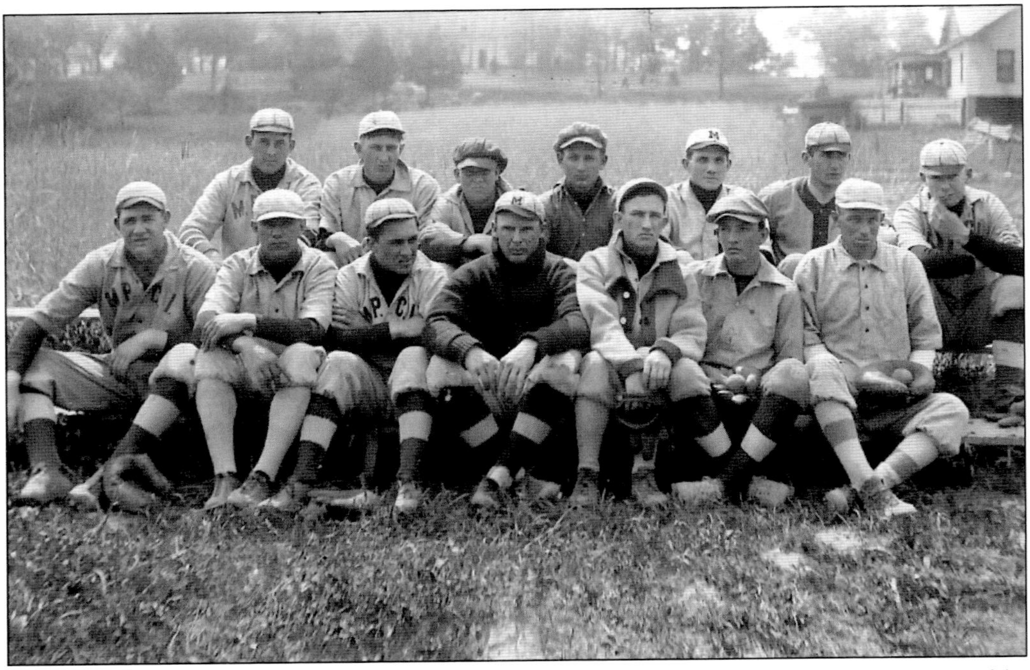

An unusual early postcard shows the Mt. Pleasant Collegiate Institute's proud baseball team. (Courtesy of the Eastern Cabarrus Historical Society Museum.)

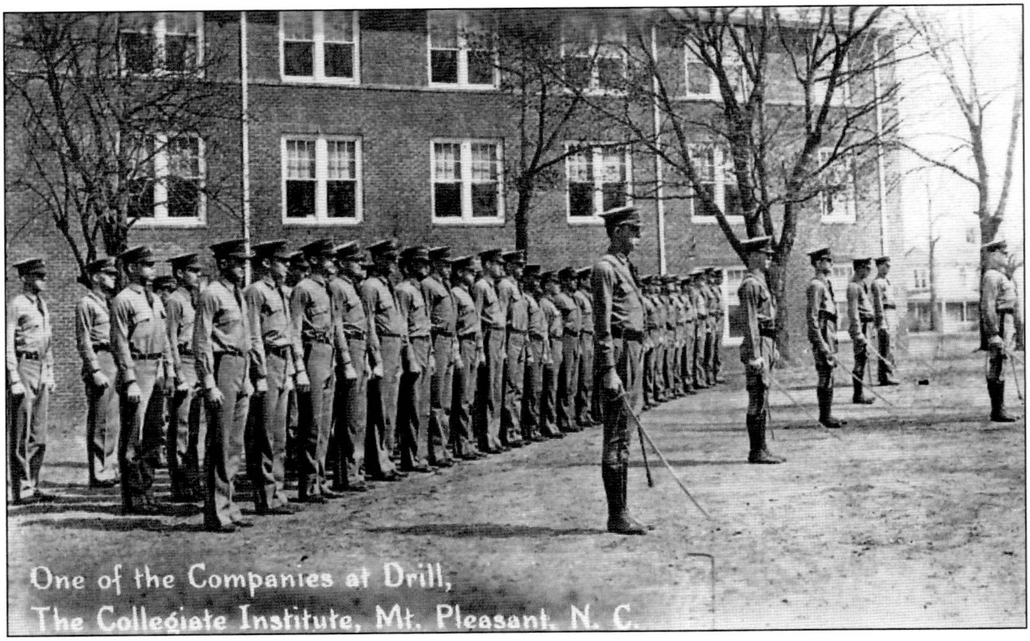

In 1907 the Institute introduced the modified military system remembered by many of the school graduates. Here the young men are "at attention" on the lawn of the Institute. (Courtesy of the Eastern Cabarrus Historical Society Museum.)

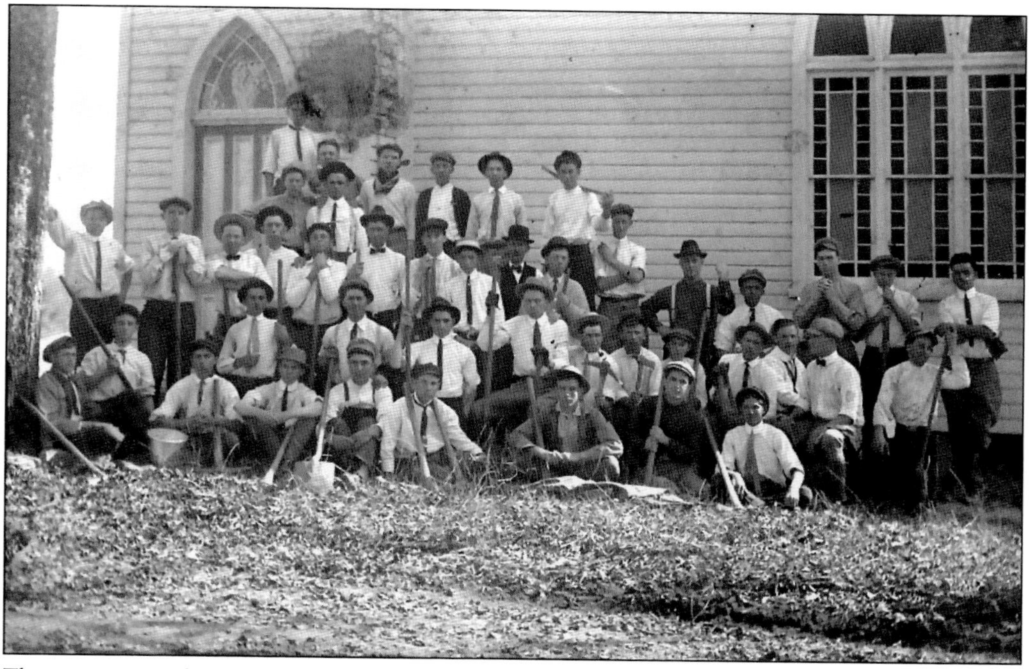

The young men of Mt. Pleasant Collegiate Institute pose for the camera as they get ready to clean up the streets of Mt. Pleasant. They are pictured in front of St. James Church of Christ located south of the school. The young men were often called on to help with different projects in and around the town. (Courtesy of the Eastern Cabarrus Historical Society Museum.)

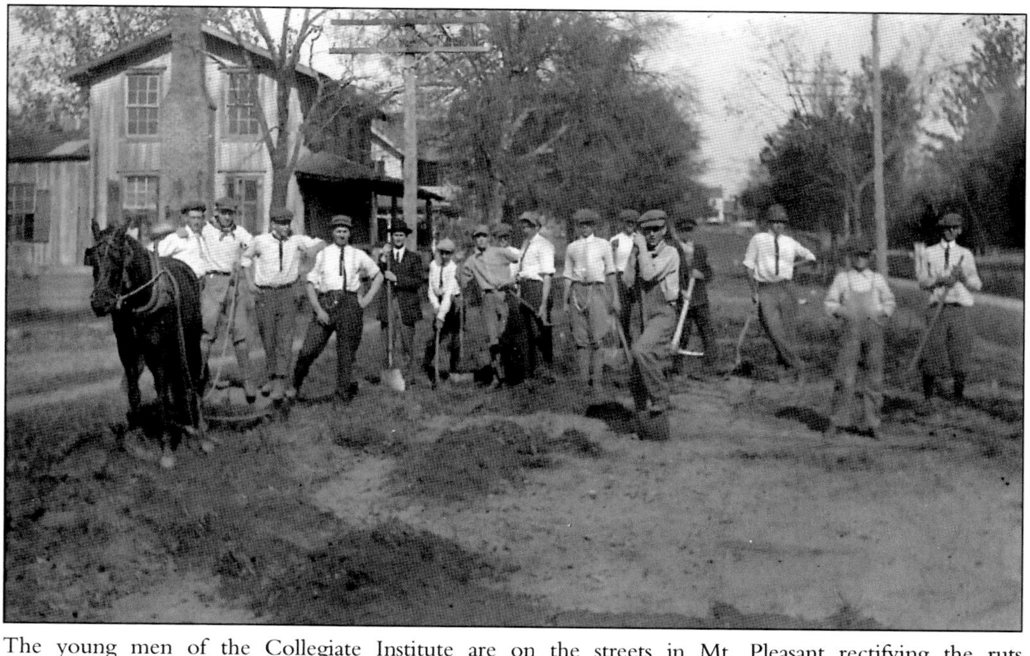

The young men of the Collegiate Institute are on the streets in Mt. Pleasant rectifying the ruts and "unpleasant droppings" left by horses. Just to the left and behind the young men can be seen the Lentz Hotel in its original location on North Main Street. (Courtesy of the Eastern Cabarrus Historical Society Museum.)

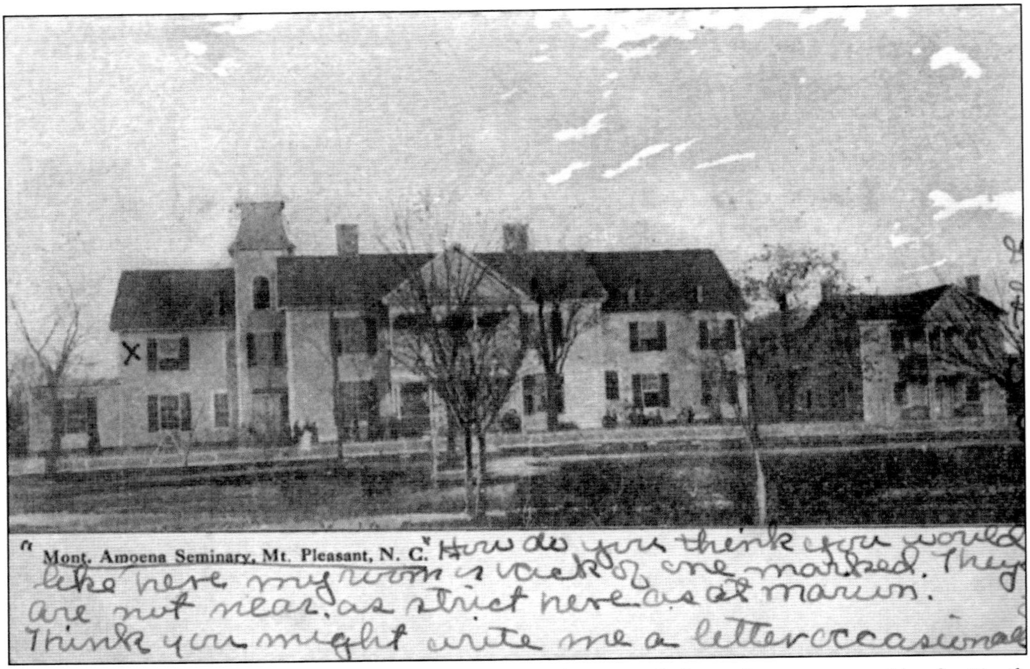

Mont Amoena Seminary was a place of higher education for young ladies and was sponsored by the North Carolina Synod of the Evangelic Lutheran Church. Built in 1859, it was located on the east side of South Main Street across from Holy Trinity Lutheran Church. (Courtesy of Wayne Chapman.)

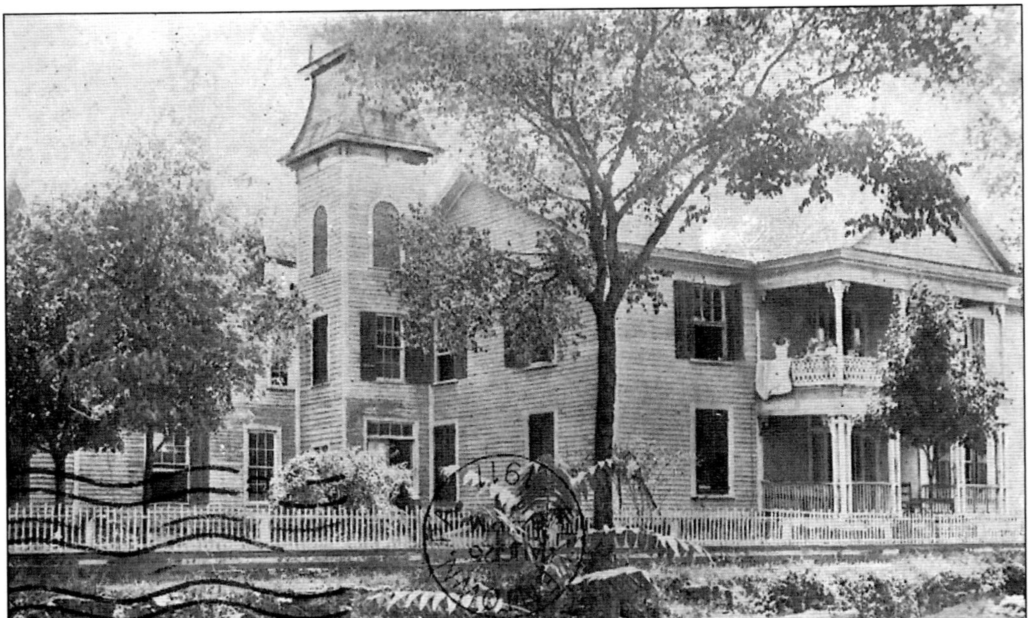

This was the two-story frame building that housed the seminary for more than 50 years. The building was destroyed by fire in November 1911. Some of the young ladies can be seen on the balcony. (Courtesy of Marian Harter.)

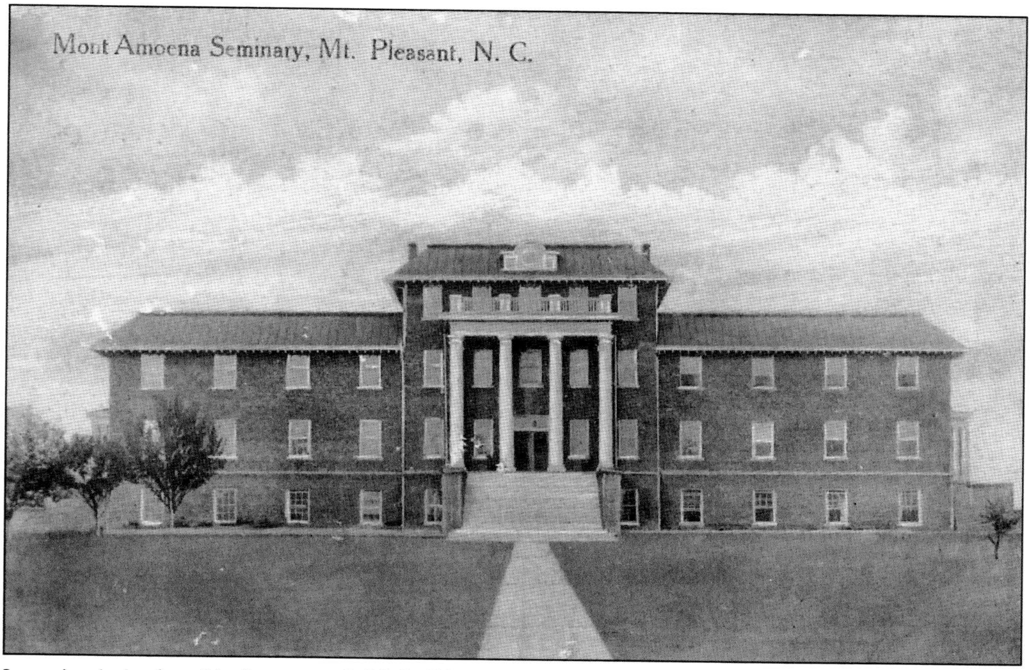

Imposing in its day, this three-story brick building with its white columned facade was the second home of Mont Amoena. This building served the seminary from 1912 until 1927 when it closed forever. (Courtesy of the Eastern Cabarrus Historical Society Museum.)

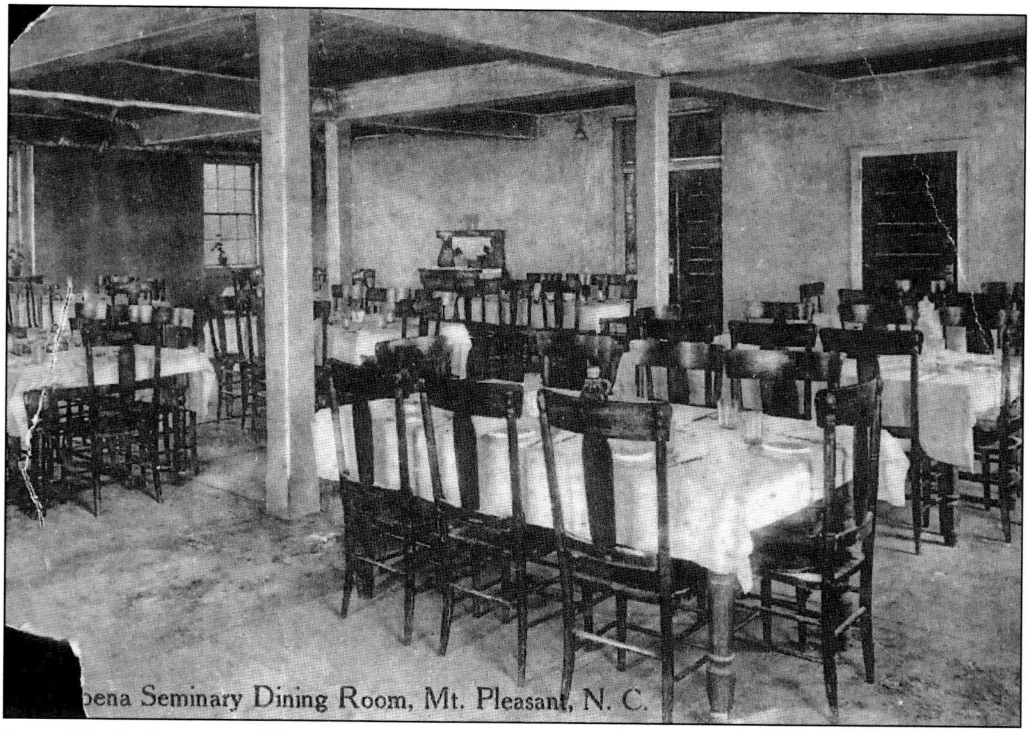

Located in the basement of the second building, this was the dining room at the Mont Amoena Seminary. (Courtesy of the Eastern Cabarrus Historical Society Museum.)

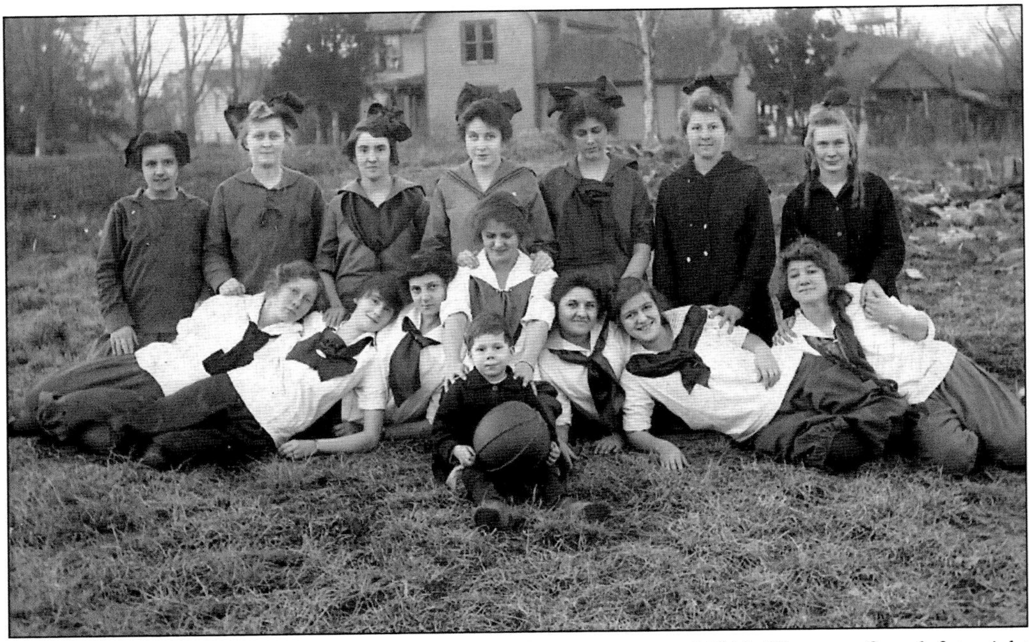

Some of the young ladies of Mont Amoena pose for the camera around 1915. They are, from left to right (first row) Rox Cauble, Annie Lee Pless, Mary Gyann, Liblian Potrea, Wannie Cress, Julian Von Oshen, and Kathrine Fisher; (second row) Amy Fisher Honeycutt, Grace Cauble, Olanthe Miller, Alma Davis, Stella Hahn, and Ruth Sloop. The young boy with the ball was Henry Lee ?. (Courtesy of the Eastern Cabarrus Historical Society Museum.)

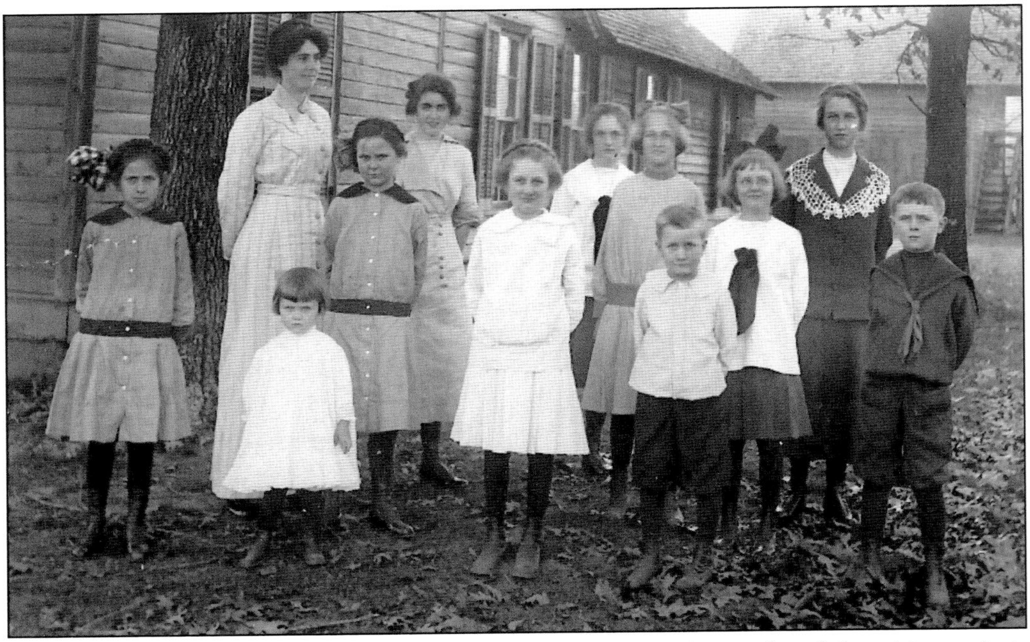

School students associated with the Mont Amoena Seminary in Mt. Pleasant, from left to right, are Janie Tucker, Annie B. Shuemaker, Julia Tucker, Helen James, Rosa James, Agnes Allman, Ruth James, Willie Allman, Brown McAllister, Alica James, Mable McAllister, and Bus James. (Courtesy of the Eastern Cabarrus Historical Society Museum.)

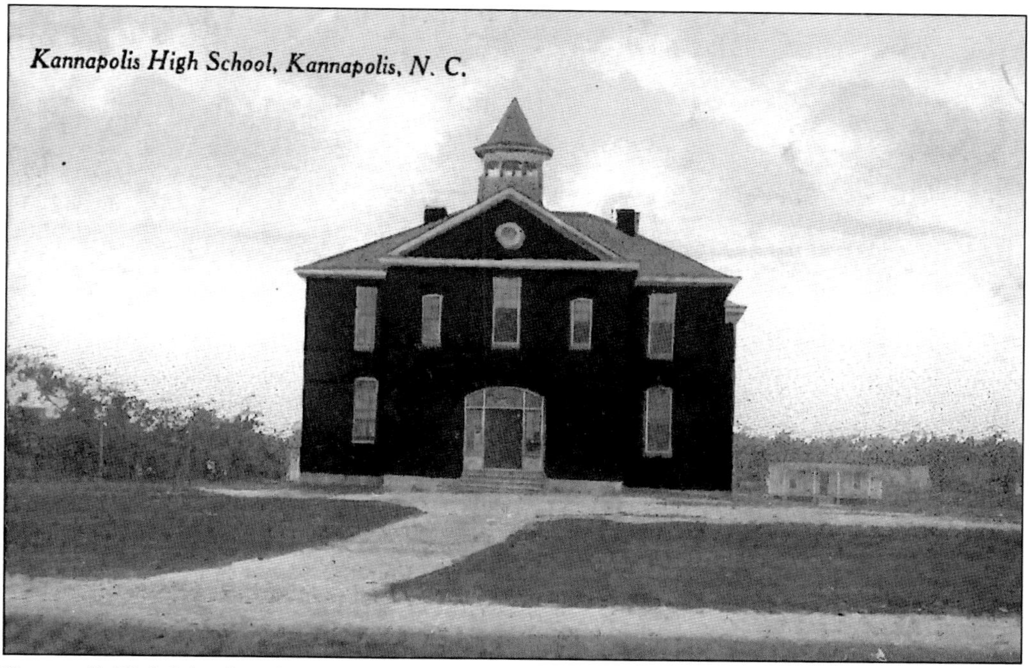

Kannapolis High School, as this early card depicts, was located on South Main Street north of today's police department. The school became South School, also known as McIver Elementary School. (Courtesy of Jim Ramseur.)

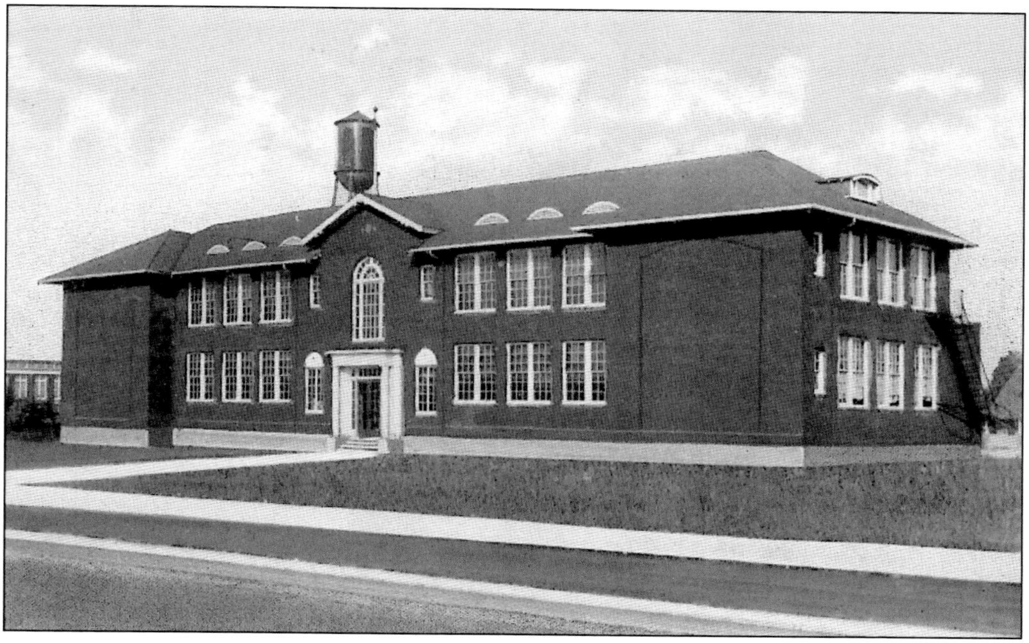

A later view of South School shows it to be quite an impressive building compared to the old school building that once stood in this location. In order to provide more classroom space the earlier structure had additions built on to it. This building was lost to fire. (Courtesy of Marian Harter.)

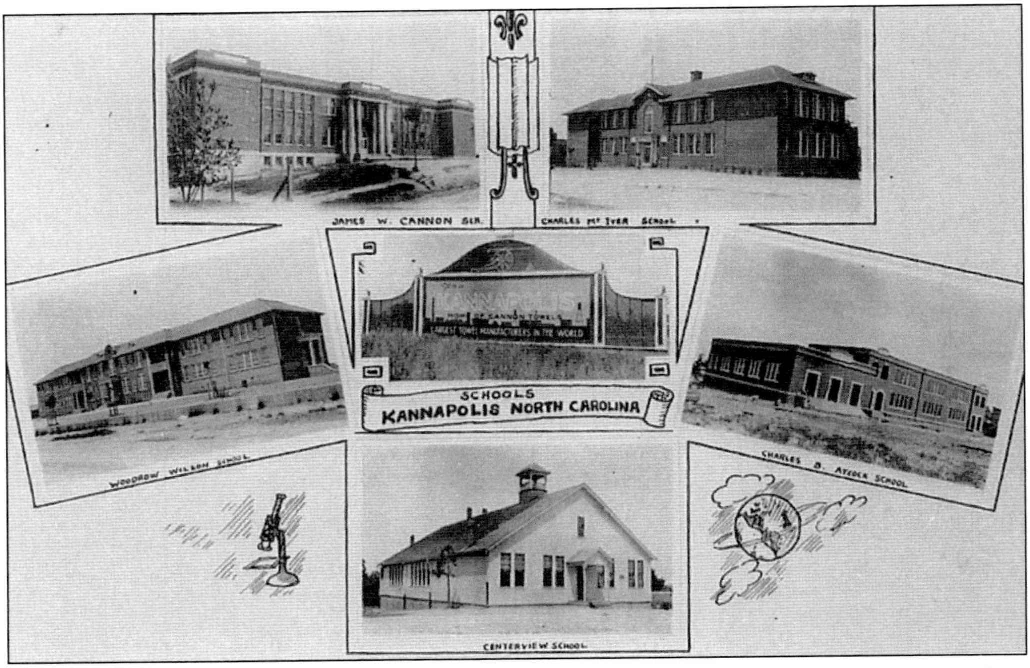

A proud grouping of schools located in Kannapolis is the subject of this postcard. Clockwise from top left are James W. Cannon, Charles McIver, Charles Aycock, Centerview School, and Woodrow Wilson School. (Courtesy of Durwood Barbour.)

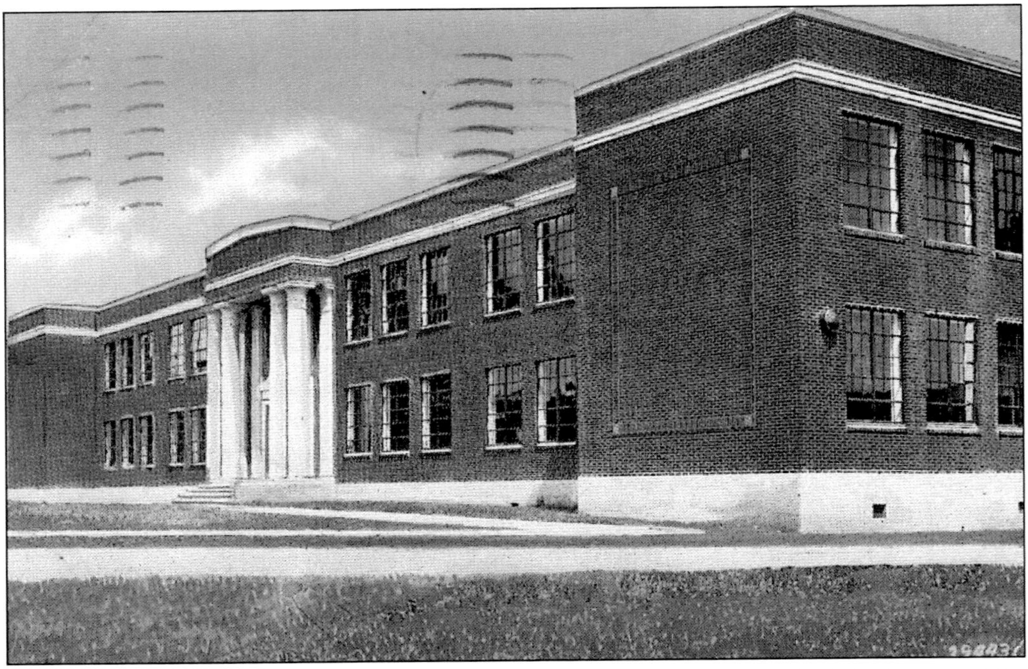

James W. Cannon High School was located on North Rose Avenue near today's high school. This building was used at one time as the junior high school and was lost due to a fire. (Courtesy of Whitley's Funeral Home.)

Nine

Government and Community Life

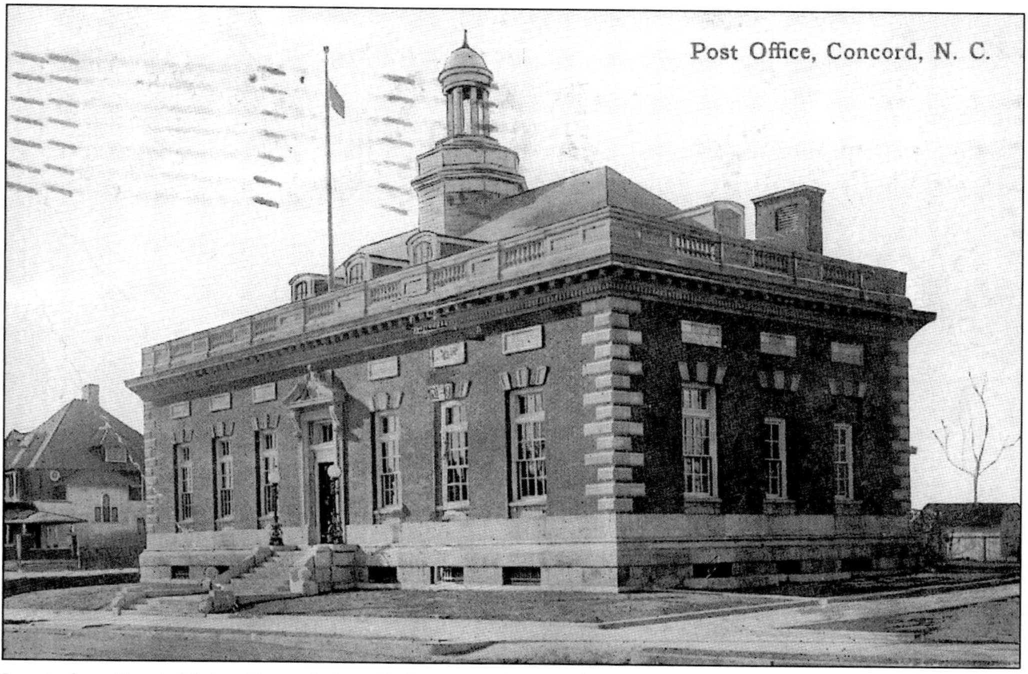

Located on South Union Street below St. James Lutheran Church was Concord's post office. First built in 1912, this impressive structure was the pride of Concord. The card is a color card and has a postmark of 1912, making this one of the first cards made of this building.

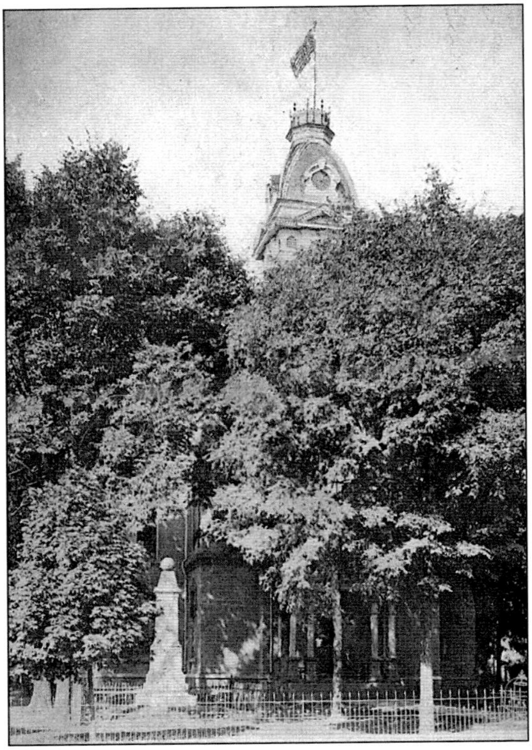

George S.H. Appleget was the noted architect from New Jersey who designed this building, the third Cabarrus County Courthouse. Construction was awarded to F.W. Ahrens, a Charlotte builder. It is thought that this image was made in the spring of 1910. Shown on the grounds in front of the courthouse in its original location is the beautiful monument to the Confederacy, which was dedicated on Thursday, May 8, 1892 in front of more than 3,000 attendees.

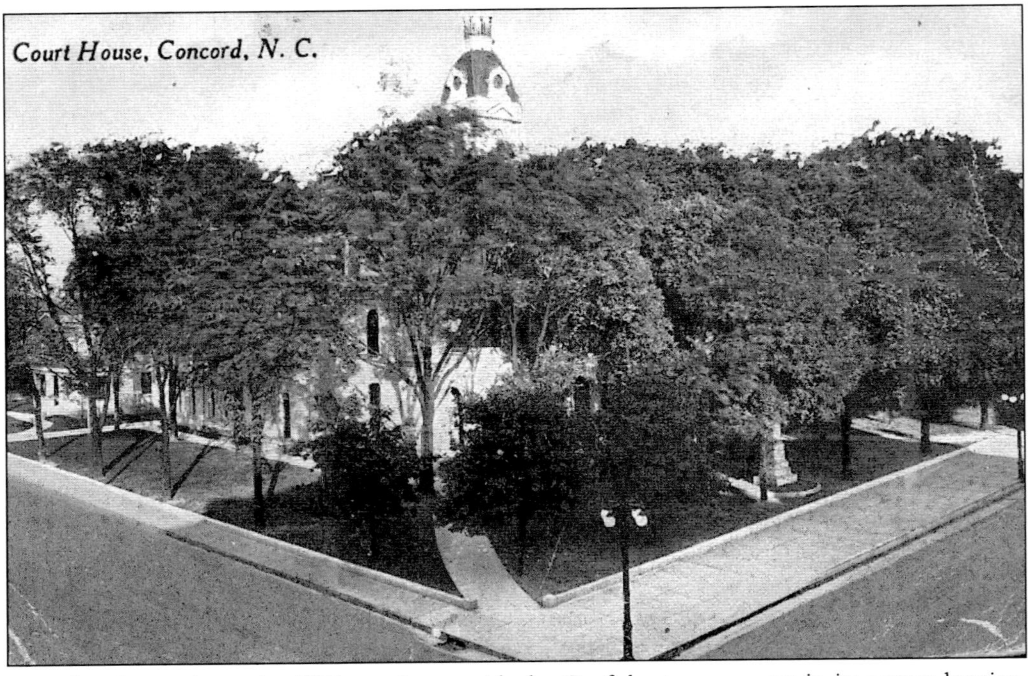

A modern image shows the 1876 courthouse with the Confederate monument in its present location. Confederate memorial services were held at this location each year on May 10 until 1966 and were resumed in 2000 by the Cabarrus Guards, the local chapter of the Sons of Confederate Veterans, and the Daughters of the Confederacy.

Built in 1903, this ultra-modern building was located on South Union Street at Barbrick Street. It housed the police station, mayor's office, tax collector's office, and city jail all on the first floor. Upstairs was the Opera House where Shakespearean plays, minstrels, vaudeville shows, local speakers, and town meetings could be held. The north side housed the fire house, recognized by the large double doors allowing passage of the fire wagon pulled by two bays.

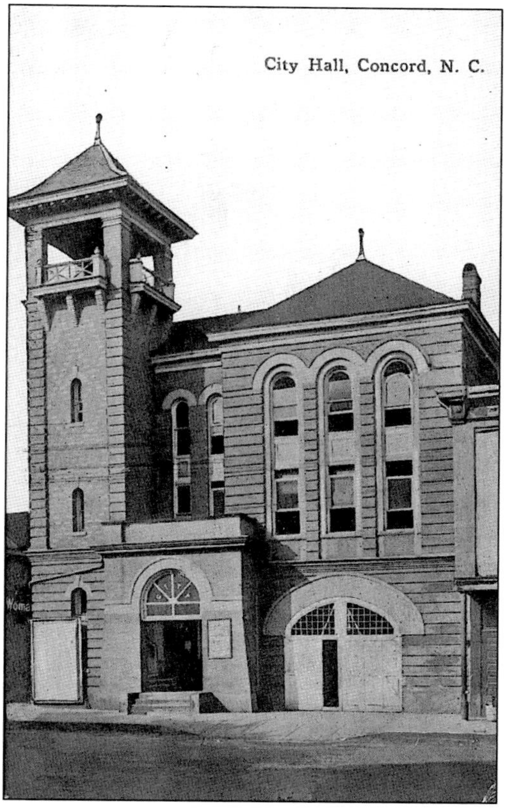

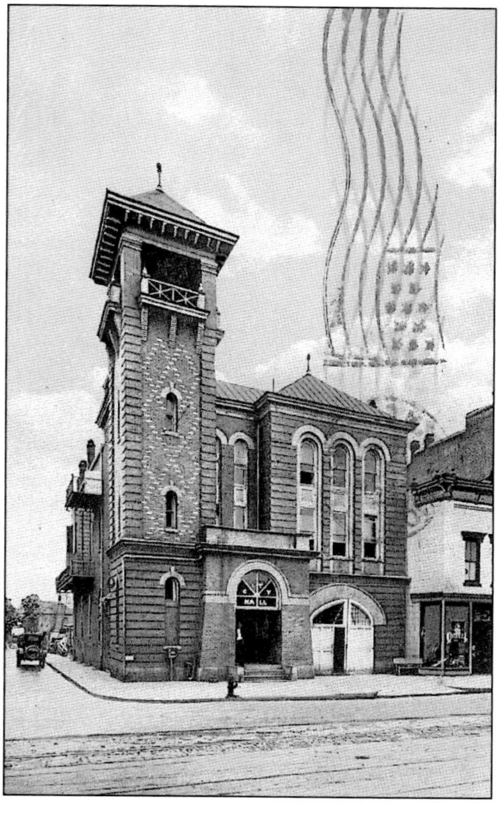

A 1920-postmarked card of city hall also shows the Ritz's Store to the north. This building underwent major changes in the 1950s and is still used today by the City of Concord.

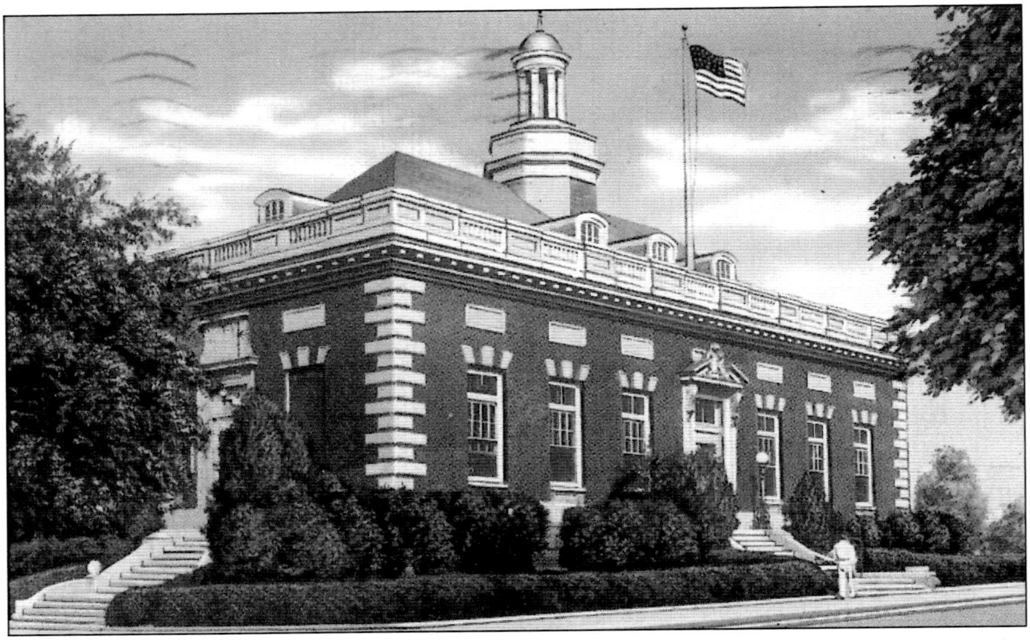

A 1938-postmarked card shows the United States Post Office. St. James Lutheran Church purchased this property and razed the building to make way for a much needed parking area.

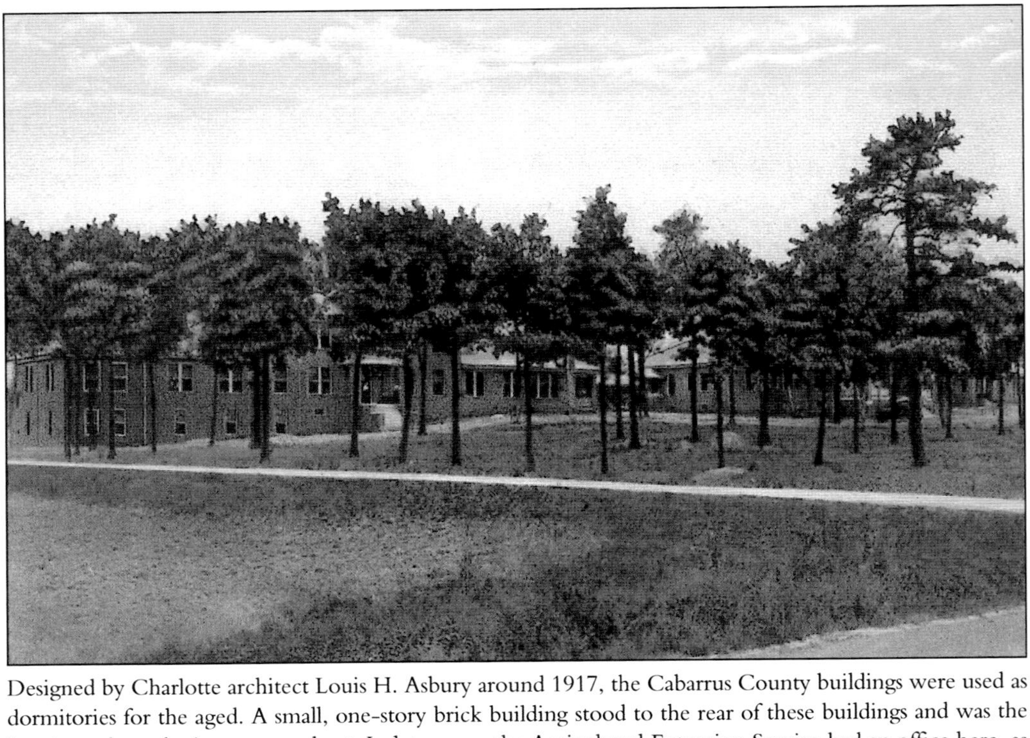

Designed by Charlotte architect Louis H. Asbury around 1917, the Cabarrus County buildings were used as dormitories for the aged. A small, one-story brick building stood to the rear of these buildings and was the location where the insane were kept. In later years the Agricultural Extension Service had an office here, as did the Cabarrus County Health Department.

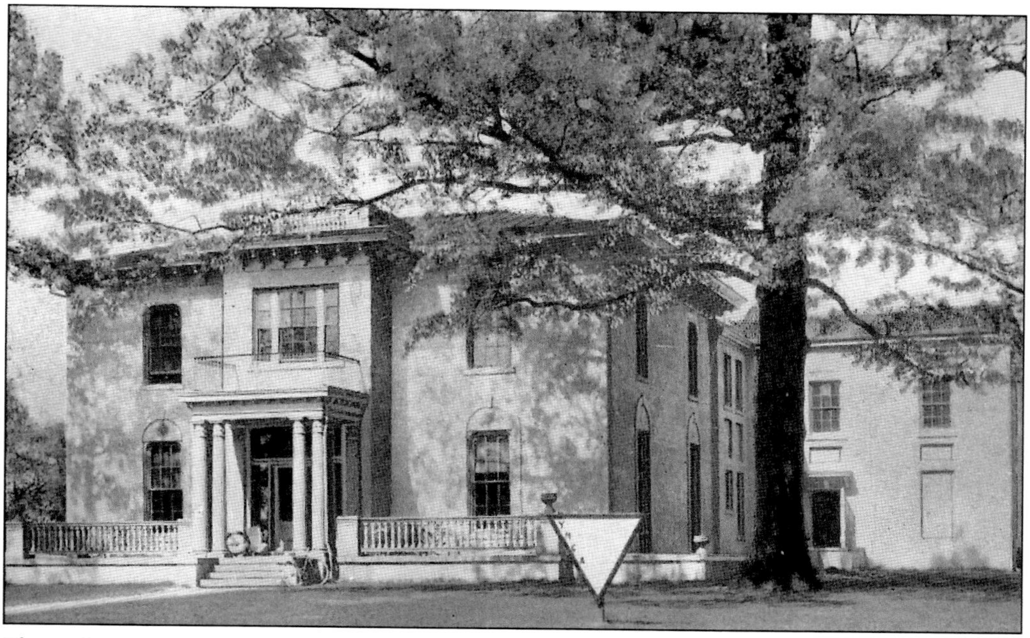

The William A. "Sandy" Smith home was built around 1869 and was located on North Union Street at Holly Lane (today's Killarney Street). Purchased in 1916 by the City of Concord, it was remodeled to add a pool and gymnasium and opened as the YMCA. In later years its name was changed to the Community Center and it housed the public library and the Memorial Hall. Memorial Hall was used by servicemen during World War II as a canteen.

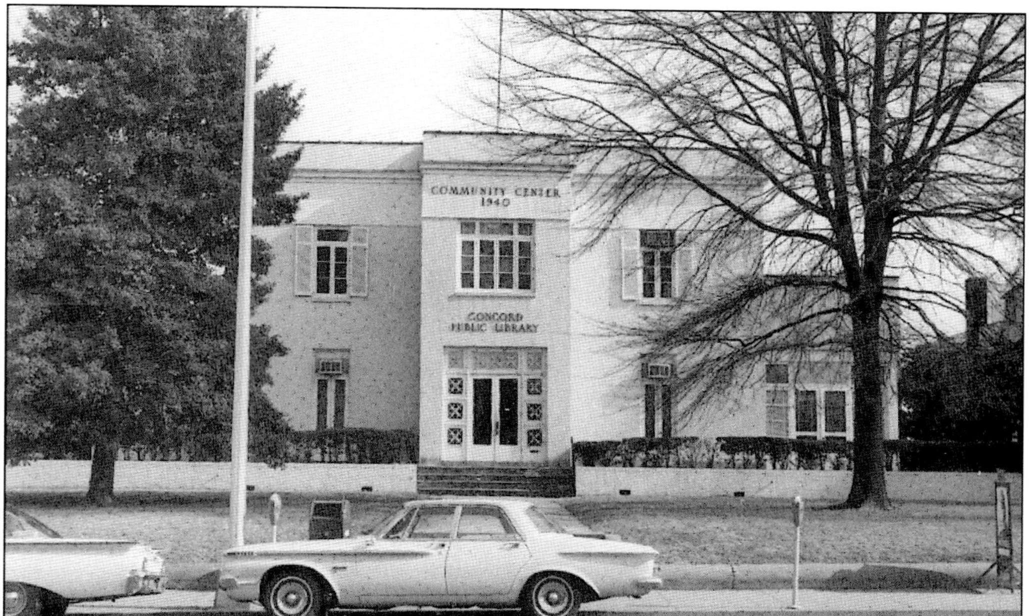

The Community Center, shown here in the early 1960s, was razed in 1977. Today, the city library has a new home across the street and south of this building and is known as the Charles A. Cannon Memorial Library.

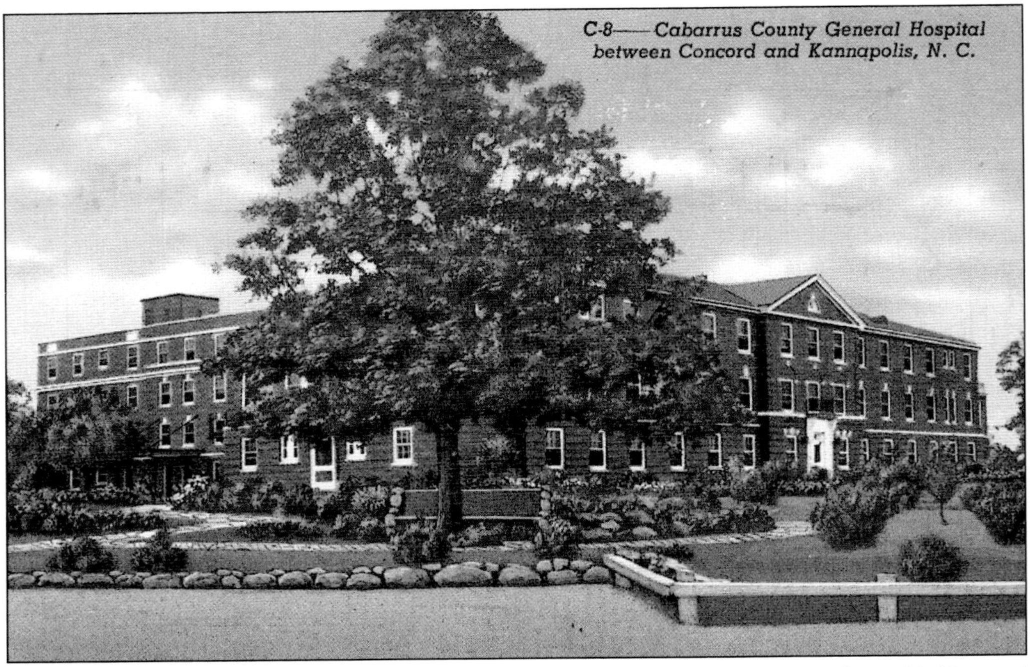

Cabarrus County General Hospital was the name given to this hospital located on Highway 29 (Concord Parkway) on the north side of Concord. The land was given by Mary Ella Bost Cannon. Her son Charles Albert Cannon helped get legislation through so the hospital could be built in 1937. It had 46 beds, 19 employees, and 8 physicians.

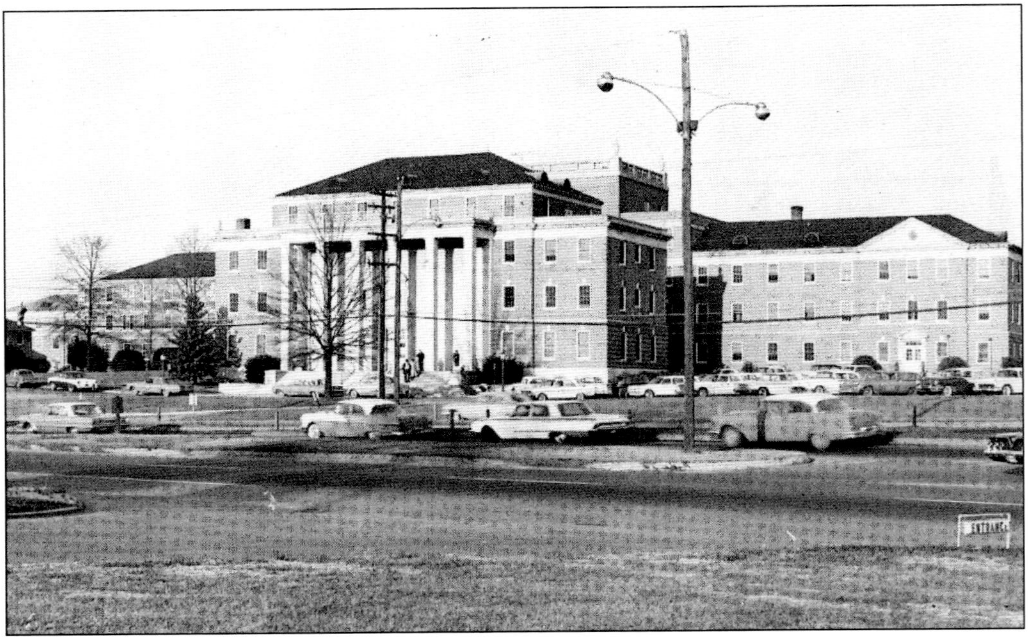

A 1960s image of Cabarrus Memorial Hospital, also the location of the Louise Harkey School of Nursing, is today known as NorthEast Medical Center. It has 457 beds, more than 200 physicians, and 2,400 employees. It is the fifth fastest-growing hospital system in the United States.

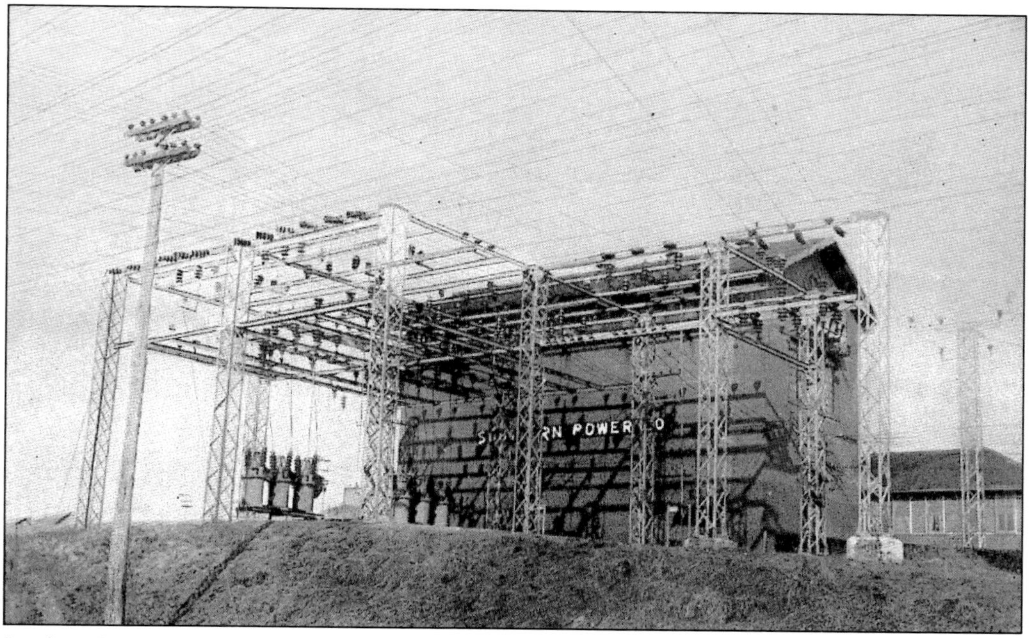

Southern Power Company was the owner of this relay station, which is thought to have been located on the west end of Academy Street. Southern Power Company is today's Duke Power Company. (Courtesy of Jim Ramseur.)

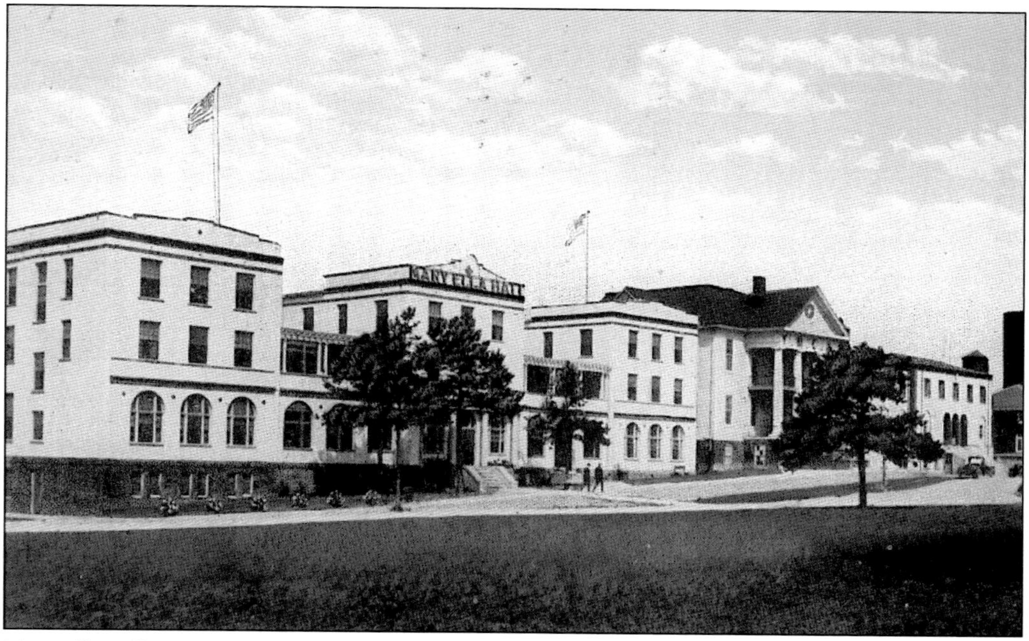

Mary Ella Hall was a boarding house completed and occupied in 1919 that honored James W. Cannon's wife. Two hundred forty residents could live there in 120 double rooms. Three separate sections were incorporated: one for women, one for men, and a center section for married couples. Seven separate meals were provided and up to 772 people were fed each day. This card shows the first YMCA on the right side of the hall. (Courtesy of Marian Harter.)

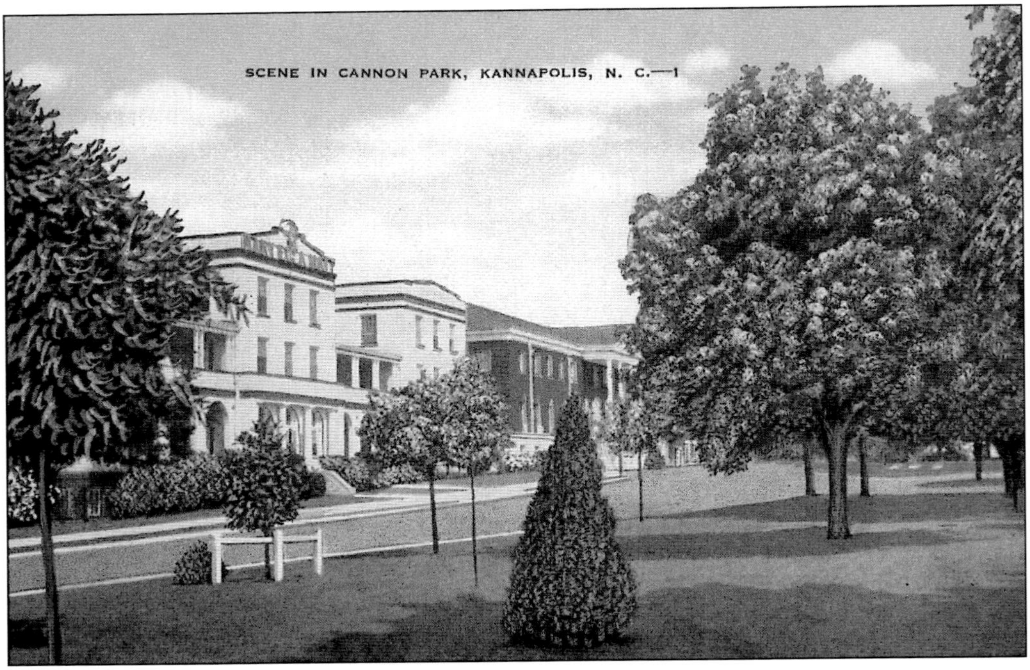

A second image of Mary Ella Hall shows the third YMCA to the right. Dr. E.E. Robinson, the Cannon Mills physician, had an office located in this building. Mary Ella Hall was demolished in 1963. (Courtesy of Whitley's Funeral Home.)

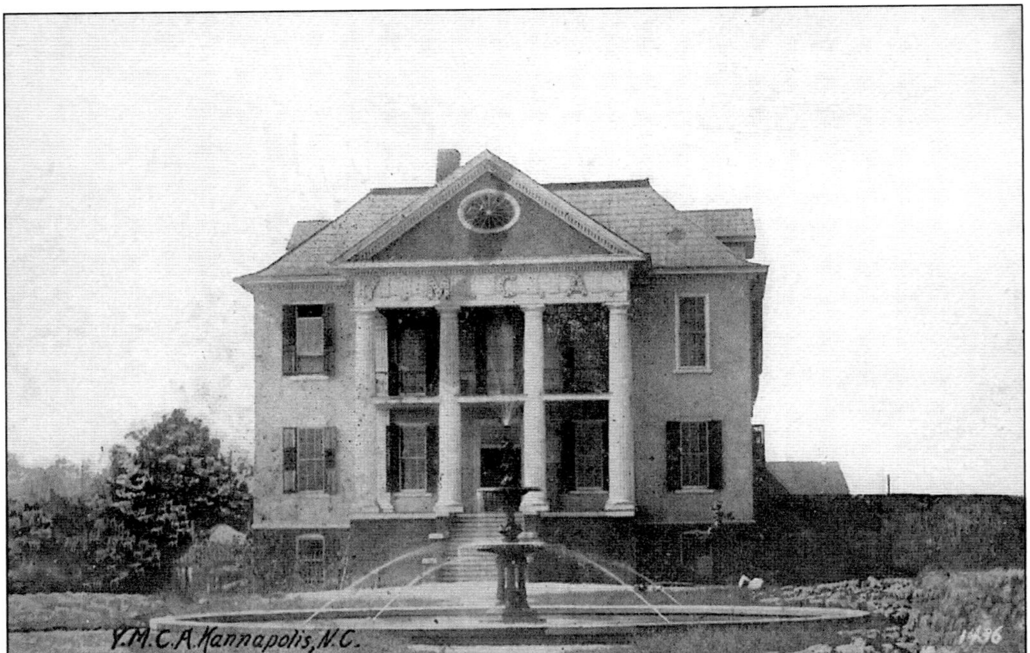

On November 5, 1908 this first building of the YMCA was dedicated to the memory of David Franklin Cannon by his brother James W. Cannon. At one time this YMCA boasted a membership of 1900 paid members making this one of the largest YMCAs in the country. (Courtesy of History Advocate of Kannapolis, North Carolina.)

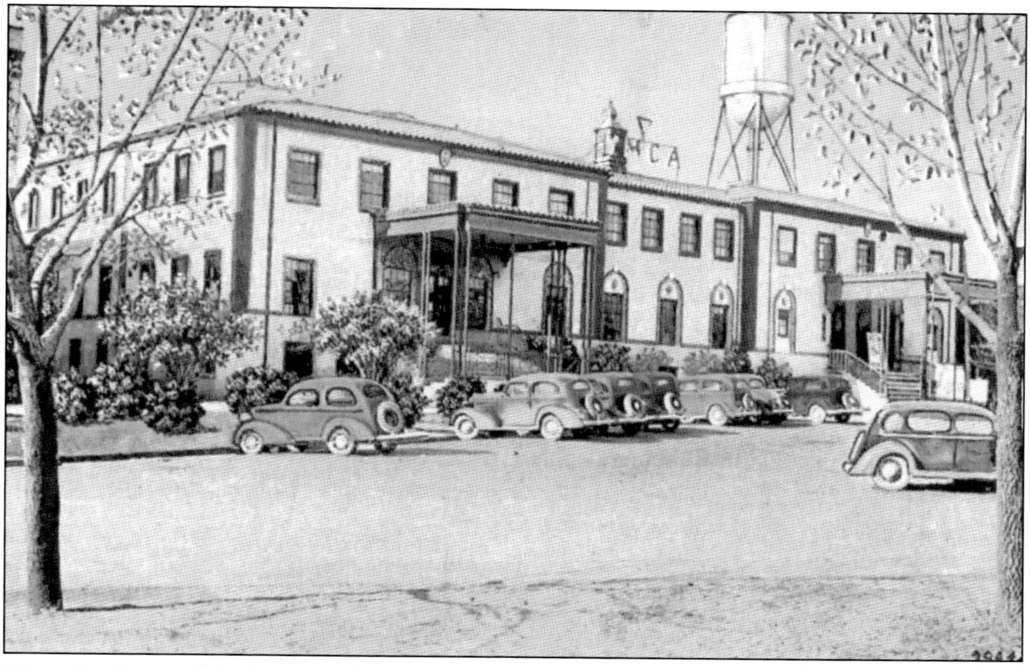

After a fire destroyed the first YMCA, a second building was erected in 1924–1925. This building was built in memory of Mr. and Mrs. James W. Cannon, and it too was lost to a fire, this time in 1937. (Courtesy of Marian Harter.)

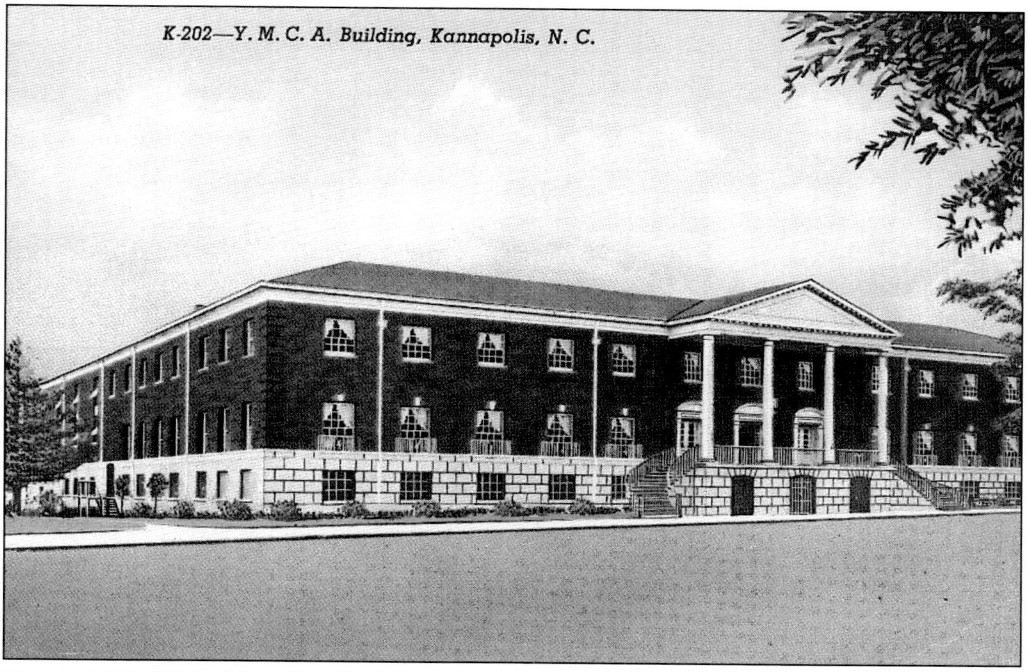

The third YMCA building formally opened in January 1940 in memory of Mr. and Mrs. James W. Cannon. This was the first building to have been arranged to serve members of the entire family including a special department for girls and women. Membership at one time climbed to 4,723. (Courtesy of Mike Coltrane.)

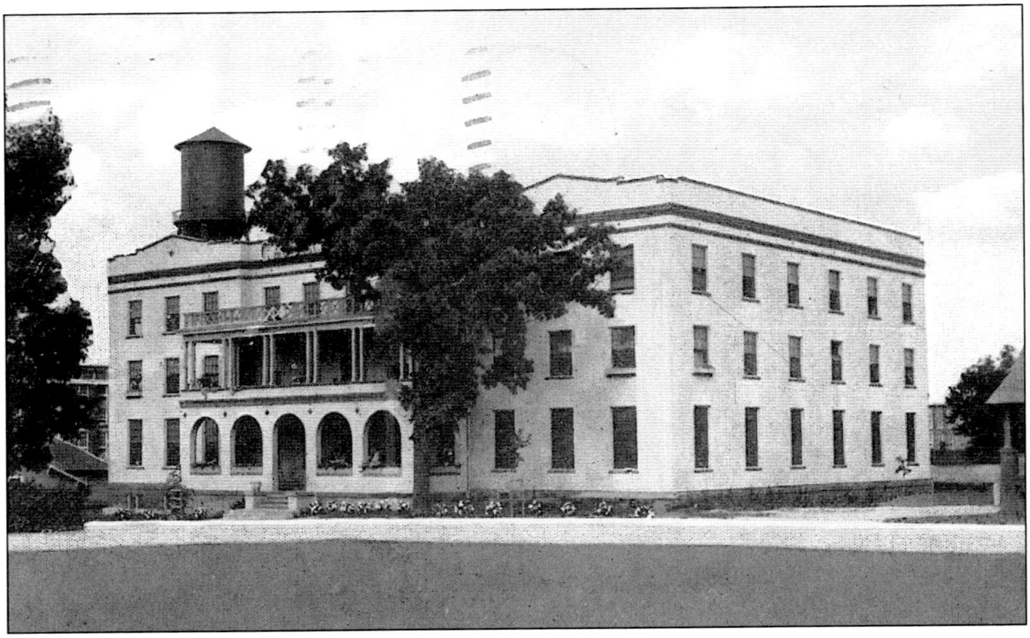

A 1936-postmarked card shows Cabarrus Hall. The building was a hotel/boarding house used primarily to house single people. Located on West Avenue near McIver School, this was a favorite place for teachers who taught at McIver to live. During the 1950s, a portion of this building was used as the Cabarrus County Health Department.

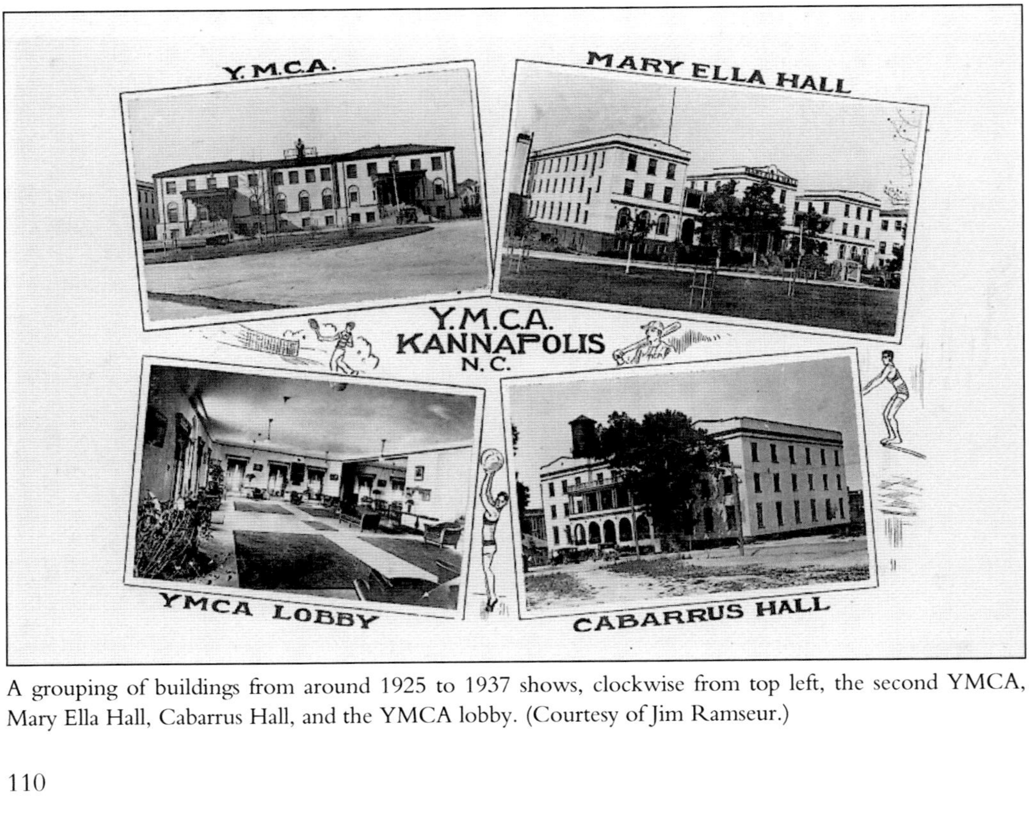

A grouping of buildings from around 1925 to 1937 shows, clockwise from top left, the second YMCA, Mary Ella Hall, Cabarrus Hall, and the YMCA lobby. (Courtesy of Jim Ramseur.)

Ten

Miscellaneous Views

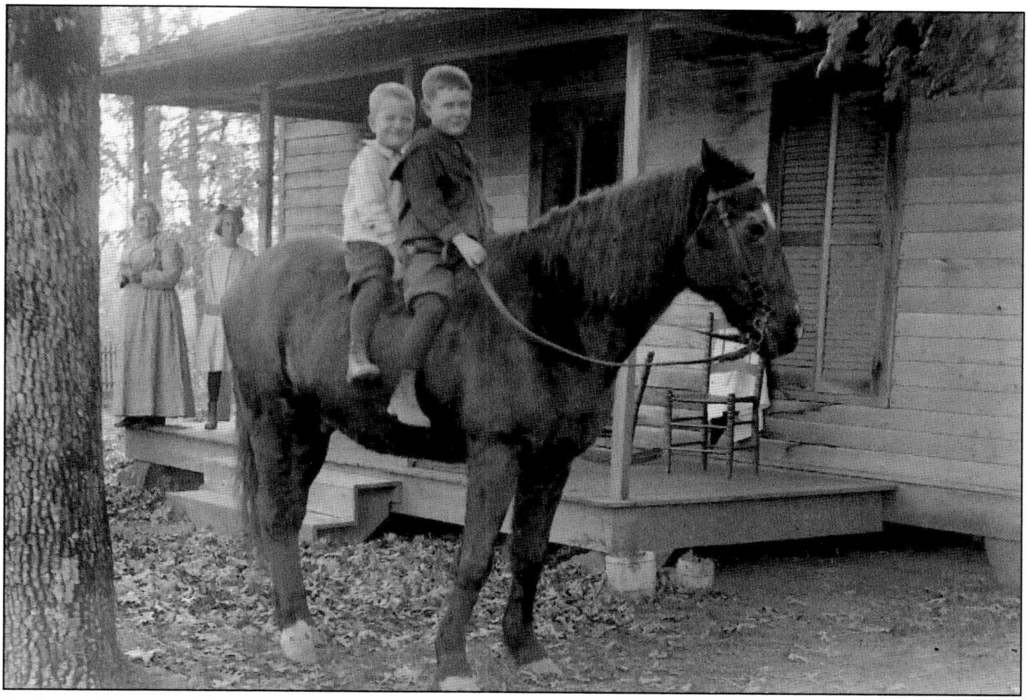

In the early 1900s life was simple for the two young boys on this mighty horse. It had to be a day to remember for Brown McAllister in the white shirt and Bus James in the dark. The older lady on the porch is unidentified, but the young girl is Willie Allman. (Courtesy of the Eastern Cabarrus Historical Society Museum.)

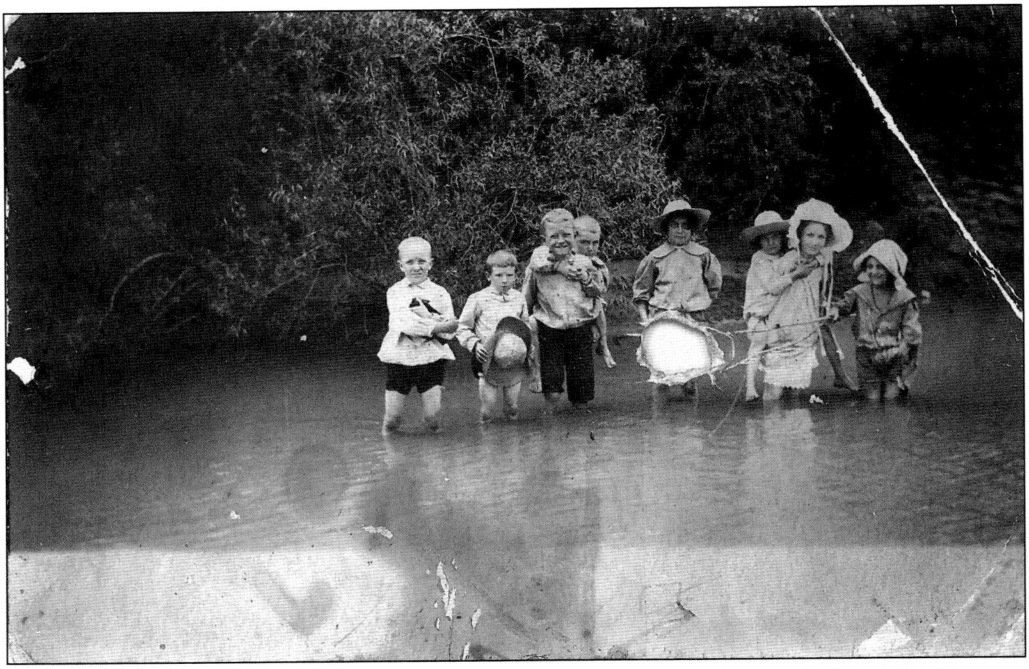

These youngsters stand in Adams Creek near Mt. Pleasant in this image made around 1902–1905. They are, from left to right, Jim Misenheimer, Miller Cook, unidentified, Mack Misenheimer, "Bill" Misenheimer, Ruby Misenheimer, Helen Misenheimer, and Bonnie Misenheimer. (Courtesy of the Eastern Cabarrus Historical Society Museum.)

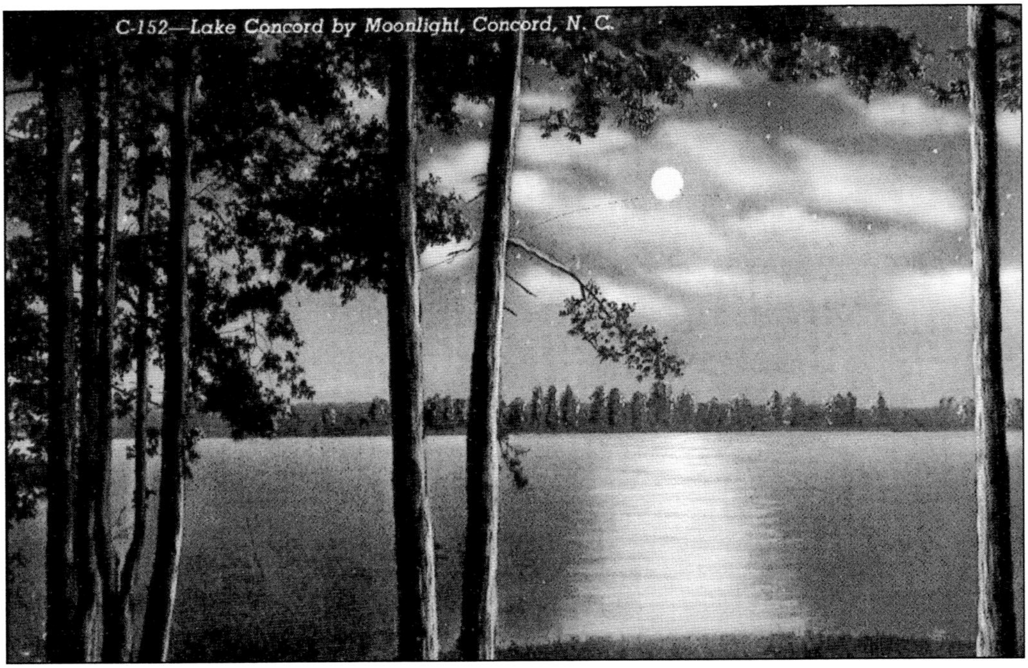

A peaceful scene of Lake Concord shows the moon reflecting on the water. The lake, with a 400,000 gallon capacity, was situated on the tributaries of Cold Water Creek and serves as the municipal water supply of the City of Concord.

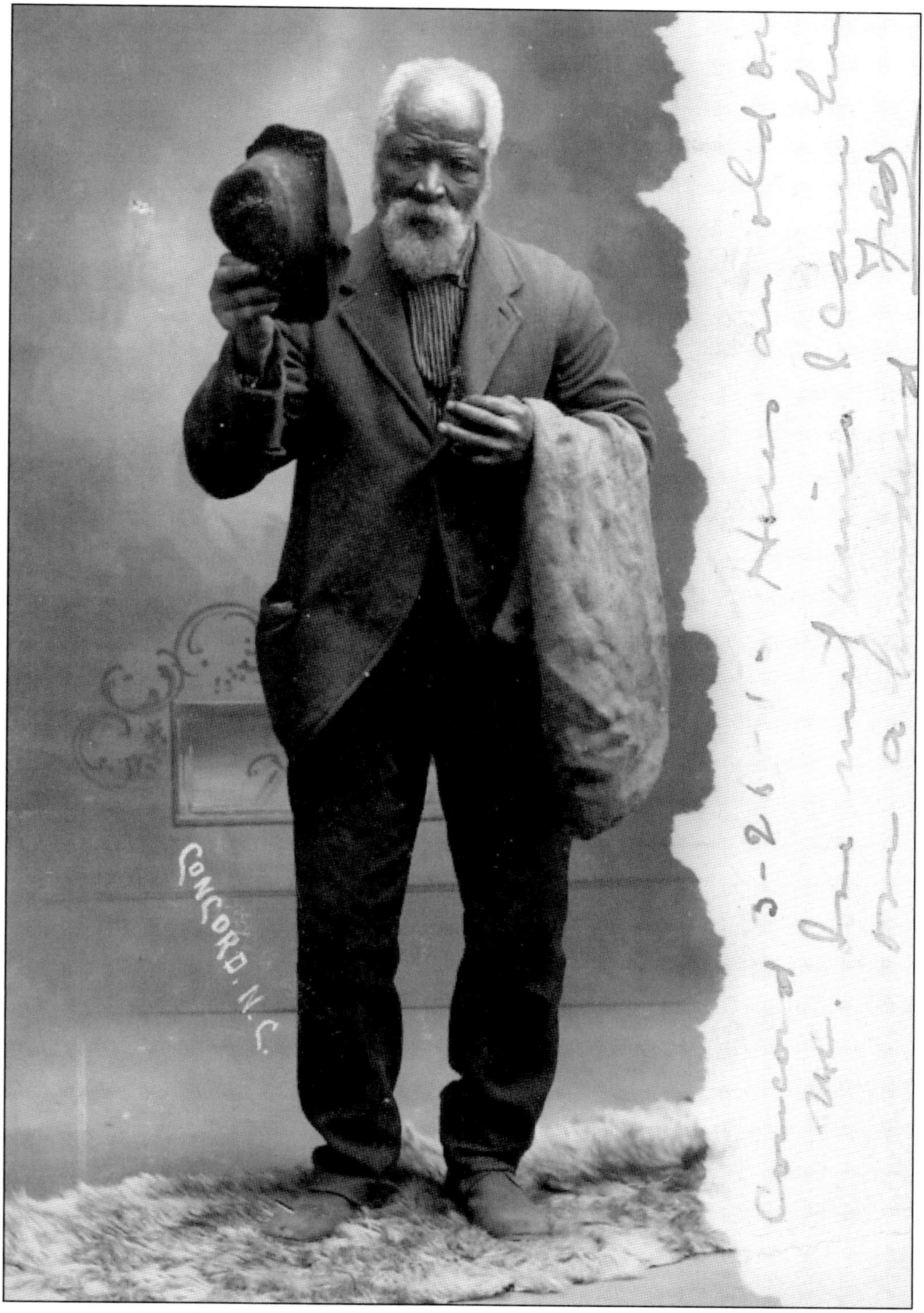

Another card sent by "Fred" is shown here, and he wrote on March 26, 1906, "Here's an old one I've meet since I came here over a hundred." Is it possible that this kindly old gentleman could have already celebrated his 100th birthday?

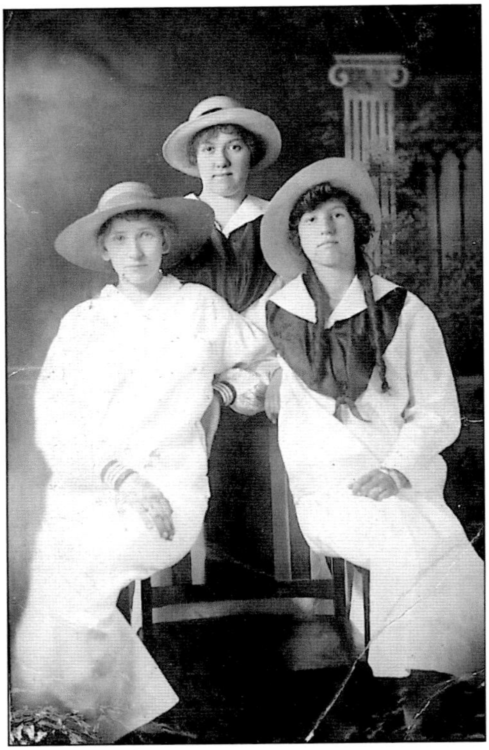

A group of young ladies from Kannapolis typical of the early 1900s are shown in this image made around 1918–1919. From left to right are Kathy ?, Merrian Goodson, and Mildred Poteat Goodson. Mildred was an excellent seamstress, and it is rumored that Mr. Cannon would seek her out if he needed "special" sewing done to give to a personal friend or favorite client. (Courtesy of James C. Poteat.)

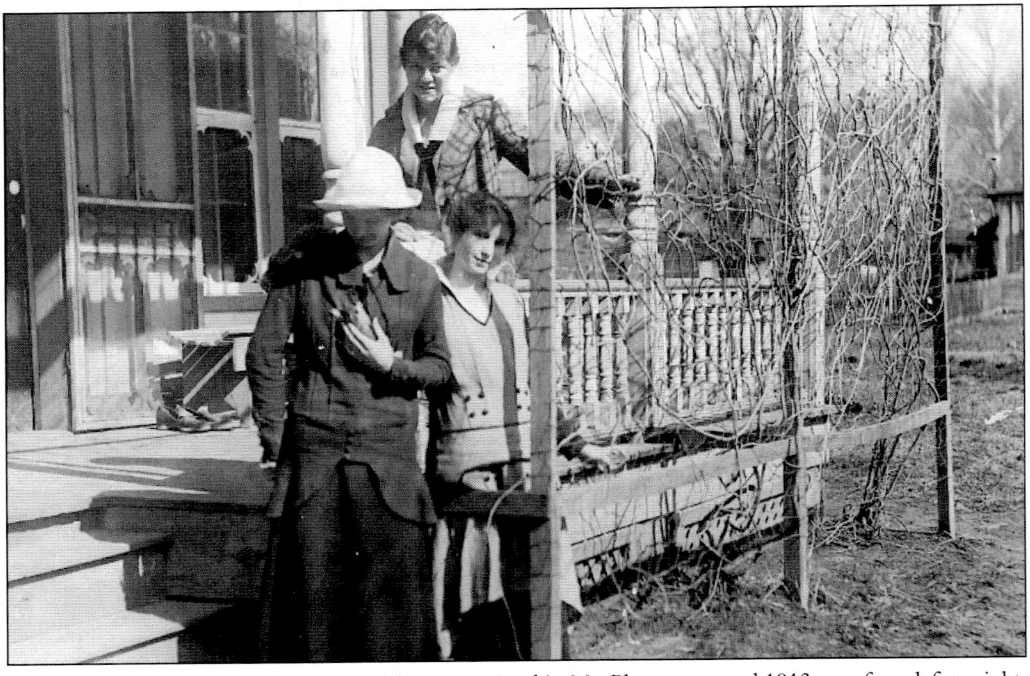

These three cousins, pictured in front of the Lentz Hotel in Mt. Pleasant around 1913, are, from left to right, Maud E. Lentz (b. November 1884), Laura Heilig Lentz (b. November 8, 1897) on the porch, and Mary E. Lentz (b. July 1897). Laura married George Bowden in 1919 and raised two children, George Jr. and Katherine. Laura died in 1977. (Courtesy of Charles G. Lentz Jr.)

Typical of many young man from Cabarrus County, Bob Goodson served his country during World War I. When he returned to Kannapolis after the war, Bob went to work at the Sears Motor Company where Mills Florist stands today. (Courtesy of James C. Poteat.)

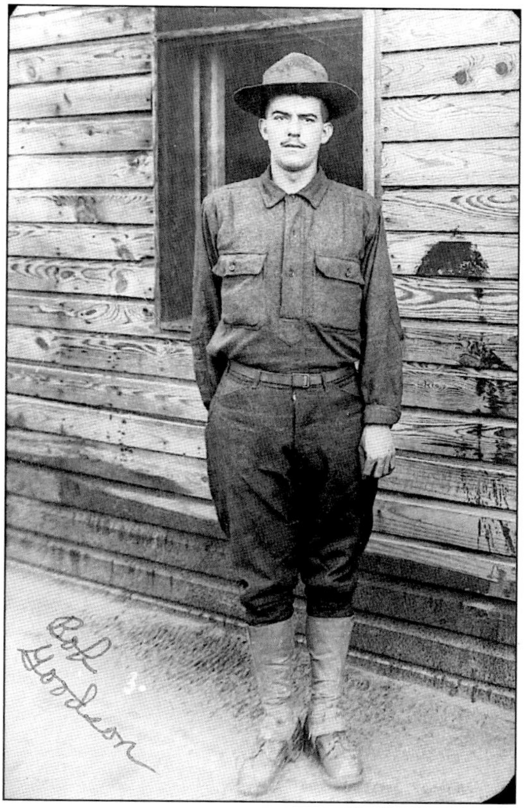

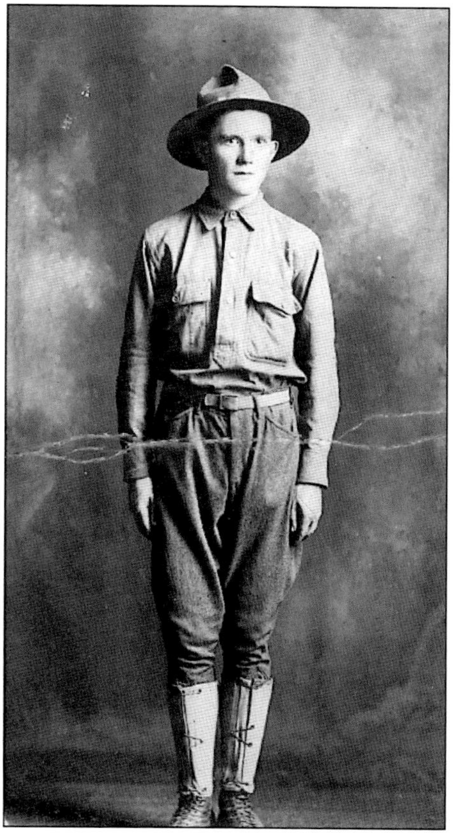

Charles Alexander Lemly was born in Cabarrus County on July 12, 1900, and he too served his country during World War I. When he returned to Kannapolis, he worked for Cannon Mills and raised three children. Charles died on March 17, 1986. (Courtesy of Norris Dearmon.)

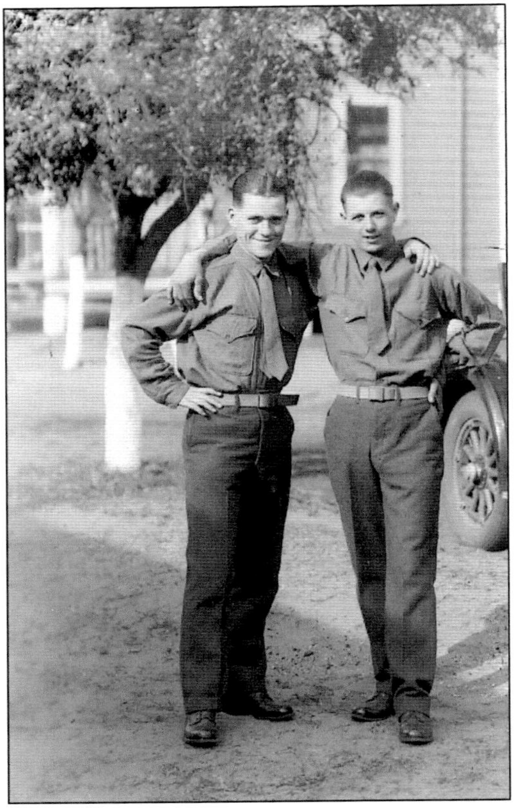

World War II began and with it came the call for young men from Cabarrus County to join the armed services. Pictured at Paris Island, the young man on the right is Ed Gilliland who enlisted into the Marines at age 15 and sent this card to his folks back in Kannapolis just before going to meet the enemies of our country. (Courtesy of James C. Poteat.)

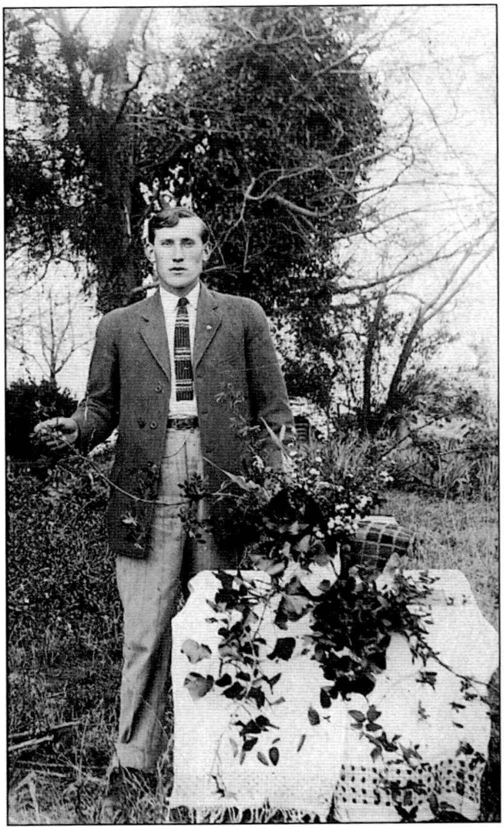

Laban J. "Labe" Chapman grew up near the Main Plant of Cannon Mills in Kannapolis and worked at the mill for 14 years. He later became a deputy with the Rowan County Sheriff's Department. His brother Ira Chapman became chief of the Kannapolis Police Department. (Courtesy of Ottis Chapman.)

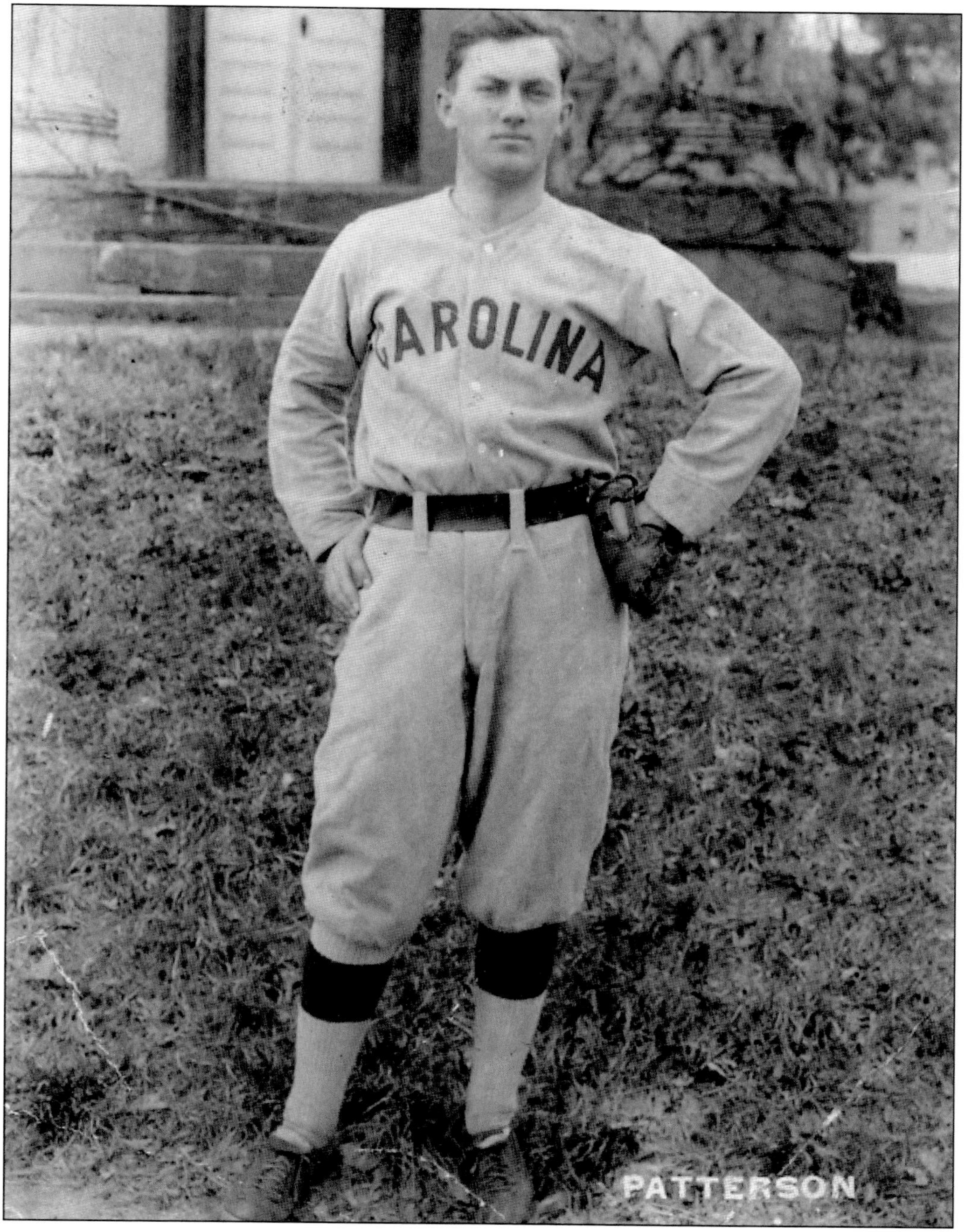

Fred M. Patterson was the son of John K. Patterson and lived at 75 North Union Street in Concord. He played ball for Cinco's, a cigar factory located in Concord, in 1911. Fred went to Trinity College (Duke University) from 1912 to 1913 and then to UNC-Chapel Hill from 1913 to 1916, where he graduated. World War I started and Fred joined up in July 1917 and was assigned with the 113th U.S. Artillery. He was sent to France where he lost a foot in combat and received the Croix de Guerre for extraordinary acts of bravery. He returned to college in Pennsylvania where he received his degree in medicine. Returning to North Carolina, he made his home in Greensboro where he practiced as a urologist. This postcard mailed from Chapel Hill to his father has a postmark of 1914. (Courtesy of Alex and Jane Patterson.)

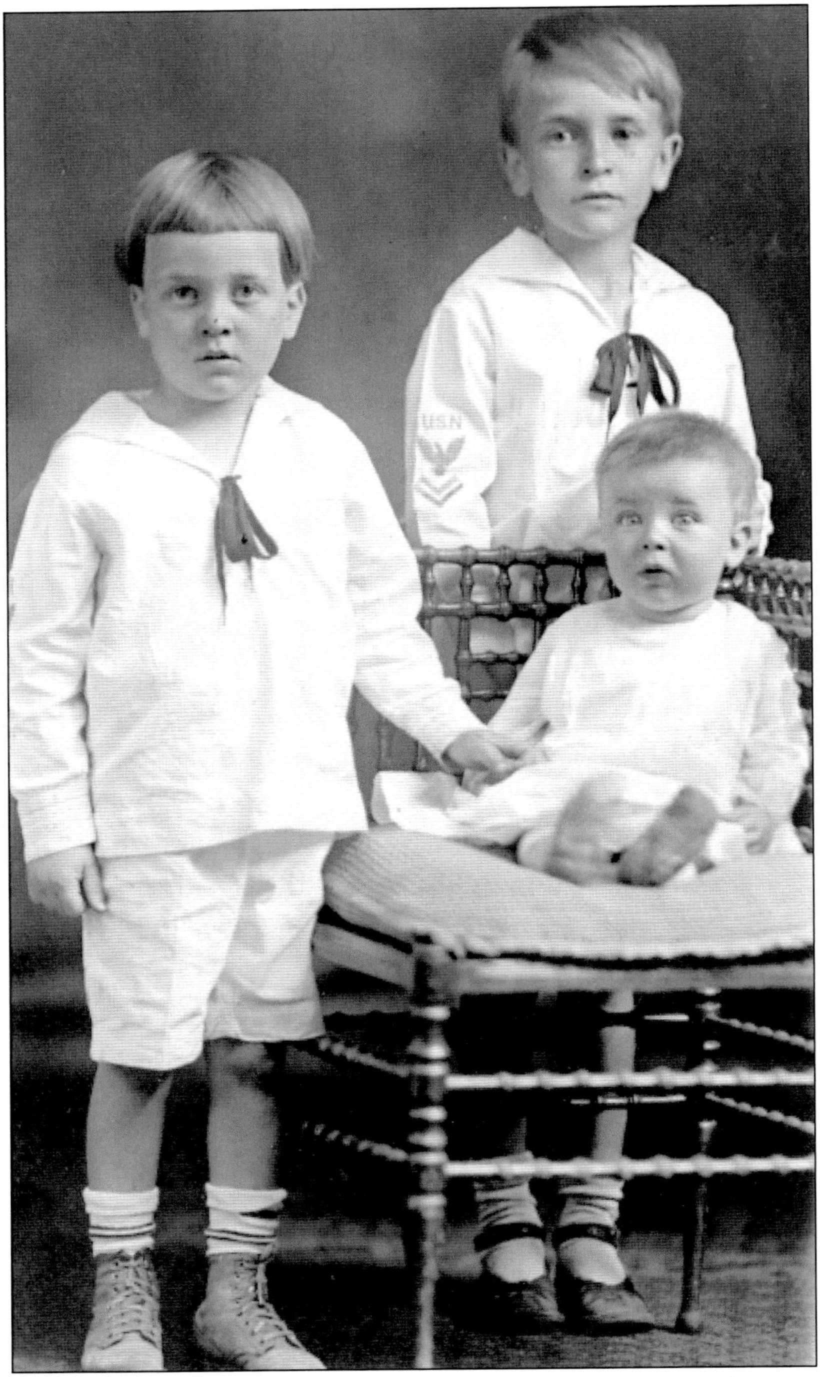

Postcards were a good way to send a picture of young ones to older relatives. Pictured in this image, from left to right, are John William Patterson (1914–1995), Lewis Allen Patterson Jr. (1911–1991), and young Frank Earl Patterson (b. 1918). These young boys were raised and worked in Concord, and they too raised their families in Concord. They were the pride of Louis Sr. and Effie Michael Patterson along with their three sisters, Dorothy, Mary, and Ann, who, along with Frank, still make Cabarrus County their home.

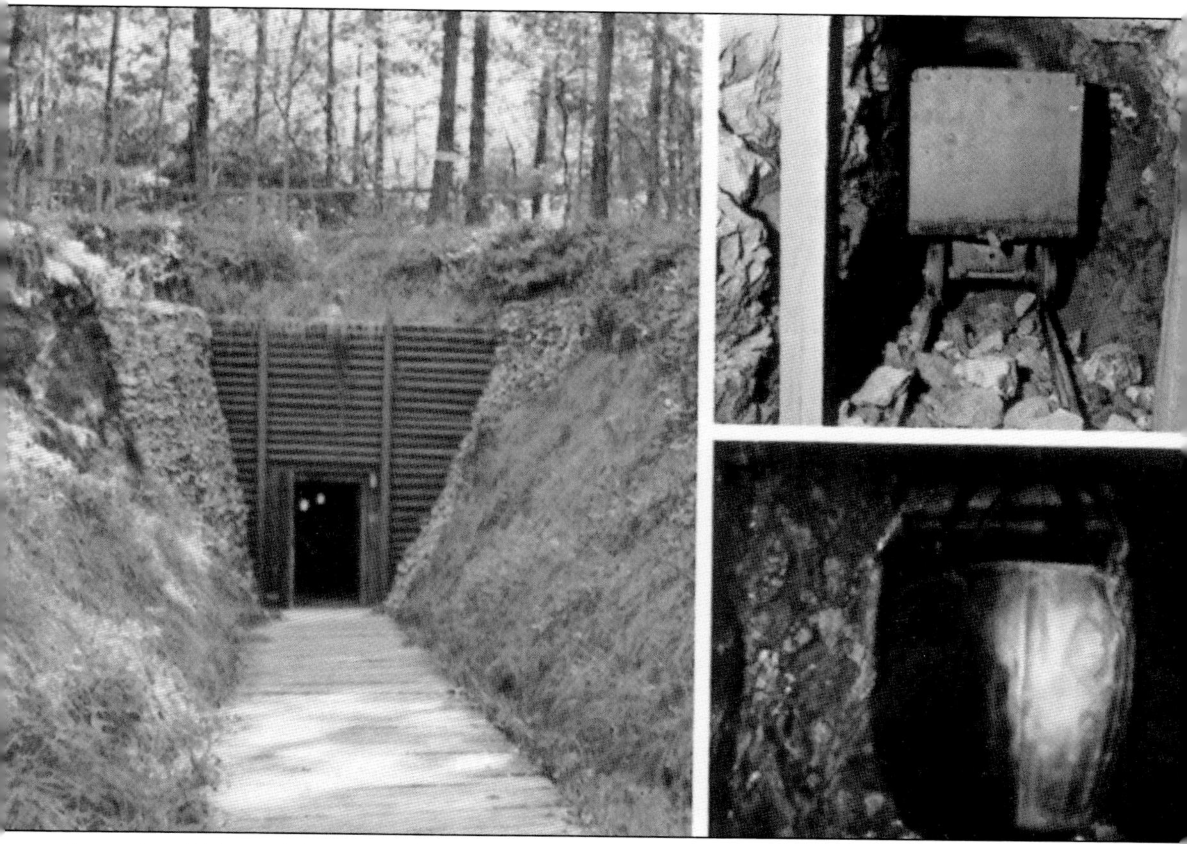

Located on Highway 200, a few miles east of Concord, is the community of Georgeville. It was near here that 12-year-old Conrad Reed was bow fishing when he found a yellow rock in Meadow Creek. Young Conrad took the pretty rock home where it was used for many years as a doorstop. On a trip to Fayetteville, North Carolina in 1799, Conrad's father carried the rock with him to show to a jeweler and learned that it was gold. After being processed, the yellow rock fetched $3,000. This was the first discovery of gold in the United States. Today the Reed Gold Mine is a state park with a museum and a gold mine open to the public. This card shows the Linker Adit (the visitor's entrance to the mine). Shown also are a Kibble ore bucket and an ore cart, both used for conveying ore to the surface. (Courtesy of the Charles A. Cannon Memorial Library.)

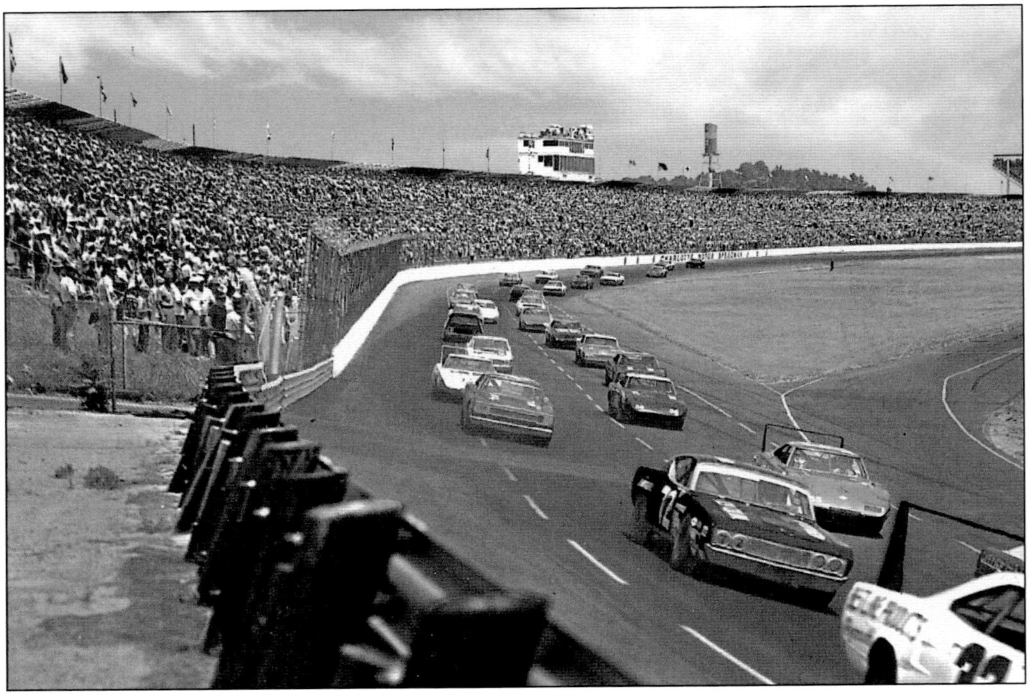

One of the most recognized attractions in Cabarrus County is Charlotte Motor Speedway (Lowe's Motor Speedway). The speedway has made much progress over the past 40 years, as shown in this postcard from the 1970s. (Courtesy of Jim Ramseur.)

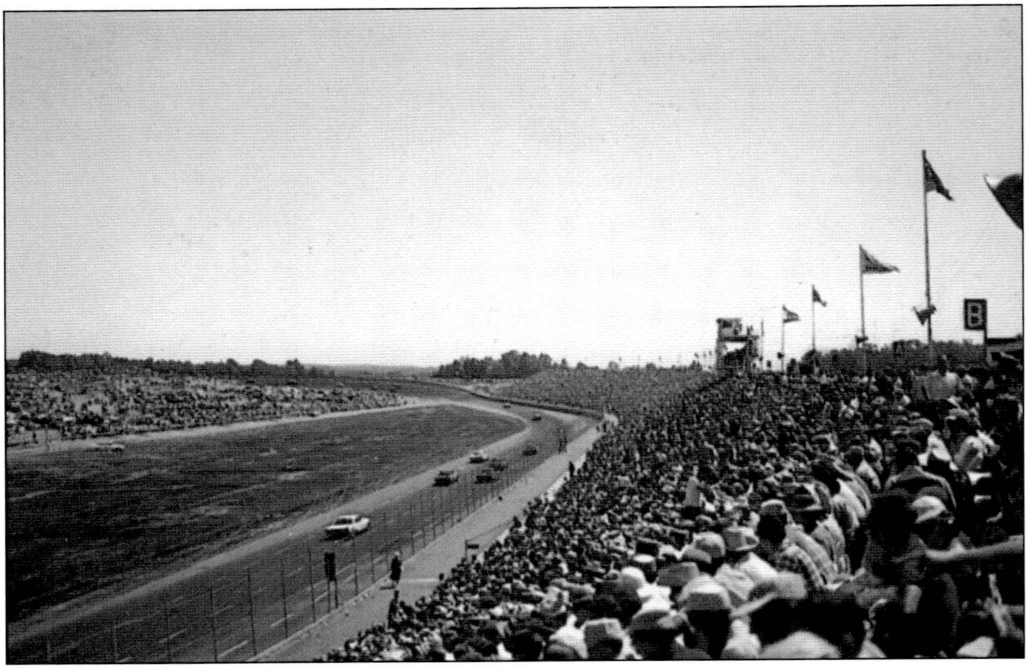

An earlier image of Lowe's Motor Speedway shows the way it looked in the early 1960s. Richard Petty, Junior Johnson, Cale Yarboro, and Glen "Fireball" Roberts are just a very few drivers who raced on this track. Fireball Roberts lost his life in a crash on this track.

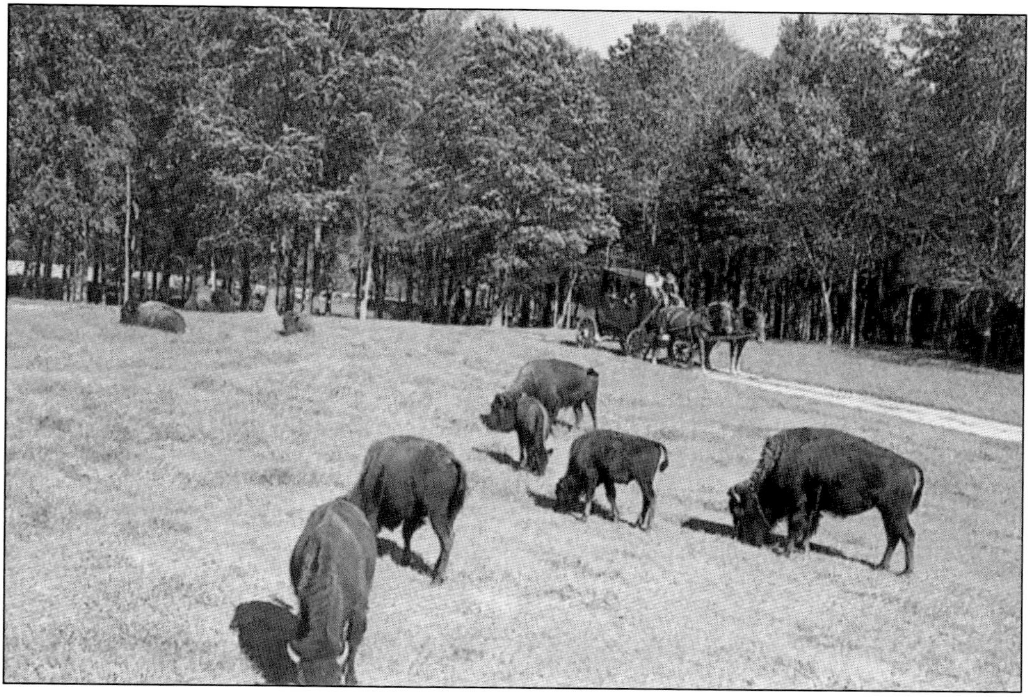

Three miles from Concord on Highway 49 was the Buffalo Ranch owned by Mr. R.B. Cook. The Buffalo Ranch was a popular attraction in Cabarrus County and had a large herd of buffalo, longhorn steers, horses, cows, and a rather large group of deer. (Courtesy of Jim Ramseur.)

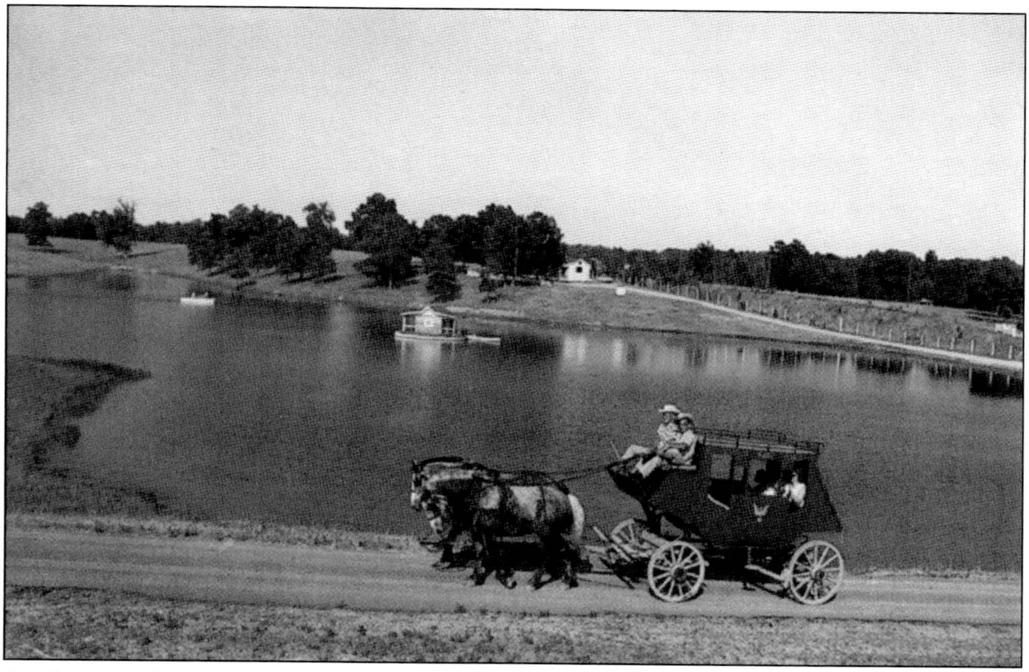

Another view shows the Buffalo Ranch with a small number of the herd grazing as a stage coach with spectators watch. Cook also owned Cook's Packing Company. (Courtesy of Jim Ramseur.)

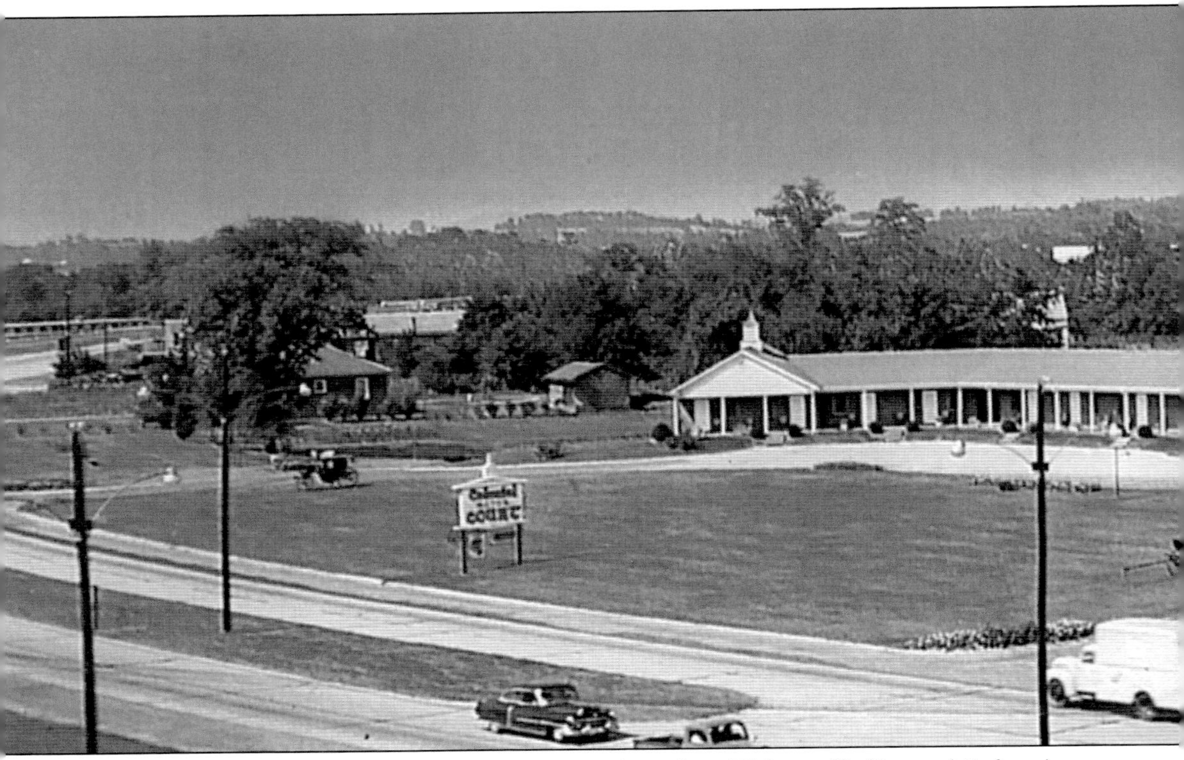

The Propst family owns the Colonial Motor Court located on Highway 29 (Concord Parkway) across from Cabarrus Memorial Hospital (NorthEast Medical Center). Seen in this unusual image is the motor court in the mid-1950s. The Colonial Court is still in operation today. Shown also is a delivery

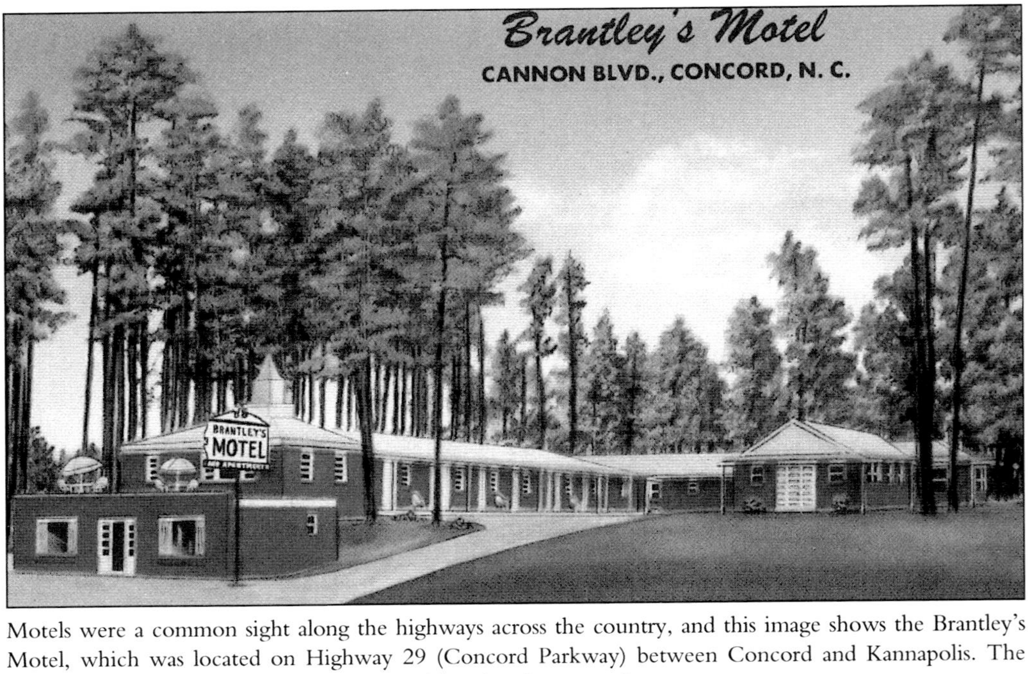

Motels were a common sight along the highways across the country, and this image shows the Brantley's Motel, which was located on Highway 29 (Concord Parkway) between Concord and Kannapolis. The motel changed names a number of times and has since been razed.

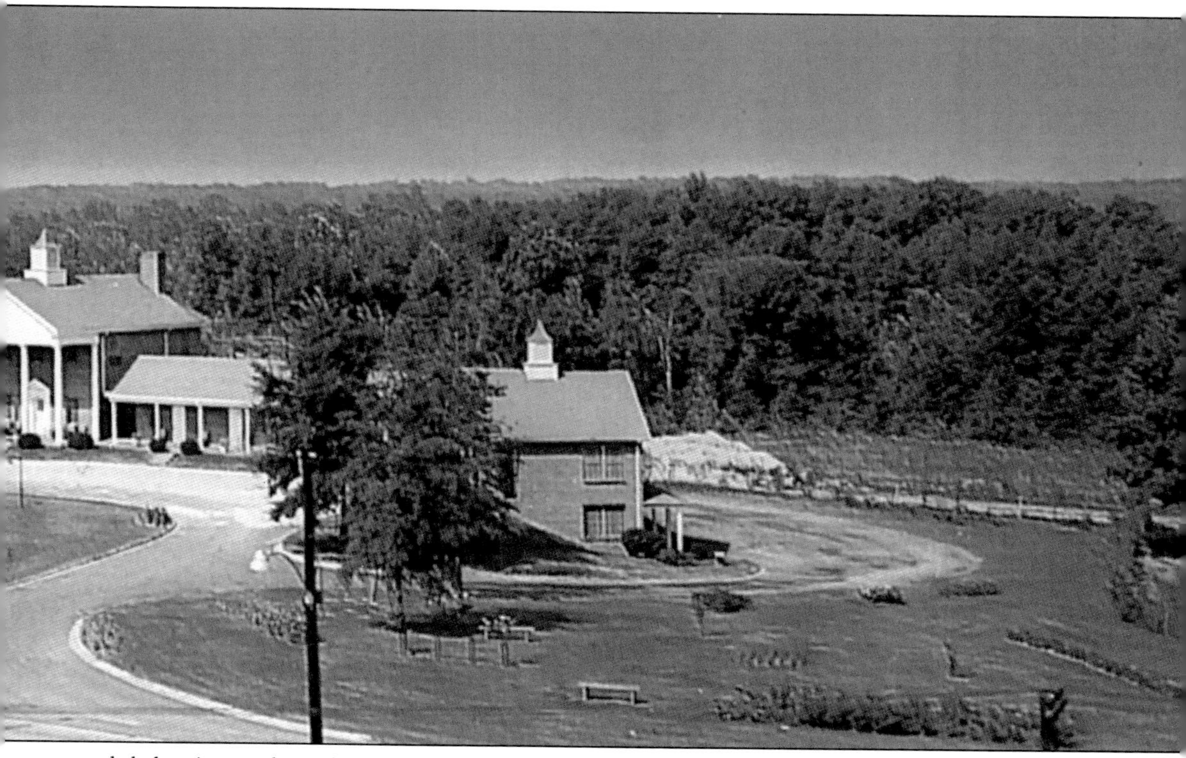

truck belonging to the Cabarrus Creamery. Robert L. Burrage was the owner of the creamery, and he started the business in 1923. It became known for wholesome milk and delicious ice cream. (Courtesy of Robert E. Burrage.)

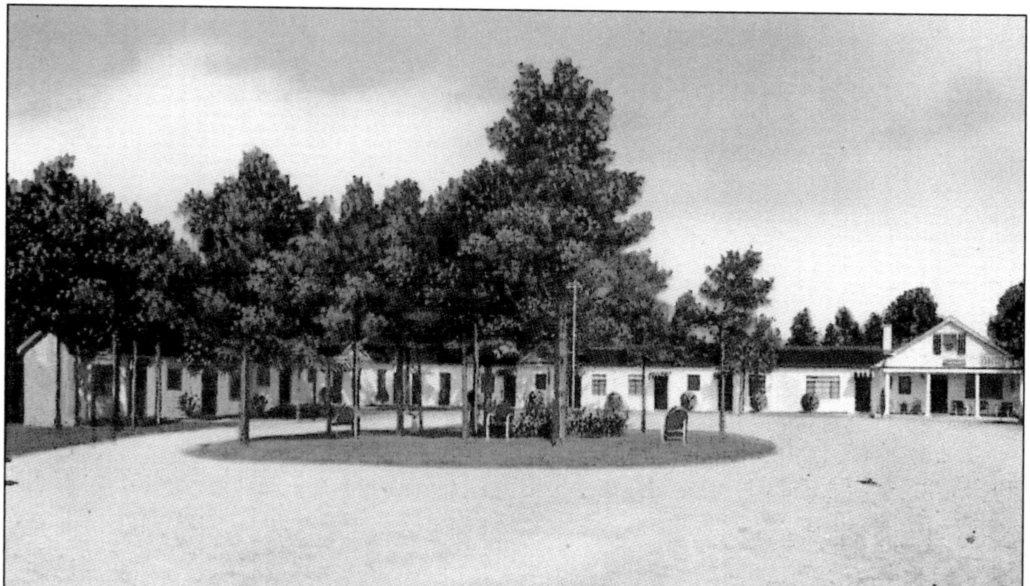

The Mayfair Motel, located on Highway 29 North (Concord Parkway), is still in operation today, although many changes have been made to it. This image shows what a typical motor lodge would look like in the late 1940s and early 1950s.

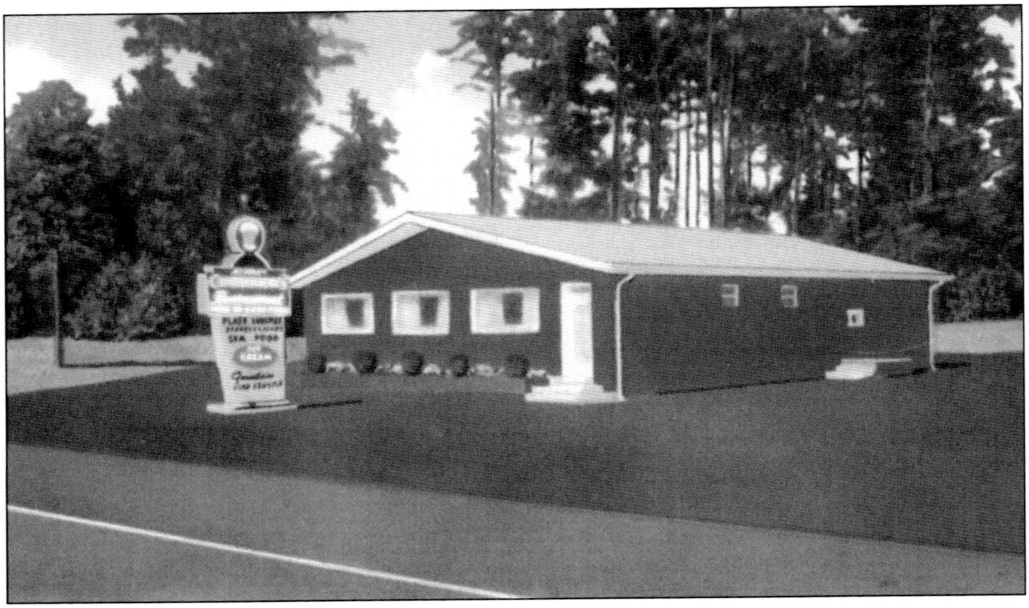

Chubirko's Restaurant was first located across from Cabarrus Hospital and later moved to this location only a short distant north and across the street from its first location on Highway 29. Local people remember the wonderful home cooking found at Chubirko's. (Courtesy of Mike Coltrane.)

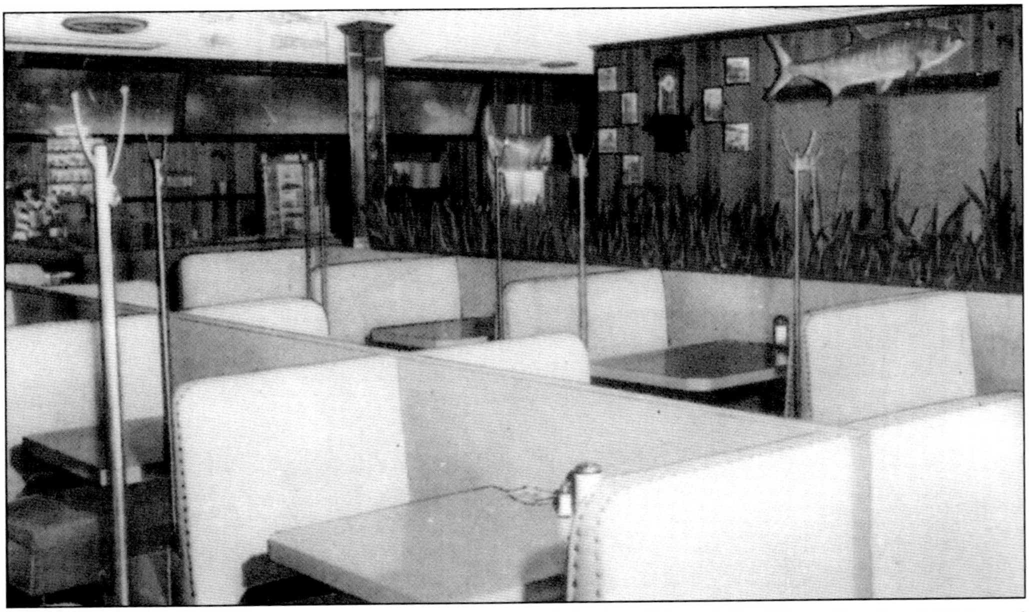

An interior view of Chubirko's Restaurant, which was "Air Conditioned For Your Comfort." This card dates to the late 1950s or early 1960s.

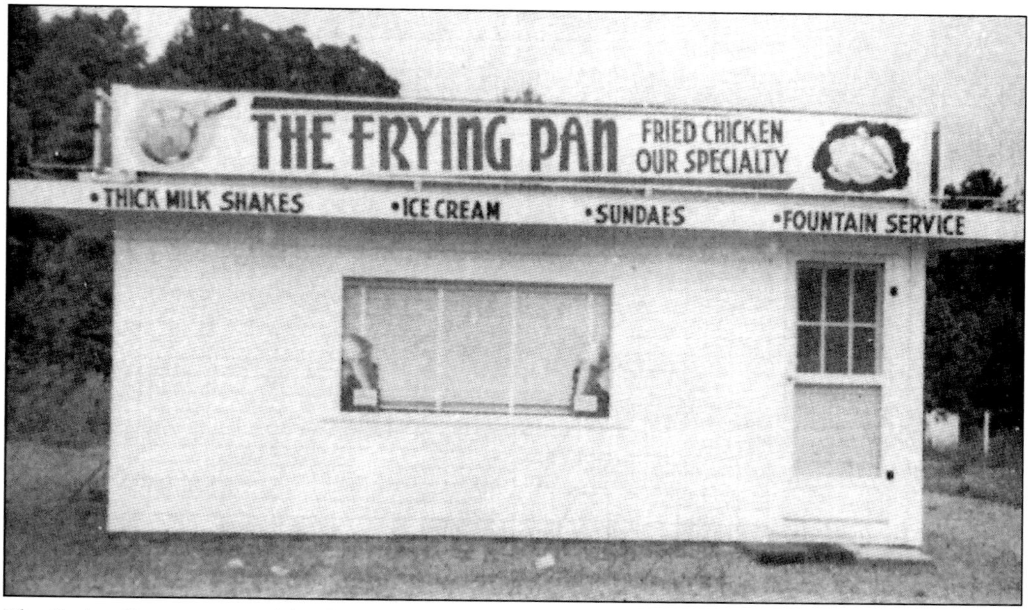

The Frying Pan was owned by Bruce R. Glover and was located on South Union Street. People still remember and speak highly of its thick milk shakes, great burgers, and wonderful fried chicken.

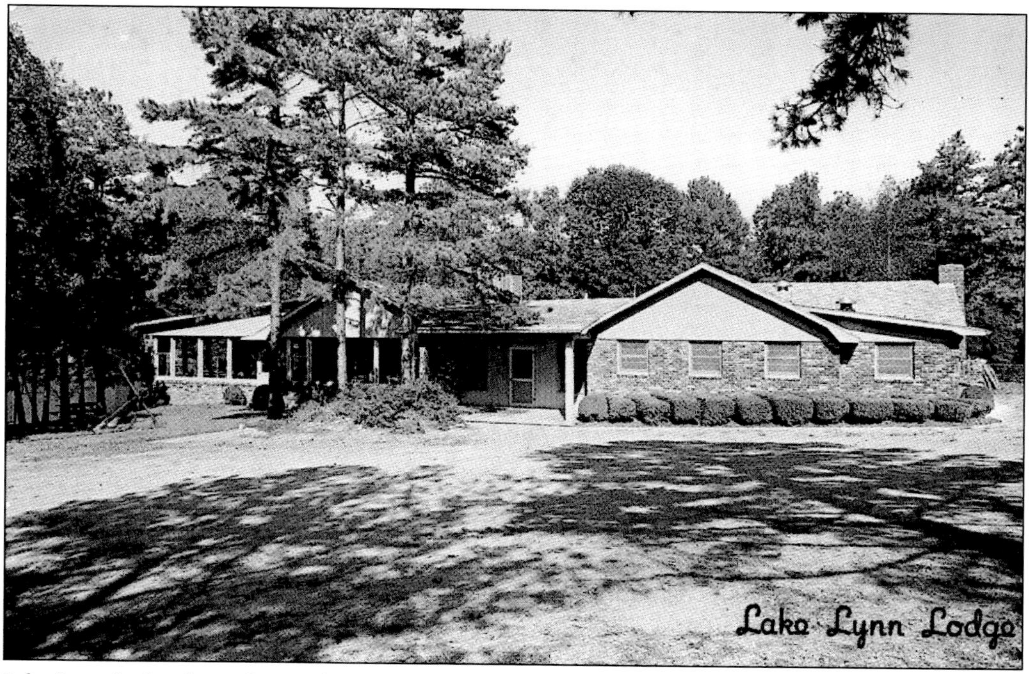

Lake Lynn Lodge, located east of Concord in a beautiful country setting, is known for its steaks, seafood, and chicken dinners, as well as its great party rooms. This restaurant is owned by the Frank Ridenhour family, who still operate it today.

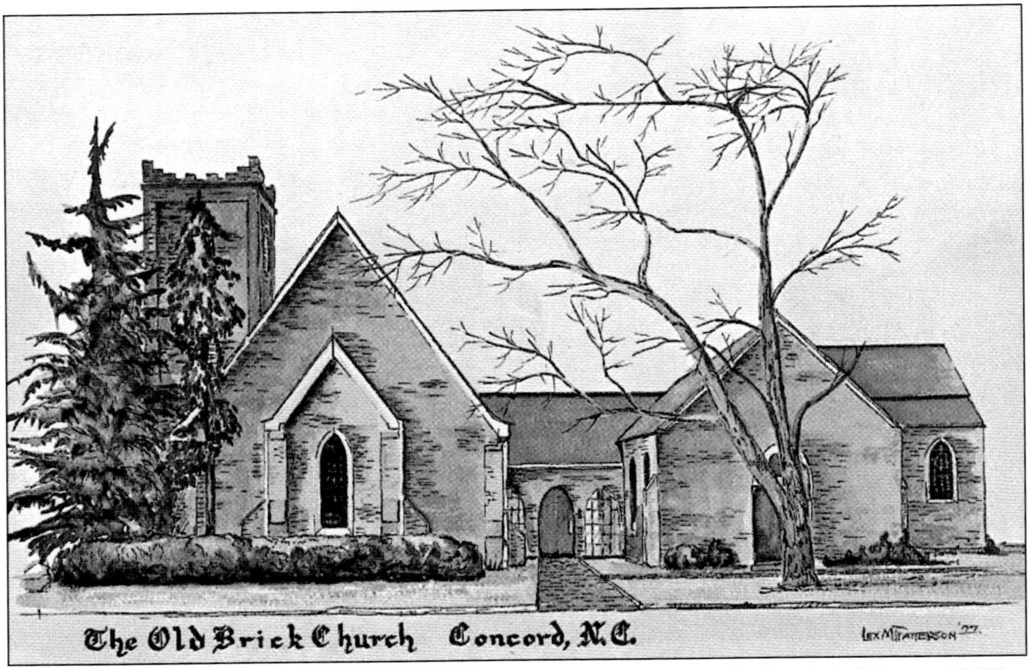

The Old Brick Church Restaurant, located in the old All Saints Episcopal Church building at 18 West Spring Street, was owned by Mrs. Francis B. Ridenhour. Ridenhour brought "fine dining" to Concord. The artist who created this card was Lex Patterson of Concord. (Courtesy of Jim Ramseur.)

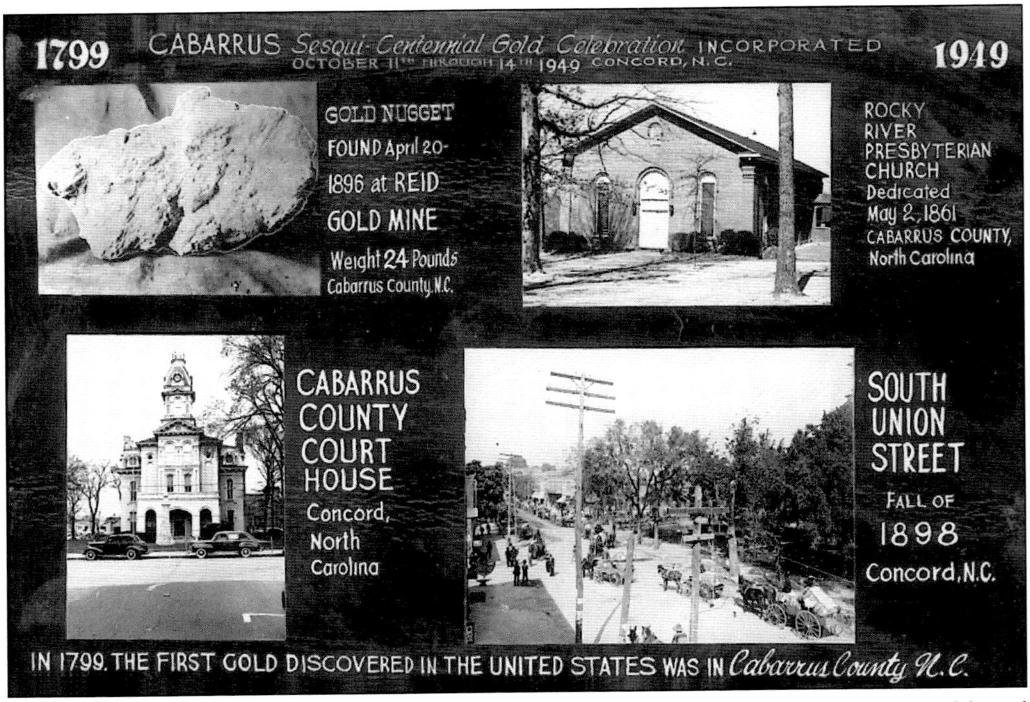

Cabarrus County had its Sesquicentennial Gold Celebration from October 11 to 14, 1949. It celebrated the first gold discovered in the United States, which was at the Reed Gold Mine. (Courtesy of Alex and Jane Patterson.)

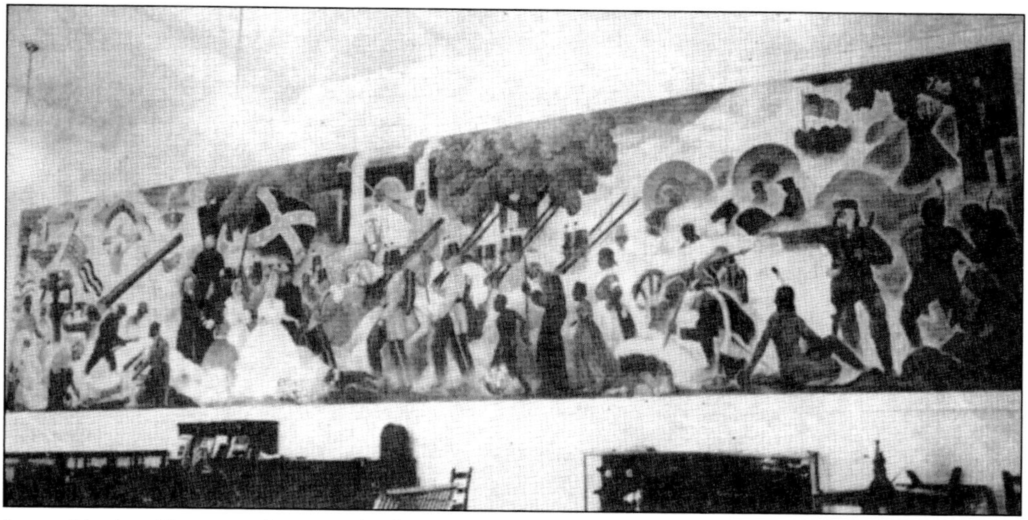

Located in the old community center in the Memorial Hall was a mural dedicated to the history of Cabarrus County, from its early Native American inhabitants to the Industrial Revolution after World War I. Painted by James McLean, this work can be found in the Cannon Memorial Library in Concord. (Courtesy of the Charles A. Cannon Memorial Library.)

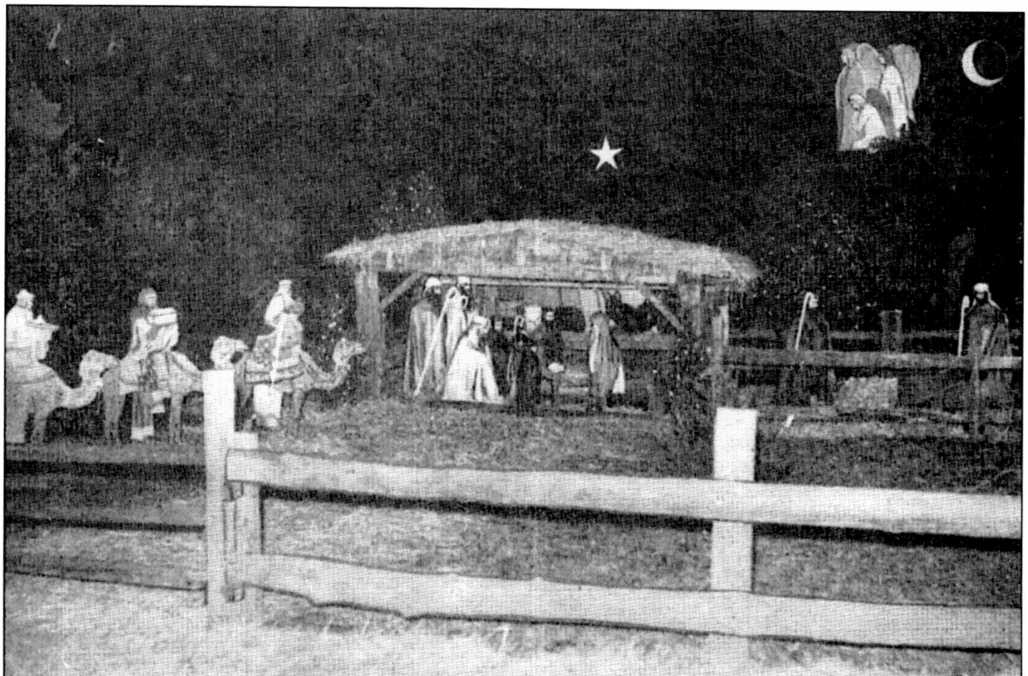

N.J. Mitchell, owner of Weddington and Mitchell Funeral Home located on West Corban Street, had a nativity scene set up beside the funeral home for all to enjoy. (Courtesy of the Charles A. Cannon Memorial Library.)

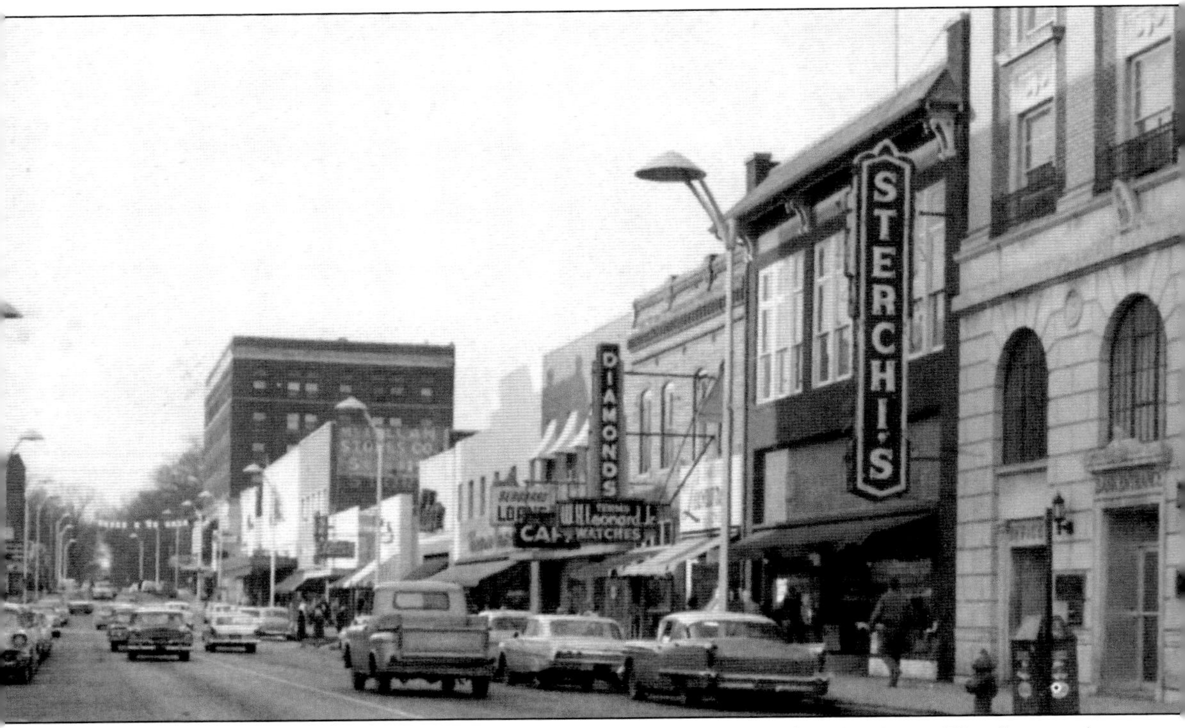

Shown here is downtown Concord in a 1960s view looking north on South Union Street. The photographer placed his camera in front of the 1876 courthouse to capture the busy little city. The facades have changed over the years. However, the hospitality still remains and people are proud to raise their families here, taking their places in the history of Cabarrus County, North Carolina.